Landscaping with Conifers and Ginkgo for the Southeast

To My Friend Kathy,
Thanks for coming out today. I hope you will soon visit.

Tom Cox
9-20-2016

UNIVERSITY PRESS OF FLORIDA

Florida A&M University, Tallahassee
Florida Atlantic University, Boca Raton
Florida Gulf Coast University, Ft. Myers
Florida International University, Miami
Florida State University, Tallahassee
New College of Florida, Sarasota
University of Central Florida, Orlando
University of Florida, Gainesville
University of North Florida, Jacksonville
University of South Florida, Tampa
University of West Florida, Pensacola

Tom Cox and John M. Ruter

Landscaping with Conifer

nd Ginkgo FOR THE SOUTHEAST

University Press of Florida
Gainesville
Tallahassee
Tampa
Boca Raton
Pensacola
Orlando
Miami
Jacksonville
Ft. Myers
Sarasota

All photos were taken in the southeastern United States by the authors unless
otherwise noted.

18 17 16 15 14 13   6 5 4 3 2 1

Library of Congress Cataloging-in-Publication Data
Cox, Thomas Wilson, 1945–
Landscaping with conifers and ginkgo for the Southeast / Tom Cox and John M. Ruter.
p. cm.
Includes bibliographical references and index.
ISBN 978-0-8130-4248-0 (alk. paper)—ISBN 0-8130-4248-8 (alk. paper)
1. Landscape gardening—Southern States. 2. Ornamental conifers—Southern States.
3. Ginkgo—Southern States. I. Ruter, John M. II. Title.
SB470.54.S68C69 2013
712.0975—dc23   2012039459

The University Press of Florida is the scholarly publishing agency for the State University
System of Florida, comprising Florida A&M University, Florida Atlantic University,
Florida Gulf Coast University, Florida International University, Florida State University,
New College of Florida, University of Central Florida, University of Florida, University
of North Florida, University of South Florida, and University of West Florida.

University Press of Florida
15 Northwest 15th Street
Gainesville, FL 32611-2079
http://www.upf.com

Contents

Introduction

 Conifers are among the most beautiful and versatile of all garden plants, yet they remain underutilized in the South. No other plant group can provide the year-round variety of color, form, and texture of conifers. We think their underuse is due in part to the belief in some circles that they are not adaptable to the southeastern climate. This book is written with the intent of introducing the reader to conifers we have evaluated and whose use we encourage in southern landscapes.

The idea of writing this book stemmed from our frustration when seeking accurate information concerning proper selection of and cultural requirements for conifers in southern climates. Our goal is to provide information about the use of conifers in a region of the United States where such information is practically nonexistent.

Our recommendations are based on our collective experience over the past 20 years in conducting trials of conifers from almost all genera. Together, we combine our knowledge of growing plants in different conditions—Tom in Zone 7b (Piedmont region) and John in 8a (Coastal Plain region). This has afforded us the opportunities to evaluate differing environmental factors as they impact growth and survival of conifers. While we have experienced some failures, we have also encountered far more successes.

As we traveled around the South visiting nurseries and growers, we found a great lack of knowledge concerning selection of conifers and about which ones are adaptable to our growing conditions. This lack of knowledge creates a problem for wholesale growers outside the South as to what conifers to recommend to retail buyers. We found that even libraries, bookstores, and Internet sites had scant information written by southern gardeners or academicians concerning conifers for the region. Authors writing about conifers are either from regions

Conifers in the garden

outside the South or from the United Kingdom, or the text is written in a foreign language. In each instance, the accounts and experiences do not line up well with the growing conditions of the South.

Reference sources referring to Zones 6–9 inclines us to think in terms of the plants' adaptability to cold temperatures with little or no thought to heat tolerance. Growing conditions in Zone 7 in Oregon or California are very different from those in Zone 7 in Birmingham, Alabama. Similarly, a Zone 6 plant may survive just fine in winter, then suddenly perish in the heat of our summer.

There is a general assumption that we are limited in our selection and that, as a group, conifers will not grow here. As a result, more common taxa such as junipers (*Juniperus*), arborvitae (*Thuja*), and Leyland cypress (*Cupressus ×leylandii*) are overplanted. Compared with other regions in the United States, this overuse has resulted in any number of "look-alike" landscapes. Traditionally, gardeners in the South have relied on the mass of spectacular spring blooms as the backbone of their landscapes. With the addition of conifers, homeowners and landscapes can enjoy 12 months of low-maintenance color.

Cox Arboretum and Gardens in the winter (photo by Cheryl Provence)

In this book we introduce the reader to genera and species that have proved adaptable as well as to many of the best cultivated varieties (cultivars) that have performed well in the southeastern United States. All photos in the book were taken in the southeastern United States by the authors; contributed photographs are noted in the list of plates.

We also cover details on a range of topics, from proper pruning techniques to insects and diseases and nursery sources. Our aim is to equip the reader with sufficient knowledge concerning *what* to buy, *where* to plant it, *how* to maintain it, and *what* to expect growthwise.

While the main focus is on selections that are commercially available, we have also included several newer selections that are worthy of wider use. After some names of commercially developed species we have added the abbreviations "PP" or "PPAF"; these stand for "plant patent" and "plant patent applied for," respectively. In including these newer selections, we hope to induce growers and nurseries to consider expanding their offerings. As you will see, it is possible to find a plant of any size, shape, and color.

Conifer trials in Tifton, Georgia

What Is a Conifer?

The term *conifer* refers to a class of primitive plants that with few exceptions bear cones. Notable exceptions to the production of cones are junipers (*Juniperus*), podocarpus (*Podocarpus*), yews (*Taxus*), and plum yews (*Cephalotaxus*). These plants bear fleshy seed cones as opposed to the more scaly cones typically associated with conifers. While the majority have needle-like leaves, such as those of pines, or flat, triangular scalelike leaves, such as those of *Chamaecyparis*, a few species such as *Podocarpus* and *Nageia* have flat, strap-shaped, broader leaves.

Conifers are members of a class of plants referred to as gymnosperms and are among the oldest living plants on earth. In addition to conifers, gymnosperms include cycads, *Ginkgo*, and *Gnetales*; these collectively were the dominant land plants in the age of the dinosaurs, and they predate modern flowering plants (angiosperms).

Unlike modern flowering plants, conifers bear their seed naked (seeds develop on the surface of the reproductive structures) and in contrast to many plants that are insect pollinated, all conifers are pollinated by the wind. The male cones have structures called microsporangia that produce yellowish pollen. Pollen is released and carried by the wind to female cones. For most species, this occurs in spring.

Conifers have their own unique evolutionary history; many are better adapted to extended periods of low rainfall than most broadleaf trees. Earliest fossil records reveal that they have existed for more than 300 million years.

Conifers comprise 8 families, 69 genera, and 630 species, though these numbers vary widely depending on the authority. These ancient plants occur on all continents except Antarctica. Compared with modern plants, which comprise between 250,000 and 300,000 extant species, conifers make up only a small portion of our current flora. In the entire history of conifers, there likely have never been more than a few thousand species.

Although the total number of species is relatively small, they are the dominant plants over vast areas of land, most notably the boreal forests of the Northern Hemisphere, but they are also dominant in similar cool climates in mountains further south, where their distribution is more scattered. Where conifers make up the dominant landscape, such as the Pacific Northwest of the United States, they form some of the most beautiful forests in the world and are an important economic element. At one time they were historically dominant in the southeastern Coastal Plains, with longleaf pine (*Pinus palustris*) being most notable.

Most conifers are evergreen trees, except for five genera that are deciduous: *Taxodium*, *Metasequoia*, *Larix*, *Glyptostrobus*, and *Pseudolarix*. Conifers vary in size from less than 1 foot (0.3 m) to more than 300 feet (89 m) in height. All the world's tallest, largest, thickest, and oldest living plants are conifers. The tallest, at 379 feet (115 m), is a coast redwood (*Sequoia sempervirens*). The largest in volume is a giant sequoia (*Sequoiadendron giganteum*), with a volume of 52,508 cubic feet (1487 m^3) and a weight of more than 1800 tons. The thickest tree, with the greatest trunk diameter at 37.5 feet (11.4 m), is a Montezuma cypress (*Taxodium distichum* var. *mexicanum*). Depending on how it's counted, the oldest tree is a *Picea abies* in Sweden (9550 years), and the oldest living tree trunk is a Great Basin bristlecone pine (*Pinus longaeva*) in California (4844 years). The tallest tree east of the Mississippi is also a conifer, eastern white pine (*Pinus strobus*).

Planting and Growing Conifers

One of the challenges in writing a region-specific text is the recognition that growing conditions vary across the region. Not all conifers that we recommend are suitable for every area of the South. For example, in a state such as North Carolina, there are at least three specific regions. Western North Carolina has higher elevation and therefore tends to be cooler. In the center of the state lies the Piedmont range, and to the east, the Coastal Plain. There is also a difference in the northern tier of the region compared with conditions further south.

What works in Huntsville, Alabama, may not be appropriate in Mobile, and vice versa. Each area has plants that flourish and others that languish. To the greatest extent possible, we have included specific recommendations on plant selection and growing conditions. The South as addressed in this book extends from Kentucky and Virginia in the north, south to Gainesville, Florida, and west to Arkansas, and includes eastern portions of Oklahoma and Texas where annual rainfall is greater than 40 inches (102 cm).

This region covers a wide swath, and growing conditions vary depending on soil type, temperature, elevation, and moisture. It is a region where the elevation ranges from sea level to 6684 feet at Mt. Mitchell, North Carolina.

To better assist you in successfully growing conifers, we have detailed what we consider best cultural practices. You have paid good money for your plants and likely have some emotional investment tied up in them. In addition, some rare gems may be available only on a limited basis. While your plant may be well suited for your particular region, unless it is provided with the correct cultural practices, it will generally not prosper. This does not have to be as difficult as it may seem at first, and the guidelines are fairly straightforward.

2

Cultural Practices

Planting

Dig a hole approximately twice as wide and just as deep as the root ball, to ensure that the roots will have an easier time penetrating the new soil. There is no need to dig the planting hole any deeper than the plant requires when placed in the hole; it should sit where the root crown is at ground level with or slightly above the soil line. Regardless of whether the plant was received balled and burlapped (B&B), container grown or bare-root, a well-planted conifer is one with the root ball resting on undisturbed soil.

For container-grown plants, the first step in planting is to visually check the root ball to see whether the roots have grown into a circular mass around the inner wall of the container. Sometimes one can simply spread the roots apart by hand; if not, submerge the plants in a pail of water for several hours and then try to untangle the ball. This will also serve to remove some of the artificial growing substrate, thus allowing more root contact with the soil. Where this is not possible, take a sharp knife and make three or four sharp vertical cuts about 0.25 inch (0.6 cm) deep and then spread the roots out. Otherwise, the main roots will continue to grow in a circling fashion and may never radiate out. The intent from Day One is to get the roots growing out, into the native soil. With conifers, we have found this to be key to their successful acclimation. Following this same logic, smaller plants generally establish more quickly as it is easier for them to get their roots into the surrounding soil.

In the case of balled and burlapped plants, dig the hole twice as wide as and no deeper than the root flare from the main trunk. Place the ball in the hole so the root flare is resting at or just slightly above ground level. Be careful to remove all twine as it does not easily decompose and will eventually girdle the plant's trunk. As long as the burlap is not made from a synthetic material, there is no need to remove it, as over time it will decompose. Make sure, however, that no burlap is left exposed above ground; otherwise it will act like a wick and pull moisture from the plant. As feeder roots are tiny and easily damaged, try to minimize any lifting of the tree by its trunk or moving it from side to side once in the hole.

In all instances, fill the hole half-full of soil and then thoroughly water. Let it settle, and then firmly pack the soil being careful not to pack too tightly. The goal is to properly seat the soil so as to remove most air pockets, yet leave space for roots to grow. On some species, it is beneficial to create a slight saucer-like depression around the outer perimeter of the root ball to act as a catch-basin for water as the plant is getting established—this should be removed after the first growing season.

We do not recommend you amend the soil unless it is so compacted that it cannot be broken apart when dry. This is seldom the case, so it is the rare exception rather than the rule. If you are going to amend, then amend the whole area, not just the planting hole. Plan to amend to one-third of the depth you till. If you till 9 inches (23 cm) deep, add 3 inches (7.6 cm) of amendment to the whole tilled area. Composted pine bark works well. Pea gravel or expanded shale can also be used on heavier clay soils. When you must amend the soil, do so with compost, not sand or peat moss. Sand binds to the particles of clay and worsens the situation (think bricks). Peat moss does not hold up well in our humid region and actually can be a deterrent to the absorption of water when it gets too dry. Another option is to incorporate well-rotted or composted manure into the soil.

As a general guideline, think of roots in the following fashion: amendments may actually encourage roots to remain in the vicinity of the planting hole as opposed to spreading into the nonamended soil. If a plant is going to adapt to our soil, then the best way to acclimate it is to get the roots spreading into native soil from Day One. Where the soil is on the acidic side, incorporating dolomitic lime with the soil may speed growth and enhance the color of certain conifers such as Colorado blue spruce (*Picea pungens*), which is native to less acidic soil. Before incorporating dolomite, you should have a soil pH test conducted and follow the recommended rates of application.

Fertilizing

One of the most commonly asked questions about conifers is when and how to fertilize. In general, fertilizer should be applied directly to the soil surface;

if you have mulched properly, you should not experience any fertilizer runoff when water is applied. The timing of application is linked to the period of active root growth. Since most conifers are evergreen, there is usually some root growth during most months of the year in the South. As a general rule, fertilizer should be applied from just prior to bud break through the end of the first flush of growth. This is the period of maximum nutrient uptake. On sandier soils in the lower South conifers respond well to an additional application of complete fertilizer in August or September.

Mulching

Assuming the plant was properly planted, other than watering, there is no step more critical than mulching to long-term health and appearance. Mulch serves a host of functions. Most significant is that it makes watering easier as there is far less runoff, particularly important on slopes. Additional benefits include the following:

- deterring weeds
- cooling the soil
- replenishing nutrients by breaking down over time
- being aesthetically pleasing
- reducing soil splash on plants during heavy rains

Mulch should be applied out to the drip line of the canopy, at a depth of 2–3 inches, with no "mulch volcanoes" around the base of the tree.

Watering

Assuming your soil drains well, conifers seem to do better with the soil slightly on the moist side. A simple method for testing how well your soil will drain is to dig a hole 18 inches (46 cm) deep and fill it with water. If it drains in an hour, drainage is good. If it takes several hours to 24 hours, drainage is fair. Longer than this means you have poor drainage or a high water table.

With noted exceptions, a good rule of thumb is that roots cannot grow in either too dry or waterlogged soil. When no moisture is available, there is nothing to drink. In waterlogged soil, there is no ability to drink. We recommend that conifers be planted in a raised bed in an area where the soil does not drain well. In their natural habitat, conifers often live in conditions of dry soil or with periods of drought, especially in summer.

Once established, conifers seldom need supplemental watering, except during times of drought. If one is looking to maximize growth, additional watering will often facilitate improved growth. This is best done in the morning to avoid losses due to evaporation. The least desirable time to water is in the evening, since sending plants into the night with wet foliage is an invitation for diseases to start. Over the past several years the South has experienced significant drought in some areas, and this combined with temperatures above 90°F (32.2°C) for an extended period has resulted in the decline of many conifers. For newly planted specimens it is important in the first two years to water the entire root ball as opposed to just the surface. One common mistake that can lead to the demise of dwarf conifers in their first two years after planting is to water only the surface soil and not the entire area surrounding the root ball. As the soilless mix from the plant's original container drains more quickly, the soil dries faster and the plant dies from lack of water.

Weeding

Like all plants, conifers do not like competition for moisture and nourishment, and this is especially true of small plants that are not yet established. In addition to mulching, weeds can be kept in check either by hand-weeding or by the use of weed killers such as glyphosate. In no case do we recommend digging around your plants to remove weeds as it has the potential to damage the fine root hairs that are the main source of nourishment. An additional deterrent is application of a pre-emergent herbicide that suppresses the growth of weed seeds.

Planting Time

As with all plants, the optimal time for planting conifers is between autumn and spring. This is especially true of larger specimens purchased as B&B or in 5-gallon and larger containers. A specimen planted in summer requires more water while its roots become established. Also, during periods of prolonged heat, larger conifers require more water and it is easy to underwater them. Smaller container-grown plants can be planted out at other times, but as previously mentioned, it is essential that young plants do not dry out.

Transplanting

Conifers in general are not that difficult to transplant. If the plant is small enough, the job is simple. Dig a circle approximately 1 foot (0.3 m) out from the drip-line and lift out the entire plant in the shovel. If you use this method, the plant will scarcely know it's been moved. With larger plants, the weight of the root ball makes this impractical. In this instance, dig the circle the same as for small plants, then gently go around the plant and pry it out of the soil. Sometimes, using your hand to tease roots out of the hole is successful. The aim here is to save as many roots as possible. Avoid trying to lift the plant by the trunk as you run the risk of destroying the tiny feeder roots. Remember, with conifers, the demand for moisture never ceases. Some root tips must always be ready to satisfy it. Further, since a conifer root cannot be safely exposed to air for more than a few minutes before it starts to harden, it is advisable to dig the new hole first. Place the newly dug plant in its new home, backfill, water well, and mulch.

The critical issue is timing. Roots grow best when the soil cools off and shoot growth has ceased, allowing energy to be sent to the roots instead of to shoots for growth. Hence, planting in spring should be accomplished before hot weather and in the fall after hot weather. The optimum time to transplant conifers in the South is September and October. Since plants still need moisture and the water hoses have been stored for the winter, waiting until December through February is not recommended unless one is gardening in those areas of the Deep South where temperatures below freezing are seldom a problem. Expecting that the plant can safely rely on Mother Nature for its moisture needs after being transplanted is an iffy proposition. Above all, water only once, or at the most, twice per week as roots cannot survive if you continue to flood the soil.

Containers

Many conifers make excellent containerized plants, and many can be effectively used indoors. Tom is growing a number of marginally hardy conifers indoors in the winter and has found them to be excellent houseplants. As a general rule, the principal factor is moisture requirements. As most indoor plants die from overwatering, good drainage is essential, and one should always make sure that the container has holes in the bottom to allow water to freely drain. The choice of soil should be an area where you don't skimp. Choose a potting mix that drains well, and take care to not leave standing water in the saucer beneath the pot. Taken to the other extreme, soil should not be allowed to become completely dry. Remember, conifers that you plan to leave outdoors must be able to survive the stresses of both winter and summer. There are two principal limiting factors: moisture and temperature extremes.

Since the roots of container-grown plants are exposed to lower winter temperatures than roots in the ground, you should select plants that are at least one USDA Zone hardier than your area. Top dressing with a 1-inch layer of mulch may provide additional protection, as would relocating containers closer to the house as a shelter from winter wind and to provide some radiant heat.

The principal culprit in summer is insufficient moisture. If you intend these plants to be somewhat carefree, select ones that are drought resistant. Again, good drainage is essential. The use of mulch is an effective measure to lessen the evaporative effects of the sun as well as retard growth of weeds that compete for moisture. Keep in mind that evergreens require water year-round, and the soil in the container should never be allowed to completely dry out. Water whenever the soil is dry to the touch, anytime the soil is not frozen.

Pruning

While there is no "one size fits all" approach to pruning conifers, three practical basics are important to understand: why, when, and where.

Why

Think of pruning for two purposes: pruning required for maintenance, and pruning to achieve desired form. As an example, the removal of a multiple leader on a cypress serves both purposes, lessening the likelihood of the tree splitting apart as it matures as well as creating a more desirable form.

When

Since conifers have differing growth cycles, it is imperative to know the characteristics of the particular genus. In the spring, some conifers such as pines produce new shoots (often referred to on pines as candles). As the growth continues, these elongate and then harden. Once that cycle is complete, growth for that year is finished (determinate growth). There are exceptions with some species. Conifers such as hemlock and spruce grow in spurts and therefore produce multiple flushes of new growth throughout the active growing season. Conifers such as junipers and cedars grow continuously until the onset of cold weather.

Conifers can also be classified into growth classes known as (1) randomly branching and (2) whorled-branching (see below for list by genus). Randomly branching conifers tend to have multiple growth spurts during the year and latent buds along the stem that will be induced to grow when the shoots are pruned. In general, conifers with whorled branching patterns have few latent buds on parts of the stem without leaves, and often the buds are programmed to grow in a single flush during the season. Because of the long growing season enjoyed in the South, many conifers produce more flushes of new growth than in regions where the season is shorter. In chapter 5's plant descriptions, we give the optimum time for pruning for each genus.

Randomly Branching Conifers

Calocedrus	*Nageia*
Cedrus	*Platycladus*
Cephalotaxus	*Podocarpus*
Chamaecyparis	*Sequoia*
Cryptomeria	*Taxus*
Cupressus	*Thuja*
Juniperus	*Tsuga*

Whorled Branching Conifers

Abies	*Picea*
Araucaria	*Pinus*
Cunninghamia	*Pseudotsuga*
Keteleeria	*Sciadopitys*

Where

Since certain conifers are less forgiving in the way they are pruned than other plants, the third component—where to prune—is the most critical. Removing individual branches is preferred to "shearing," since shearing can often leave dead tips that are unsightly. Below is a list of some of the more commonly encountered species with recommendations for pruning.

Abies (firs): Pruning cuts can be made anywhere there are visible buds or internodes along the branch, even where there are no live needles.

Cedrus (cedars): Same as for *Abies*.

Cephalotaxus (plum yew): No special requirements as long as all cuts are made within the zone of living foliage.

Chamaecyparis (false cypress): No special requirements as long as all cuts are made within the zone of living foliage.

Cryptomeria (Japanese cedar): No special requirements as long as all cuts are made within the zone of living foliage.

Cunninghamia (China fir): It is best to make all cuts at a branch node or collar. China fir will form new buds anywhere it is cut. In fact, it is one of the few conifers that will resprout on a tree that has been completely cut to the ground (coppiced).

Cupressus (cypress): No special requirements as long as all cuts are made within the zone of living foliage.

Ginkgo: No special requirements except to make all cuts at a branch node.

Juniperus (juniper): Junipers are one of the most forgiving of all conifers when it comes to pruning. Cut back anywhere along the plant as long as you leave some green needles. All cuts should be made at a node or by removing the branch back into the canopy where the cut cannot be seen.

Keteleeria: Make all cuts at a branch node or collar, Keteleeria will form new buds anywhere it is cut. In fact, it is another one of the few conifers that will resprout from cutting the tree nearly to the ground.

Metasequoia (dawn redwood): No special requirements except to make all cuts either at a branch node or at a collar.

Picea (spruce) Similar to *Abies* (fir) above, but because of its propensity to produce latent buds, it is more capable of budding back on old wood.

Pinus (pine): Pines are normally pruned to influence future growth. There are two approaches to pruning pines. For most gardeners, the simplest and most forgiving is a method referred to as candle pruning. This involves partial removal (normally half) of the cluster of candles from the new spring flush. Timing is the crucial element as the candle should be able to be easily snapped in two. It is recommended that this be done with fingers as opposed to using pruners. The cut will be cleaner, reducing the risk of inducing disease. This is an excellent method to control size and increase density as well as reduce the internodal length between branches, especially in the five-needle species. This forces the tree to grow a number of smaller branches at various angles.

Unlike other members of the Pinaceae family such as *Abies*, *Picea*, and *Tsuga*, pines usually produce only one flush of growth per year. When this is over, the tips of the new shoots develop a terminal bud to set the stage for the following year's growth.

The second method entails pruning branches and requires a bit more attention to detail. As a general rule, no cuts should ever be made where there are no green needles. Cutting a branch back and leaving no needles will result in the death of the branch. Always prune back to green needles, thus allowing new buds to form, which will subsequently develop new branches. It is recommended that you make cuts only where the current season's needles are present. Some nurseries employ a process called shearing; unless skillfully done, this technique can turn needle tips brown. Pruning or removal of branches is the preferred method for the homeowner. Limit pruning in the summer; exposed cuts can attract bark beetles.

Poor pruning
on *Pinus strobus*

Platycladus (Oriental arborvitae): Same as for *Chamaecyparis*.

Pseudolarix (golden larch): Same as for *Metasequoia*.

Sequoia (coast redwood): While we recommend making all cuts at a branch node or collar, coast redwood will form new buds anywhere it is cut. In fact, it is one of the few conifers that will resprout after being cut completely to the ground (coppiced).

Taxus (yew): Perhaps the easiest of all conifers when it comes to pruning. Since yews will form new buds anywhere on old wood, no special skills are necessary.

Taxodium (bald cypress): Same as for *Sequoia*.

Thuja (arborvitae): Same as for *Chamaecyparis*.

Tsuga (hemlock): Same as for junipers except the cuts do not have to be made at a branch node.

Soils and the Southern Climate

Understanding the dynamics between soil type and the southern climate will go a long way in helping you understand the cultural requirements of many conifers. Our combined growing experience leads us to the following conclusions regarding conifer adaptability. For those who garden in heavy clay soil, root survival under wet, hot summer conditions is the principal limiting factor in growing conifers. In areas such as the coastal plain and east Texas, where the soil drains more freely, adequate water during the hot summer months is more critical. In the early stages of trials, far more conifers were lost in July and August than in any other months. As summer temperatures rise in the South, respiration rates increase, creating a requirement for more oxygen as a factor in root survival. Further exacerbating this situation are our nights when the temperature does not cool down, resulting in further respiration losses. Heavy rains in the summer on our poorly drained soils during this period can create sometimes fatal conditions. Peak oxygen demand when plants are waterlogged in poorly drained soil quickly creates anaerobic conditions where roots cease to function, thus creating conditions conducive to root rot.

It is important to distinguish this condition as unique to southeastern United States soil types. Soils in the Southwest and West tend to be much drier during periods of high temperature, and central and northeastern states are cooler during periods of heavy rain. This is a poorly understood factor by most growers, particularly when it comes to choice of rootstock when grafting conifers. Further, container products from Pacific Northwest growers comprise predominately a coarse-textured medium that ensures rapid drainage, and this medium is sometimes made with ground Douglas-fir bark that does not break down well in southern soils. We recommend you remove as much of this medium as possible and place the roots in the native soil where they will be growing.

An overlooked factor in growing plants in the South is soil pH. Almost all conifers will grow in the varying pH of southern soil types. Understanding the pH of your soil will help to optimize growth and appearance. Typically because of heavy rain amounts, Southern soils tend to be on the acidic side as rain leaches minerals such as calcium, magnesium, and potassium from the soil. As one moves westward and rain amounts begin to lessen, the soil becomes less acidic. As an example, the soil pH around Dallas, Texas, averages around 8.0, and 185 miles southeast in Nacogdoches, Texas, the average is 5.0. In the lower south around Tifton, Georgia, where John conducts his research, soil pH is 4.2–5.0, and where Tom gardens in Canton, Georgia, it ranges from 4.0 to 5.5.

Sulfur- or acid-forming fertilizers can be used to lower the pH, while dolomitic limestone can be used to raise the pH. Limestone should be incorporated before planting as surface applications do not move very far into the soil, and you end up with a high pH in the top 0.5–1 inch of soil. Alkalinity and pH of irrigation water can also influence soil pH. John has noted that even moderately alkaline irrigation water can result in the pH under drip emitters to increase, thus causing iron chlorosis. In his trials using drip emitters, the pH has risen to 7.2 over several years, while two feet away, the pH may still be less than 5.0.

Conifers and the Southern Climate

Conifers are very adaptable plants but even they are limited by diverse, ever-changing climate in the southeastern United States. Plant hardiness can be influenced by environmental factors such as temperature, radiation, day length, rainfall, soil moisture, and in some parts of the South, snow. For the Southeast, the number of days above 90°F (32.2°C) ranges from about 10 to 100; the number of days below freezing is roughly similar, and rainfall ranges from 40 inches (102 cm) in the west to more than 65 inches (165 cm) along the Gulf Coast.

Most plant growth occurs in an optimum temperature range usually from the low 70s to 85°F (22–29°C). Growth is limited by temperature extremes above or below the range. The USDA Hardiness Zone map (http://www.usna.usda.gov/Hardzone/) was designed to designate zones of cold hardiness for plant survival in all areas of the United States. The zone areas addressed in this book coincide with hardiness Zones 6a–9a. Each zone is subdivided into sections (a) and (b) representing 5°F differences in average minimal winter temperatures.

For example, the average annual minimum temperature for Zone 6a is -10 to -5°F (-23.3 to -20.5°C), whereas the minimum winter temperatures for Zone 8b can be expected to be between 15 and 20°F (-9.4 and -6.7°C). In January 1985 temperatures dipped to -24°F (-31.1°C) with a wind chill of -50°F (-45.5°C) in Knoxville, Tennessee (Zone 7a), making the city an equivalent of Zone 4b for one day. Almost all the Deodar cedars were killed outright. The *Taxus* remained green below the snowline (about 1 foot, 0.3 m), and *Metasequoia* did not leaf out until early June that year. While snow can be a good insulator and protect plants from damage, excessive wet snow or freezing ice can wreak havoc on conifers that are not adapted to handling such conditions (many of the cypresses fall in this category).

The other extreme, high temperatures can also limit growth. To help address this, the American Horticultural Society (AHS) created the Plant Heat-Zone map (http://www.ahs.org/publications/heat_zone_map.htm) in 1997. This map is based on the average number of days per year above 86°F (30°C). Twelve zones have been demarcated, ranging from fewer than one day per year to greater than 210; the southeastern region covered here ranges from AHS Zone 2 (1–7 days) on some of the higher elevations in the Appalachian mountain range to roughly Zone 9 (about 120–150 days) in the Coastal Plain region. While Tifton, Georgia, and Virginia Beach, Virginia, are in USDA Hardiness Zones 8a and 8b for winter temperatures, Tifton is in AHS Zone 9, while Virginia Beach is in AHS Zone 6 because its climate is moderated more by the Atlantic Ocean.

High nighttime temperatures need to be considered as well. In the Coastal Plain region it is not uncommon to have temperatures in the low 80s at 10 p.m., a situation that influences the carbon balance of a plant. During the day, if the temperatures are in the 90s (32+°C), the plant struggles to make sugars from photosynthesis because of the high temperature. Then, at night if the temperature remains high, the plant respires off most of the sugars made during the day, leading to a neutral or negative carbon balance with nothing remaining for growth or defense compounds. After several months of this, the plant dies from starvation or other induced stresses. A general rule of thumb is that the temperature

Winter browning on *Cryptomeria japonica* 'Mushroom'

decreases 3°F (about 1.5°C) for every 1000-foot (298 m) increase in elevation. In Canton, Georgia (1200 feet, 357 m), Tom experiences cooler nighttime temperatures than John does for his collections in Tifton at 365 feet (109 m).

Solar radiation often ties in well with temperature stress. In summer, with long days and cloudless skies, photoinhibition can occur as a result of chronic exposure to sunlight. In the winter, browning of certain conifers such as *Cryptomeria* and *Thuja* is related to the development of a carotenoid pigment, rhodoxanthin, produced by the plant to protect itself from too much light on bright winter days when the temperatures are too low for photosynthesis to perform efficiently. Day length can also influence plant growth. Some conifers, such as Douglas-fir, respond to length of day in the summer to initiate and stop growth. A selection from southern Canada might have a critical day length period of 16 hours, whereas the longest day in the Coastal Plain region is only 14 hours. In such cases, a selection from Arizona might perform better than one from further north.

Rootstock Selection

In the world of dwarf conifers, grafting is a common production method. Grafting is used to more quickly produce a marketable plant that combines aerial portions of the desired plant with the root system of a compatible rootstock. Commercial growers in the Pacific Northwest, Midwest, and Northeast have traditionally used rootstocks that work well in their areas with little or no emphasis on the South. This has led to the quick demise of some plants that were shipped in on rootstocks that are incompatible with our growing conditions. Early in the learning curve, Tom recalls purchasing a large Spanish fir (*Abies pinsapo* 'Glauca') from a Pacific Northwest grower of specimen conifers. Tom reasoned that because this species of fir is native to a warm climate, it might adapt well in the South. Despite excellent drainage and sound horticultural practices, the plant did not survive longer than one month. It was later learned that the rootstock was balsam fir (*Abies balsamea*); thus the plant was doomed for a sudden death when it left the shipping dock. Had the plant been produced on a compatible rootstock such as *Abies firma*, the chances of survival would have been greatly increased.

Assuming the graft will produce a commercially viable plant, as a general rule growers select rootstock based on two factors: cost and availability. As in the example above for firs, the use of rootstocks such as *Abies balsamea* or *A. fraseri* is quite common, but neither will prosper in most areas of the South. Exceptions

Table 1. Climatic Data for the Southeastern United States

City and state	Days above 90°F (32.2°C)	Days below 32°F (0°C)	Annual rainfall (inches)
Asheville, N.C.	9	98	47.6
Athens, Ga.	51	50	49.7
Baton Rouge, La.	84	23	60.9
Birmingham, Ala.	53	57	54.6
Charleston, S.C.	53	32	51.5
Gainesville, Fla.	81	13	51.8
Houston, Tex.	98	18	46.1
Knoxville, Tenn.	29	73	47.1
Lexington, Ky.	19	94	44.5
Little Rock, Ark.	73	57	50.9
Richmond, Va.	42	84	43.2
Tallahassee, Fla.	91	34	65.7
Tulsa, Okla.	72	76	40.6
Tupelo, Miss.	65	53	55.9

Source: www.climate-zone.com

are elevations above 2200 feet (655 m), where the growing conditions are different. Otherwise, if you desire to grow a fir in the South, look for one grafted onto *Abies firma*, or a species on its own roots that might be more adapted to Zones 6 and portions of 7. Other grafted conifers that can be problematic are spruce, pines, and Lawson cypress.

Taking these one at a time, most spruce are grafted on Norway (*Picea abies*) which is generally adaptable. An even better rootstock would be *Picea orientalis* or *P. omorika*. The least desirable are *P. glauca*, *P. engelmannii*, and *P. pungens*.

In the case of pines, most two- and three-needle species are grafted on Scots pine (*Pinus sylvestris*). We have found this species adaptable as a rootstock in Zones 6 and 7. High-elevation pines and western coastal species such as *P. contorta, ponderosa, radiata*, and *jeffreyi* should not be used. While not much research has been conducted, more evaluations should be conducted of native pines such as *P. elliotii* and *taeda*. In the five-needle category, the common rootstock is *P. strobus*. We have discussed this with several southern producers who have begun to graft pines. Thus far they are having success with *P. strobiformis*, which is generally better adapted to the warmer portions of our region.

Given the prodigious number of magnificent cultivars of Lawson cypress (*Chamaecyparis lawsoniana*), no conifer is more frustrating to lose. The principal culprit is *Phytophthora lateralis*—a disease that has caused the demise of many Lawson cypress on the West Coast over the last two decades. New research using varieties grafted onto resistant root stock has been developed by Oregon State University and is marketed under The Guardian™ Series. Some West Coast growers are using this and the results look promising. John has had success with the cultivar 'Yvonne' growing on Guardian™ rootstock in Tifton.

Some nurseries are using *Chamaecyparis pisifera* 'Boulevard' and *C. pisifera* f. *squarrosa* rootstocks for dwarf forms of Lawson cypress, such as 'Minima Glauca', 'Nestoides', or 'Lutea Nana'. Tom has been conducting trials of several and remains skeptical about long-term compatibility because of the tendency of the grafted cultivar to grow faster than the rootstock. Over a period of years, the graft union does not hold up, especially with larger-growing selections.

In conclusion, we continue to provide feedback to conifer producers in hopes that the South might receive more attention with respect to the use of compatible rootstocks. We are optimistic, especially in light of the continued embrace of conifers in our region. Also, southern growers have recently begun to learn more about how to graft conifers. While using an appropriate rootstock is promising, not all species are adaptable to the Southeast. For example, John has tried *Abies alba* and *A. spectabilis* grafted onto *A. firma* as a rootstock without success. Tom has had similar experiences; thus one cannot say with absolute certainty that as a rootstock *A. firma* is a panacea for growing firs in the South.

3

Insect Pests

Insects and spider mites can cause considerable damage to conifers in the southeastern United States. Some insects, such as sawflies, chew foliage; bark beetles bore holes in trunks; and spider mites have piercing mouthparts to suck the plant juices out of foliage. Effective management requires proper identification of the pest causing the damage. The descriptions below cover some of the more common insect and mite pests of conifers in landscape settings.

Bagworms (*Thyridopteryx ephemerae-formis*)

> Bagworms are found mainly on *Cupressus ×leylandii*, *Juniperus*, *Platycladus*, *Taxodium*, and *Thuja*.

Female bagworms are wingless and remain in the characteristic "bags" for life. They produce one generation of offspring per year. Eggs overwinter in the female bags and hatch in April and May. Once the larva hatches, it constructs from leaves, twigs, and silk a bag that can reach 2 inches (5 cm) or more in length. Tree damage is caused by larvae feeding on the needles. Bagworms can be controlled by picking the bags off host plants or by treating them with an insecticide when the larvae are hatching. Bagworms pose a greater problem in the upper south than in the Coastal Plain region.

Cypress twig gall midge (*Taxodiomyia cupressiananassa*)

> The cypress twig gall midge feeds on all three varieties of *Taxodium distichum*: bald cypress, Montezuma cypress, and pond cypress.

Globose to spherical galls are created by the small adult fly that lays its eggs in developing foliage in the spring. As the larvae develop, the galls enlarge up to

Gall of the cypress twig gall midge

1 inch (2.5 cm) in length. Galls appear as whitish oblong swellings on the foliage in the summer. Insects overwinter in the galls that fall from the trees in the winter. Chemical control is not generally required. Certain lines of bald cypress are known to have resistance to this pest.

Pine beetles—Black turpentine beetle (*Dendroctonus terebrans*)

Black turpentine beetles feed on all species of pines native to the southeastern United States.

Among the five common species of native pine bark beetles in the southeastern United States, the black turpentine beetle is largest: up to ⅜ inch (0.9 cm) long. Adults are dark brown to black. This beetle attacks fresh stumps and trunks up to a height of 10 feet (3 m). Attacks can be identified by masses of pitch up to the size of a half-dollar. Multiple generations can occur yearly. Insecticides can be utilized to control pine beetles. Consult with your local Cooperative Extension Service or state forestry officials for control guidelines.

Pine beetles—Ips engraver beetles (*Ips* spp.)

Ips beetles are considered secondary pests that attack weak or stressed pine trees.

Damage from
pine beetles

Three different Ips species of varying size occur in Georgia. They can be identified by the appearance of a "scooped out" rear end with four to six spines. En-
graver beetles usually attack the upper portion of trees first, then spread up and
down the trunk. Egg galleries under the bark are Y- or H-shaped and radiate
from a central chamber.

Pine beetles—Southern pine beetle (*Dendroctonus frontalis*)

The southern pine beetle will attack and kill all southern pines, but
slash pine and longleaf pine can be more resistant.

Bark beetle damage on *Pinus bungeana*

The most destructive of the pine bark beetles in the southern United States is the southern pine beetle. Populations fluctuate from year to year. In off years, southern pine beetles attack damaged or stressed trees, but in years with high beetle populations, healthy trees are quickly infested and killed. Adults are about ¼ inch (0.6 cm) in length. Adults make S-shaped galleries in the tree and can fly up to two miles. Several populations can occur per year.

Pine sawflies (*Neodiprion* spp.)

Eleven species of sawflies exist in the Southeast, attacking most species of pines. Black-headed (*N. excitans*) and red-headed (*N. lecontei*) sawflies are commonly seen in south Georgia.

Pine sawfly larvae

Sawfly adults are wasps that deposit eggs in small slits in the needles of pine trees. The larvae damage trees by defoliating them and can be identified by head and body color as well as by patterns of stripes or spots on the body. Sawflies are often found in colonies of up to 100 or more per branch. Pine sawflies are easy to control with insecticidal products available to homeowners.

Pine tip moth (*Ryacionia frustrana*)

> The most widely distributed species among pine tip moths, the Nantucket pine tip moth causes damage to most two- and three-needled pines under a height of 15 feet (4.6 m). Five-needled pines appear to be resistant to this pest. Loblolly and shortleaf pines are its preferred hosts.

Adult pine tip moths emerge in early spring, mate, and lay eggs on new pine buds and shoots. Larvae hatch and begin to feed on the shoots. As they feed, they spin a protective web that gradually becomes covered with pitch. Webbing among the shoot tips is a sign of tip moth infestation. The larvae pupate inside hollowed-out shoot tips, which then die back. Dead shoot tips can be

Early damage from pine tip moths

found in early May in south Georgia. Three to four insecticidal sprays per year are recommended for Christmas tree farms in Georgia to control this pest. On small trees the damaged shoots can be pruned out and thrown away.

Spider mites—Spruce spider mite (*Oligonychus ununguis*)

> Spider mites attack many conifer species. They are found most often on *Abies, Juniperus, Picea, Pinus, Thuja,* and *Tsuga*.

Related to spiders, spider mites are not true insects. They are cool-season pests that feed on conifer needles by sucking the juice out of plant cells. Peak feeding occurs in the late spring and fall. While feeding generally occurs at first on older needles and on the interior foliage, the mites soon move to newer growth. Under ideal conditions a generation can be completed in two to three weeks. Heavy infestations can result in bronzing of the foliage, followed by needle drop. Webbing can be seen on the foliage when pest densities are very high. Spruce spider mites are most active when daytime temperatures are in the 60s and 70s F (15–25°C), with adults becoming inactive when temperatures regularly remain in the mid-80s (28–30°C). Treat trees with summer oil or miticides as needed for

Spider mite damage on *Juniperus chinensis*

control. Insecticidal oils are not recommended for "blue" conifers, as they will dissolve the waxy cuticle that makes the plant blue, turning a blue spruce green!

Woolly adelgid—(*Adelges* spp.)

> The hemlock woolly adelgid (*A. tsugae*) attacks hemlocks (*Tsuga* spp.) while the balsam woolly adelgid (*A. piceae*) attacks firs (*Abies* spp.).

Small aphid-like insects with piercing mouthparts, many adelgids secrete from their pores a white fluffy or waxy coating, which shows up as a crust in infested trees. The hemlock woolly adelgid survives only on *Tsuga* spp. and was first reported in North Carolina in 1995. It is killing native hemlocks throughout the eastern United States. Research at the U.S. National Arboretum has shown that

Hemlock woolly adelgid

T. chinensis has resistance to this pest; unfortunately this species will not cross with our native *T. canadensis*. Hemlocks usually die within four to ten years of infestation. The balsam woolly adelgid is destroying Fraser fir forests (*Abies fraseri*) in the Appalachian mountain range. Systemic insecticides containing imidacloprid show promise for treating individual trees against both pests.

4

Disease Problems

Why do conifers die? There are many answers to this question. Sometimes it is because we plant them too deeply or prepare the planting site poorly. Improper care can also kill a conifer. Overwatering and overfertilization can induce root rot problems. Environmental stressors such as drought, freezing temperatures, or high night temperatures can damage plants. Plant diseases can also be the culprit.

All the conifer diseases covered here are caused by fungi. For a fungal disease to be successful, several conditions must be met. Fungal diseases often occur on stressed or damaged plants, but first, a pathogen capable of causing a disease must be present. Second, the environment must be right (high humidity, poor air circulation, wet foliage). Finally, a susceptible host must be present. The descriptions below identify common fungal diseases of nursery and landscape plants and make basic recommendations for disease control.

Canker—Bot canker (*Botryosphaeria dothidea*)

Affects *Cupressus ×leylandii*, *Cupressus*, and *Thuja*.

An opportunistic fungal pathogen that attacks stressed or damaged trees, *Botryosphaeria dothidea* infects a limited number of branches where damage, such as a pruning wound, has occurred. Individual branches turn brown to rust color, and a deep canker forms at the site of infection. With Bot canker, needles usually remain attached to an infected branch even when a hand is run along its length. Once Bot canker has occurred, pruning is the best way to deal with it. Individual infected branches can be removed by making pruning cuts at least 9 inches below the canker. (Be sure to discard or destroy infected branches.) The best times to prune are winter and summer, when the disease organism is inactive. Plant pathogens can be spread by pruning tools, so do not cut into active

Bot canker on
Leyland cypress

cankers when pruning. Be sure to clean pruning tools with isopropyl alcohol or a mild bleach solution between uses (or better, between cuts) in order to avoid spreading this, or any, fungus. Fungicides are not effective for controlling Bot canker. Keeping plants healthy and stress free is the best defense.

Canker—Seiridium canker (*Seiridium* spp.)

Affects most *Cupressus* spp., particularly Leyland cypress.

Seiridium canker symptoms are similar to those of Bot canker. Like Bot canker, Seiridium canker tends to infect numerous branches, yellowing or browning

Seridium canker
on *Cupressus*

the foliage and often causing damage to a significant portion of the tree. Unlike Bot cankers, Seiridium cankers are shallow and readily ooze sap. Also, when brushed, the needles easily fall from Seiridium-infected branches. Control measures are the same as those for Bot canker. While heavy fertilization and severe pruning of established trees should be avoided, maintaining adequate soil fertility and keeping trees well irrigated during times of drought will help reduce damage from canker organisms.

Cedar apple rust (*Gymnosporangium juniper-virginianae*)

> Affects *Juniperus virginiana*. Alternate hosts are apple, hawthorn, and pear.

Cedar apple rust becomes apparent when immature, green, first-year galls known as "cedar apples" develop on red cedars. During the second year, the

Cedar apple rust on *Juniperus virginiana*

galls turn dark brown. In the spring, the second-year galls give rise to yellow-orange fingerlike projections known as teliohorns that release spores during rainy weather. The wind-borne spores then infect the alternate hosts to complete the disease cycle. Cedar apple rust can be controlled by both mechanical and chemical means. Infected or deformed red cedar branches should be removed and discarded or destroyed. Fungicides can be applied if necessary. Immunox® fungicide is effective and available to homeowners for treatment of ornamental crabapples. The best control method is to remove nearby alternate hosts.

Cercospora needle blight (*Passalora sequoiae*)

> Affects *Cryptomeria, Cupressus* spp. (Arizona cypress and Leyland cypress), *Juniperus virginiana,* and *Platycladus.* Monterey cypress (*Cupressus macrocarpa*) should not be grown in the South because of its susceptibility to this disease.

Cercospora needle blight is a common pest of Leyland cypress in Christmas tree farms and in hedgerows that receive regular sprinkler irrigation into the foliage. Needle browning begins in the interior, basal part of the plant and spreads outward. As the disease progresses, all needles except for current

Cercospora needle blight on Leyland cypress

growth die out. In Georgia, the fungus sporulates from late May through Thanksgiving. For disease control in commercial settings, fungicidal sprays are required every 10–14 days. In both commercial and landscape situations, spray must be applied with significant force to reach and successfully treat the interior of the tree. Limiting overhead irrigation and maintaining good air circulation among trees can also help inhibit the spread of the disease.

Eastern gall rust (*Cronartium quercuum*)

Affects various species of *Pinus*, the alternate host being oaks (*Quercus*).

This disease is characterized by spherical galls on the stems of pine trees. Galls increase in size each year and, in spring, bright yellow-orange spores form on the gall surface. Witches' brooms (a deformity characterized by a dense mass of shoots that grows from a single point on a branch) are often seen in conjunction with the galls. Infected branches should be pruned out of ornamental pines in the landscape and discarded or destroyed. If required, fungicides can be used in nursery settings.

Fusiform rust (*Cronartium quercuum* f. sp. *fusiforme*)

>   Affects primarily *Pinus taeda* and *P. elliottii*, though other species
>   of southern pines can be infected. Oaks are the alternate host.

Fusiform rust is the Number One disease of pines in the Southeast. Infection can occur both in seedlings and in mature trees, with mortality especially

Damage from fusiform rust canker on *Pinus elliottii*

pronounced in trees less than nine years old. Galls on young trees are often spindle shaped (hence "fusiform"—swollen in the middle and tapered on each end), accompanied in the spring by the appearance of bright yellow-orange spores. On older trees, galls appear as large sunken cankers on one or more sides of the tree trunk. Limbs, branches, and stems often break at the site of the gall or canker. Registered fungicides can be used to control the disease in seedling nurseries. In both commercial and landscape situations, use of genetically resistant trees is strongly recommended. Because both eastern gall rust and fusiform rust spread by wind-borne spores from oaks to pines, it may be useful to avoid planting in the vicinity of heavy oak populations.

Phomopsis blight (*Phomopsis juniperovora*)

> Primarily affects *Cupressus ×leylandii* and *Juniperus* spp., though it is sometimes seen on *Cupressus arizonica* and *C. sempervirens*.

Phomopsis tip blight is a warm weather disease of junipers and cypresses. Infection often strikes lower foliage first, starting at the shoot tips and then moving into the canopy. (This is the reverse pattern of infection from that exhibited by Cercospora needle blight.) Overall, the best way to manage Phomopsis blight is to plant disease-resistant juniper cultivars. In the landscape, plant junipers where there is good drainage, plenty of sunlight, and good air

Phomopsis blight on 'Gold Rider' Leyland cypress

circulation. In nursery production settings, regular application of fungicidal sprays every 10–14 days may be necessary, just as it is for controlling Cercospora needle blight. Also, because 'Nick's Compact' and 'Old Gold' junipers are highly susceptible to tip blight, they should be avoided in commercial situations.

Phytophthora root rot (*Phytophthora* spp.)

> Affects *Abies, Araucaria, Cedrus, Cryptomeria, Juniperus, Picea, Pinus, Taxus, Thuja,* and *Wollemia.*

A soilborne disease, Phytophthora root rot can be very damaging to container- and field-grown conifers. The roots of diseased plants are often reddish brown

Phytophthora root rot on *Cryptomeria*

in color, not healthy and white. Foliar symptoms often start with yellowing, followed by complete plant dieback because of sparse, damaged roots and stem girdling by the fungus. Early signs of Phytophthora can be confused with nutrient disorders or drought stress. Phytophthora is most active where substrates and soils are warm and overly moist. In the landscape, grow plants in well-drained areas with good air circulation. In commercial nurseries, avoid overwatering and heavy fertilization, which often induce the disease. Proper production practices, planting of disease-resistant selections, and use of chemical fungicides can all be used to manage root rot. *Abies firma*, Momi fir from Japan, is the most root rot–resistant species of fir and is used as an understock for grafting other species.

Pitch canker (*Fusarium moniliforme* var. *subglutinans*)

> Affects most native species, but is most common on slash pine
> (*Pinus elliottii*).

Pitch canker usually infects trees older than 10 years but can infect them at any age. The windborne fungus typically enters trees at damage or insect feeding sites. The disease is usually first signaled by the appearance of red or flagging terminal shoots that develop in the fall and persist through the following spring. Infected shoots also often have depressed cankers that exude abundant pine pitch. Damaged foliage often remains on the tree for quite some time, because dead shoots get matted in the pitch. On larger stems the disease appears as large, resinous cankers deeply soaked with pitch. At present, there are few proven methods for controlling pitch canker. New pine plantations should not be established near infected stands. In commercial and landscape situations, disease-resistant seedlings should be used whenever available, and care should be taken to avoid or minimize tree damage.

Redfire (*Phyllosticta* spp.)

> Affects *Cryptomeria*.

Redfire is most prevalent on plants with juvenile foliage or on container-grown plants that receive overhead irrigation. John has lost several compact forms to this disease in south Georgia. Affected leaves and stems turn a reddish rust

Redfire disease on *Cryptomeria japonica* 'Ikari'

color as they die. The use of disease-resistant cultivars is, so far, the best control method.

Always consult your local Cooperative Extension Service or state forestry commission for pesticide recommendations and appropriate control measures.

5

Conifers and Ginkgo and Their Cultivars

Our focus is on gardenworthy conifers and selected cultivars that have been evaluated and deemed suitable for the South. This book is not intended to be a compendium of all the cultivars within each genus. Moreover, we have purposely omitted several lesser-known species that are not commercially available because of their rarity. In some instances we mention new introductions that may require a little Internet research to locate. Because of their small numbers and unique characteristics, these might be considered "collectors' plants." Our specific aim is to offer a view of some of the better selections that is more comprehensive than the short descriptions that typically appear in nursery catalogs. Thus, we enumerate plant attributes, size at maturity, and cultural requirements, as these can differ depending on the cultivar. A prime example is *Picea orientalis*, which should be grown in full sun while the yellow cultivar 'Skylands' prefers afternoon shade.

Throughout this chapter we make reference to the term "witch's broom." By definition, witch's brooms are tightly congested formations of twigs and foliage that can occur on conifers. They are often, but not always, caused by insects or other biological pests, or they may develop as the result of a genetic mutation. When cuttings are taken from these genetic abnormalities, new cultivars can be propagated. The new plant will retain the characteristics of the original mutated plant.

Abies Fir

The firs are members of the pine family and consist of some 50 species, subspecies, and varieties. Since most firs are native to mountainous (montane) and subalpine regions, they do not prosper in locations where the summers are long and nighttime temperatures warm. Most firs are happiest in regions where temperatures are cooler than those experienced in most of the South. Depending on where one gardens, several firs have proven adaptable. In areas such as north Georgia, north Alabama, western North Carolina, eastern Tennessee, and southwest Virginia—where elevations can exceed 1000 feet (305 m) and the nights are cooler—the list is larger. In all areas covered in this book, *Abies firma* (Japanese momi fir) has demonstrated that it is at home and grows quite well.

Below we discuss several firs that have shown various levels of tolerance to southeastern climates. If you are is willing to experiment and can provide the right growing conditions, you may be rewarded with a beautiful tree. With the noted exception of *A. firma*, we have found that in the South, firs prefer some afternoon shade and soils that are not too acidic (Tom adds limestone to the soil at the time of planting) or that are poorly drained. One collector in north Georgia has had great success over a 15-year period with *A. fraseri* (Fraser fir), *A. balsamea*

var. *phanerolepis* (Canaan fir), *A. homolepis* (Nikko fir), and *A. nordmanniana* (Caucasian fir). All are planted on north facing slopes at an average elevation of 2100 feet (640 m). Despite having no supplemental water for 15 years, all have grown large and look healthy.

Abies firma Momi Fir

Commonly referred to as momi fir, this species is native to central and southern Japan and grows naturally at lower altitudes than most firs—which might partially explain its wide adaptability. It is the largest of all Japanese firs, reaching heights up to 150 feet (46 m). In the southern United States it reaches heights of around 40 feet with widths of around 10 feet (12 × 3 m). It is adaptable throughout the Southeast, and nice specimens can be seen at the Atlanta Botanical Garden, the J. C. Raulston Arboretum in Raleigh, North Carolina, and the Cox Arboretum in Canton, Georgia. All are in

Abies firma

excess of 20 feet (6 m). A nice specimen grew at the State Botanical Garden of Georgia, reaching a height of about 30 feet (9 m) before being removed from under a power line.

While it will take some dry conditions, the plant is happiest with supplemental watering during the summer months. In its native habitat, the summers are wet. The only known drawback is its tendency to initiate bud break early in the spring; consequently, new growth may be burned by late spring frosts. While this can produce a briefly unsightly appearance until a new flush of growth replaces the old, this damage does not seem to affect the overall health of the plant.

Over the past several years, a few growers have begun to realize the commercial potential of *A. firma* as the root stock on which to graft highly ornamental cultivars that would not normally grow in the South. Most of these are custom grafted in small numbers; with some searching, they can be found in local nurseries that specialize in conifers. As a group, they are some of the most desireable plants we have found in the plant world. The variations are seemingly endless, and we could write an entire book on the numerous beauties.

It is almost a certainty that any fir purchased via mail order or from a large chain nursery will not be grafted onto *A. firma*. No matter how tempting it may be to purchase from such outlets, be careful. Don't be too intimidated to ask questions. If the seller can't identify the rootstock, we recommend you find a seller that can.

It may be useful to know that J. C. Raulston was the first to promote this species and was experimenting with the late Jean Iseli (Iseli Nursery, Boring, Oregon) to use *A. firma* as the understock for firs that otherwise could not live in the South. The Atlanta Botanical Garden has a beautiful *Abies koreana* 'Silberlocke' that is reported to be on *A. firma* rootstock. In trials where we believed that other species such as *A. pinsapo* (Spanish fir) might work in the South, the plants we received were all grafts on either *A. balsamea* or *A. fraseri,* and neither of these understocks is suitable for most areas. As more growers begin to recognize the potential demand for firs grafted onto *A. firma*, the South will one day be able to enjoy a wider variety of these beautiful plants.

Abies homolepis Nikko Fir

Like *Abies firma*, *A. homolepis*, commonly referred to as the Nikko fir, is native to central and southern Japan. In the altitude continuum, it grows at somewhat higher elevations, from as low as 2300 feet (700 m) to as high as 7000 feet (2150 m). In the cooler portions of the South, from north Georgia and north Alabama through Chattanooga, Tennessee, east into Asheville, North Carolina, and above into Louisville, Kentucky, and across to Richmond, Virginia, *A. homolepis* may be a viable landscape plant. In Canton, Georgia, Tom has a plant that has shown good vigor for more than five years. This is a species that deserves more trials to determine its southern adaptability. At maturity this tree can reach a height of 50 feet with a spread of 30 feet (15 × 9 m).

Abies koreana Korean Fir

A beautiful tree native to the summits of South Korea's highest peaks, Korean fir is rarely seen growing on its own roots in the southeastern United States. The species has produced some of the most breathtaking cultivars of any conifer, and all of these are grafted. Korean fir is notable for its attractive dark green foliage, featuring bright silvery undersides and purple, upright cones. Its needles grow like a bottlebrush nearly all around the shoot. John has vivid memories of seeing this species growing in the wild on Mt. Hallasan, Cheju-do Island, South Korea, in 1998. Tom has had good success with this species for more than five years, but growth has been very slow. The species performs best when grown in raised beds with excellent drainage in Zones 6a–7a.

Abies koreana 'Kohout's Icebreaker'

Known mostly in the United States as Icebreaker, this highly rated selection was found by the famous German plantsman, Mr. Joerg Kohout. It was derived from a witch's broom on an *A. koreana* 'Silberlocke' in Joerg's display garden.

Abies koreana 'Kohout's Icebreaker' (photo by Joerg Kohout)

New plants sometimes have a way of surprising us, and this hitherto unnoticed broom brushed against his leg as he was walking among his display plants. Like the parent, it has needles that curl upward to reveal silvery white undersides. Its expected final size is 3 feet × 3 feet (0.9 m). When grafted onto *A. firma*, this is a great addition to a mix of smaller conifers and is definitely a conversation piece. As we go to press, this cultivar is one of the most sought-after plants by those in the know and is a plant destined for greatness.

Abies koreana 'Silberlocke'

This is still the gold standard for Korean fir selections and is highly sought by all who see it. As with 'Kohout's Icebreaker', its needles are curved upward, revealing their contrasting bright silvery undersides. A show stopper in the garden, this well-known plant was discovered in 1986 in Germany by plantsman Gunter Horstmann, whose nursery specialized in conifers. All who see it in Tom's arboretum stop to marvel at its unique appearance. This upright selection is slow growing and can be expected to reach a height of 10 feet, with a width of 6 feet (3 × 1.8 m).

Abies nordmanniana Nordmann or Caucasian Fir

A narrower species than *A. homolepis*, Nordmann fir grows at a similar altitude. Occasionally, old specimens are seen growing in upper portions of the South (mostly Zone 6), and where one can find a plant growing on its own roots, the species may be adaptable at least as far south as Zone 7b. It is native to the mountains of Turkey, Georgia, the Russian Caucasus, and northern parts of Armenia. There are two subspecies, subsp. *nordmanniana* and subsp. *equi-trojani* (syn. *bornmuelleriana*), with the latter being more glabrous. Neither should be treated as particularly drought tolerant. Nordmann fir is frequently grown as a Christmas tree in the cooler sections of the United States. It casts deep shade and should reach a height of 50 feet with a width of 20 feet (15 × 6 m). When compared with other firs in the South, one of the distinguishing characteristics of Nordmann fir is that all its needles point forward, with those on top covering the shoot. Nice specimens grow at Yew Dell Gardens in Kentucky and at the State Arboretum of Georgia in Braselton. Two of the best trees are located at Don Shadow's nursery in Winchester, Tennessee.

Abies nordmanniana 'Golden Spreader'

Simply put, this is one of the great dwarf conifers for year-around color and texture. 'Golden Spreader' meets all the qualifications of what is desirable in

a dwarf conifer: it is low growing with a spreading habit, has golden yellow color (yes, even in the South) and interesting foliage. That said, one must be careful when purchasing this cultivar as it will always be grafted, and unless specifically listed as being on *A. firma* rootstock, it will not be a long-lived plant in the South. 'Golden Spreader' should be obtained only from the number of specialty nurseries in the South that carries it custom grafted. The tree is 3 feet high × 5 feet wide (0.9 × 1.5 m) at maturity—not a fast grower. It is best sited where there is afternoon shade to avoid leaf burn.

*Abies
nordmanniana*

Araucaria

All species of Araucaria are native to the Southern Hemisphere. They have a wide disjunctive population range, all the way from New Guinea, Australia, New Zealand, Norfolk Island, and New Caledonia to southern Brazil and Chile. One of the species, the famous Norfolk Island pine (*A. heterophylla*) is a popular indoor plant in the South. Owing to their origins, most Araucaria are subtropical to tropical and therefore not mentioned in this book. Only three species are discussed as having any landscape potential. If you consider yourself a collector or are looking for something totally unique in the landscape, the Araucarias fit that niche—no other plant resembles them.

Araucaria angustifolia Parana Pine

Although not a true pine, this species is referred to by the common name parana pine. It is native to southern Brazil and the northeast region of Argentina. Like a number of plants that originate from this region, the parana pine has proved to be hardier than one would imagine. There is a huge tree growing at the Atlanta Botanical Garden in Georgia, in a somewhat protected area just outside the entrance to the conservatory. It often elicits heart palpitations in visitors when they first see it. On a recent visit to Aiken, South Carolina, Tom was shown a stunning specimen growing at a home site by Bob McCartney, owner of Woodlanders Nursery. *A. angustifolia* is also growing well at Armstrong College in Savannah, Georgia, in Tifton, Georgia, and at the Steven F. Austin State University Arboretum in eastern Texas. Tom has successfully grown this species for four years at his arboretum, where it has survived temperatures as low as 12°F (-11°C).

Araucaria angustifolia

Araucaria araucana Monkey Puzzle Tree

For those in the South who have tried to grow the monkey puzzle tree, no plant has proven more frustrating. Originating in Chile and Argentina, where it can attain heights of 100 feet (30 m), this is perhaps the most unique looking of all conifers. In youth, the plant is remarkable for its nearly perfect symmetry. Its long spidery branches grow right to the ground, and its overlapping leaves are sharp pointed. As the tree matures, it sheds its lower branches. Its common name is derived from the idea that it would puzzle a monkey to climb the tree.

It appears that the main obstacle to growing the monkey puzzle in the South is not so much warm temperatures as the fact that the confluence of soil conditions, temperature, and moisture encourages root rot. The plant is hardy at least in Zone 7 if not in colder zones. Absolutely breathtaking specimens are seen growing in places such as Berkeley, California (the UC–Berkeley Botanical Garden), Portland, Oregon, the United Kingdom, and New Zealand. A plant survived for more than five years at the Unique Plant nursery in Chapel Hill, North Carolina, until it was blown over in a storm. It was situated on a berm created by adding topsoil and PermaTill (expanded slate aggregates) to facilitate better drainage. The best specimen we have seen is located in a private collection in Aiken, South Carolina. We discussed the issue with noted conifer expert Ron Determann of the Atlanta Botanical Garden, and he believes the plant's success is a factor of root compatibility and, that unless absolutely perfect growing conditions are provided, the plant will be short lived. He believes the plant is best grafted onto *A. angustifolia*. In conclusion, if you must have this plant, our best advice is to site it on a slope in full sun, in well-drained but adequately moist soil. Be careful not to overwater, and then keep your fingers crossed.

Araucaria bidwillii Bunya Pine

The bunya pine is native to Australia and may be suitable in Zones 8a through 9. The species does have landscape potential in warmer portions of the South and should be grown in more trials. The foliage shows winter damage when temperatures dip into the upper teens for several hours, but plants quickly recover in the spring. The species is performing well in John's trials in Tifton.

Calocedrus Incense-cedar

This genus comprises four species, one from the west coast of North America (California and Oregon) and three from Southeast Asia. It is monoecious, with inconspicuous yellow male cones and yellowish green female cones. Both are formed on different branches of the same tree. All species have scalelike foliage on flattened sprays, with the upper side green and the underside having visible stomatal markings, the most vivid occurring in *C. macrolepis*.

They are usually propagated from seed that requires a period of cold stratification; incense-cedar is difficult, but not impossible, to propagate from cuttings. Named cultivars are often grafted onto seedlings of this species or onto seedlings of the closely related northern white-cedar (*Thuja occidentalis*). They require well-drained soil in full sun or partial shade. Once established, all are fairly drought tolerant.

Calocedrus decurrens

Calocedrus decurrens California Incense-cedar

The California incense-cedar is found south from Oregon along the western slopes of the Cascade and Sierra Nevada ranges into southern California. The hyphenated common name signifies that this is not a true cedar. All parts of the plant are strongly aromatic.

Like a number of trees such as the western red-cedar (*Thuja plicata*) and the coast redwood (*Sequoia sempervirens*), whose origins are the coastal portions of the Pacific Northwest, incense-cedar is a surprise in terms of adaptability to the South. Here in the South, trees are slow growing but long-lived; even under the best of conditions, incense-cedar is a slow-growing tree. Two trees were documented as being planted before the Civil War in Marietta, Georgia. Sadly, we have learned that one finally died in 2008. It had been awarded the "largest in the state" designation. These trees exhibited the red, fibrous, deeply furrowed bark characteristic of this species. There is also a handsome specimen at Maymont estate gardens in Richmond, Virginia, that is reportedly more than 100 years old. While not common, incense-cedars are found thriving as one drives through the South. Yet another example of their longevity in the South are two trees at the old fairgrounds (now rose garden and theater) in Raleigh, North Carolina. These are documented as being more than 75 years old. Nice specimens also grow in the Georgia towns of Athens, Augusta, Blairsville, and Tennille. A dwarfish form was recently observed at the Lovett Pinetum in Lufkin, Texas, that has survived more than 10 years.

At maturity, the tree grows to around 60 feet (18 m) tall, forming a narrow cone shape 8–12 feet wide (2.4–3.7 m). Its ¼–½-inch (0.6–1.3 cm) dark green leaves form dense flattened fanlike vertical sprays. All really old incense-cedars observed seem to reach a certain size and then apparently almost stop growing. In Zone 7, the species seems to do quite well once it becomes established but requires a generous amount of water the first several years.

While its leaves are somewhat similar to those of certain *Chamaecyparis* and *Thuja* species, the flattened vertical form of the foliage makes it somewhat easy to identify. At one time *Juniperus virginiana* (eastern red-cedar) was the principal source of wood used in the manufacture of pencils in the United States. Now the principal source is incense-cedar. This species grows best in Zones 6–7b.

Calocedrus decurrens 'Aureovariegata'

This cultivar has highly irregular, variegated foliage, with mottled golden yellow blotches throughout what otherwise is the ordinary green of the species. The mottling is quite irregular, with some branches being almost all yellow and others much less so or completely green. The contrast between the yellow and dark green is more curious than ornamental, and we find the plant difficult to incorporate into the landscape. Expect this cultivar to reach 30 feet (9 m) at maturity.

Calocedrus decurrens 'Berrima Gold'

This cultivar is a plant that nearly everyone who sees it, in a catalog or in the landscape, wants to own. It is light gold to yellowish green in spring and summer, turning a pleasing golden orange in fall and winter. As is the case with some other rare beauties, this cultivar is not one that can simply be purchased and then placed in the ground. For starters, it requires partial shade to prevent its suffering sun scorch; in placing it in the shade, however, one sacrifices some of the bright gold color. It is also slow to establish a good root system. For readers living in the cooler portions of the South, when this plant is properly sited, it is exquisite and sure to brighten the landscape throughout the seasons. Expect a growth rate of approximately 6 inches (15 cm) per year after it has been in the ground for several years. As this is a smaller selection, expect a final size about 8 feet tall and 4 feet wide (2.4 × 1.2 m). Not recommended south of Zone 7b.

Calocedrus decurrens 'Maupin Glow'

While somewhat similar in appearance to 'Berrima Gold', 'Maupin Glow' is not nearly as bright and will accommodate more sun. Its leaves in the upper portions of the tree are bright yellow while the lower ones are more greenish. Also, like 'Berrima Gold', the plant is slow to establish and is best restricted to cooler portions of the South. This fine selection was discovered by Greg Rigby near Maupin, Oregon, and should mature at a height of about 8 feet with a width of 4 feet (2.4 × 1.2 m).

Calocedrus decurrens 'Pioneer Sentry'

This narrow, upright bright green form was found growing at Portland Cemetery in Oregon. At maturity, expect a height of around 40 feet with a width of

5 feet (12.2 × 1.5 m). This plant appears to be well worth searching out if one is seeking an unusual evergreen vertical accent. At least one nursery in the South, Hawksridge Farms of Hickory, North Carolina, lists this cultivar in its catalog.

Calocedrus formosana

Calocedrus formosana
Taiwan Incense-cedar

The Taiwan incense-cedar is endemic to northern and central Taiwan. It is most closely allied with *Calocedrus macrolepis* but differs in having more slender branchlets. In the summer months the foliage is a bright green, but as the months get colder, the foliage turns an unattractive brown. A plant growing at Cox Arboretum has survived three winters with temperatures as low as 12 degrees (-11°C) with no apparent damage. We project that the plants will grow no taller than 40 feet tall (12.2 m) in the South. This plant has performed very well at several sites in Zone 8a–8b in southern Georgia and is also growing well in eastern Texas, where great specimens can be seen at the Lovett Pinetum and Mast Arboretum at Stephen F. Austin University.

Cones on *Calocedrus formosana*

Calocedrus macrolepis Chinese Incense-cedar

The Chinese incense-cedar is endemic to southwestern China, Vietnam, and eastern Myanmar (formerly Burma). It differs from its Taiwanese counterpart by having much wider branchlets and retaining its lustrous green color throughout the winter. We suspect that provenance plays a deciding role in the zone hardiness of this species. There are at least two distinct forms we have observed. One from Iseli Nursery has wide flat sprays that are a bright green, and the plant has a broad growth habit. The other, from Camellia Forest in Wake Forest, North Carolina, is more upright, and the foliage is a dull green and not as wide. The Atlanta Botanical Garden has propagated a number of plants from seed, and some have an interesting bluish cast when young. Those we have grown in trials lost this hue with age. While pictures from China show the plants to be exceptionally upright in form, many grown in the South are more oval in appearance. *C. macrolepis* should perform well in Zone 8 but is, at best, only marginally hardy in Zone 7.

A fourth species, *C. rupestris*, was discovered in 2004 in north central Vietnam. It was growing on karstic mountains and is reportedly the most recently discovered conifer in the world. While this species has grown well in John's trials for three years and Tom is also growing it in a sheltered location, the plant is not in the trade, so we have elected not to cover it in any detail.

Calocedrus macrolepis

Cathaya argyrophylla

Native to southern China, this monotypic genus is found growing in the provinces of Guangzi, Guizhou, Hunan, and southeast Sichuan. It is found on steep, narrow mountain slopes on shallow limestone soils.

For those rare occasions when it can be located, *Cathaya* is worth searching out, even though it can be prohibitively expensive. This is a plant for the serious collector or for botanical institutions that have interest in the preservation and display of rare plants. It is considered by some to be the holy grail of conifers. Adding to its allure is the fact that *Cathaya* is an ancient plant that was living 10–30 million years ago, as documented in fossil remains found in Europe. Further owing and contributing to its rarity, the Chinese allow no material to be collected from their native trees. Nonetheless, several years ago Iseli Nursery in Boring, Oregon, apparently received some seed from a Chinese source and

Cathaya argyrophylla

raised a number of plants. These were then distributed to their top customers. Several made their way to the South, where the mortality rate has been high. Attesting to its adaptability when afforded the right conditions, the most magnificent specimen in the South (and perhaps in the United States) is growing at Plants Delight Nursery in Raleigh, North Carolina. Another beautiful specimen is growing in a large container at Bannister Creek Nursery in Duluth, Georgia.

As has been documented, the plant is tricky to grow. The first clue to successfully growing this plant would seem to run contrary to its native adaptation to limestone soils, because it prefers acid soil and requires good drainage. Where it grows in China, the soil is very shallow and the area experiences heavy summer rains. This high rainfall serves to leach certain minerals from the soil, thereby rendering it acidic. For optimal growth, the addition of calcium is beneficial, best done by incorporating gypsum into the backfill soil at the time of initial planting.

Current evaluation of grafting Cathaya onto *Pinus elliottii* (slash pine) and *Keteleeria davidiana* is under way. We have also heard that an individual in the Northeast has been grafting Cathaya onto *Pseudotsuga menziesii*. While early results are encouraging, it will be a number of years before a determination of rootstock suitability can be offered.

Cedrus Cedar

As a group, the true cedars are some of the most graceful plants in the southern landscape. Depending on the taxonomist, the number of recognized species is between two and four, with the rest treated as subspecies. We have elected to highlight the three species that are the most regularly encountered as well as the most commercially available. All species grow into large trees, but there are numerous cultivars that remain small. It is not uncommon to drive around the region and find many old trees, particularly *C. deodara*, that have stood the test of time.

All true cedars are native to northern Africa, Asia Minor, and the Himalayas. They are the only evergreen conifers in which the leaves on second-year and older shoots are borne in dense whorls on short spur-shoots. Like firs (*Abies*), their cones are erect and break apart on the tree but spend two years ripening. What we in the South commonly refer to as cedars are actually one of the following: *Juniperus virginiana* (eastern red-cedar), *Chamaecyparis thyoides* (Atlantic white-cedar), *Calocedrus decurrens* (incense-cedar), or *Thuja plicata* (western red-cedar)—technically, none is a true cedar.

If one is planting the straight species, a place of prominence is needed to adequately display its elegance and grandeur. Since myriad cultivars are available in different sizes, shapes, and colors, they lend themselves well to any number of mixed plantings. Once established, all seem to prosper as long as the soil is well drained. They will tolerate moderate shade but fail to achieve peak performance. Once established, all are fairly drought tolerant.

In cultivation, it is not always easy to discern the three species, and sometimes there are intermediate characteristics, particularly on older specimens. Generally speaking, the leaves on *C. deodara* are the longest and on *C. libani*, the shortest. This trait is not always reliable, however, as it is not uncommon to find considerable overlap. One mnemonic that aids in identification is as follows: (1) Atlas = ascending, (2) *deodara* = descending, and (3) Lebanon = level. This device is most often useful when comparing new branch tips. Our observations indicate that *C. atlantica* is less spreading than *C. libani* and the crown is more densely upright and pointed. Also, pollen cones of *C. atlantica* release their pollen in September, whereas pollen of *C. libani* is released in October.

Cedrus atlantica Atlas Cedar

This tree, commonly called the Atlas cedar, is native to the Atlas Mountains of Morocco and Algeria. Atlas cedar can form a large conical tree over a period of many years. It is slower growing in the South than other species. Experiments have shown that in areas where the soil is acidic, the species will benefit from a liberal application of lime at the time of planting. While this species adapts well to hotter and drier climates, it performs best in Zones 6 and 7 and is not recommended south of Zone 8a. While the tree can reach a height of 130 feet (40 m) in its native habitat, its most likely height in the South is 30 feet with a width of 20 feet (9 × 6 m). When compared with the other true cedars, *C. atlantica* is said to develop a more densely upright branching habit, a characteristic that varies from tree to tree. It is sometimes difficult to discern differences between it and *C. libani* and, in fact, some botanists treat it as a geographical subspecies. Several years ago, the American Conifer Society (ACS) held its national meeting in Knoxville, Tennessee, and one of the meeting sites was the Knoxville Botanical Garden, former home of the Howell Nursery going back more than 200 years. There were several large cedars planted in a field, and differing opinions were offered by the aficionados as to whether these were *C. atlantica* or *C. libani*. After much discussion, it was agreed that these were *C. libani*.

Cedrus atlantica 'Glauca Fastigiata'

In growth habit 'Glauca Fastigiata' stands out from other cultivars. The branching is more ascendant and, as it ages, it does not seem to take on the rounded pyramidal form commonly seen on other upright Atlantic cedars. Its color is a rich powder blue. This is a beautiful specimen with all the attributes for a smaller garden where a vertical accent with year-round color is desired. After 20 years, expect the tree to be 30 feet tall × 6 feet wide (9 × 1.8 m). This selection was introduced into cultivation in 1972.

Cedrus atlantica 'Glauca'

This is one of the two common cultivars most readily offered in garden centers. In nature, 'Glauca' is a naturally occurring form; some texts refer to it as var. *glauca*, as differentiated from the green form, called var. *atlantica*. Its habit is uniformly stiff with ascending branches, and over time it forms a large pyramidal tree. The year-round foliage is a striking gray blue, which is enhanced by a higher pH soil. Throughout most of the South, an application of dolomitic lime will facilitate growth and enhance the blue color. 'Glauca' is very slow growing for the first several years and will benefit from supplemental watering until it's established. After about two years all one needs to do is keep it mulched and then sit back and admire its beauty. Its size is the same as for the species.

Cedrus atlantica 'Glauca Pendula'

This is the other Atlas cedar most regularly found in garden centers. Along with its steely blue color, the most dramatic effect of this cultivar is its extremely pendulous growth habit. When properly staked, the plant can form a blue fountain of foliage that lends itself to a number of unique landscape applications. Since this cultivar is essentially prostrate in form, you get to be the artist in the way you train it. Many growers train it into a serpentine plant that never looks quite natural in the landscape and that, from our viewpoint, is difficult to site properly. Since conifers with steely blue color really stand out as a rule, a well-grown

Cedrus atlantica 'Glauca Pendula'

specimen will be curtain-like or resemble, as some would say, a "living water-fall." In this technique, the plant becomes broadly weeping, forming irregular and spreading mounds. Nice specimens grow at Duke Gardens and at Sandhills Community College in Pinehurst, North Carolina. This plant originated as a selection in the United States in 1900. A newer selection worthy of seeking out is *C. atlantica* 'Blue Cascade', which we rate as superior to 'Glauca Pendula' in form and intensity of blue foliage color.

Cedrus atlantica 'Sapphire Nymph'

This is one of the very few *Cedrus* cultivars to originate in the South. Well-known nurseryman Pat McCracken from Zebulon, North Carolina, introduced it. He relates that the parent tree is still alive but the witch's broom died years ago. The first graft of this plant is at Pat's garden in Tennessee and is now 1 foot tall × 6 feet wide (0.3 × 1.8 m). For some unexplained reason, 'Sapphire Nymph' is more widely available in Europe, where it is incorrectly listed as 'Saphir Nymph'. Several specialty nurseries in the United States also list it this way. Its color is bright blue (like the cultivar 'Glauca'). 'Sapphire Nymph' originated from a witch's broom found growing on a *C. atlantica* 'Glauca' at the University of Tennessee Agricultural campus in 1985.

Cedrus atlantica 'Silberspitz'

This is an upright and narrow form of the Atlas cedar that can be likened in growth rate to *C. deodara* 'Snowsprite'. In about 10 years' time, it forms a shapely,

Cedrus atlantica 'Sapphire Nymph'

conical tree, reaching approximately 12 feet (3.7 m). The silvery white new growth later turns more silvery blue. Several specimens growing at Just Add Water Rare Plant Nursery in Conyers, Georgia, are indeed beautiful plants. It should be considered among the top-tier conifers. 'Silberspitz' was introduced in 1992.

Cedrus deodara

This native of the western Himalayas is by far the most common of the true cedars in the South. Owing to its long-time popularity, many old estates feature this tree. Some stunning mature specimens can be found in the towns of Abbeville and Aiken, South Carolina, that must be at least 75 years old. Beautiful specimens can be seen throughout the South. Many trees in south Georgia are flat topped where their central leaders were killed by cold winters in 1983 and 1985. Most trees in Knoxville, Tennessee, were killed by -24°F (-31°C) weather in 1985. *C. deodara* fares better in the southern coastal plain if given regular fertilization. While *C. deodara* is the least hardy of the true cedars, it is perfectly adaptable throughout all regions of the South (Zones 6–9a). Given adequate moisture and full sun, it will grow relatively fast and can eventually attain a height of 50–60 feet (15–18 m) in the landscape. A review of a number of prominent nursery catalogs reveals a stunning array of cultivars. We counted 99. One has to wonder if there is really that much difference among them all. Here we list those that we have evaluated and know to be both distinctive and good performers.

Cones on *Cedrus deodara*

Cedrus deodara 'BBC'

Bracken's Best deodar cedar was selected by South Carolina nurseryman Ray Bracken for vigor, consistency, and pyramidal form. This majestic tree tops out at 60 feet tall, with a width of 30 feet (18 × 9 m). While this cultivar is on the blue side, if one is selecting for blue color, there are much better cultivars to choose from. That said, because this is a clonal selection, it lends itself well to situations where uniformity of matched plantings is desired. It is becoming more widely available as more southern growers are planting it.

Cedrus deodara 'Blue Snake'

This form, which originated in the Netherlands, can assume any number of habits. Depending on the form one seeks, 'Blue Snake' can be shaped as a compact mounding shrub with long, weeping, gray-blue needles or staked to lengthen vertically to a desired height. With the latter form, which we find more aesthetically pleasing, the plant can be trained to grow upright and then allowed to weep. Over time the lower branches creep along the ground in skirt-like fashion, further adding to its uniqueness. If trained to cascade over a waterfall, it makes a perfect complement to moving water, especially when water-loving plants such as Japanese iris are added as companion plants.

Cedrus deodara 'Bush's Electra'

This introduction from the late Richard Bush of Canby, Oregon, is widely considered one of the best in terms of intensity of blue color. Its form is also reliably conical, further adding to its beauty. Those who have grown it report that it is a slower-growing selection of deodar cedar. According to respected nurseryman Don Howse of Porterhouse Nursery in Sandy, Oregon, it seems to grow at about three-quarters the rate of the species. Over many years, one might anticipate a tree of full size. This is likely the same cultivar as 'Electra' and 'Electric Blue'. Nurserymen have shown a preference for this selection since it is so full and well branched. It also makes a fine specimen for containerized tree production.

Cedrus deodara 'Divinely Blue'

As a young plant, 'Divinely Blue' is similar to 'Feeling Blue', but as the plant matures, it begins to assume a mounding habit. It should be considered among the better blue forms, and its dense foliage is also an asset. It is not a fast grower (3–6 inches [7.5–15 cm] per year) and will remain well behaved. For space considerations, plan on a mature specimen being 6 feet tall × only 3 feet wide (1.8 × 0.9 m). It was named for Bill Devine, a retired propagator from Angelica Nursery in Maryland.

Cedrus deodara 'Feeling Blue'

This is a prostrate spreading form with striking blue needles. In 10 years it should get to be about 2 feet high and 6 feet wide (0.6 × 1.8 m). This cultivar is often grafted onto a standard or can be trained to form a powder blue ground cover. As the foliage is quite thick, the plant's use as ground cover is quite effective. According to various reports, on some occasions the plant can produce a leader, but this can easily be removed to maintain a prostrate habit. It was selected at H. C. Trimp and Sons Nursery of Boskoop, Netherlands, and introduced in 1987.

Cedrus deodara 'Gold Cascade'

This is a relatively new cultivar from Australia that holds its striking gold color better than any other *C. deodara* we have evaluated. A side-by-side comparison with similar dwarf forms shows this to be the best of the gold forms. It is a mounded compact grower with a distinctly pendulous habit. It should mature to around 5 feet high × 5 feet wide (1.5 m). Here in the heat of the South, the plant will lose some of its vibrant color as summer gets into full swing. As with 'Feeling Blue', this cultivar is often grafted onto a standard, which perhaps accentuates the best form, especially if the graft is made at about 1–2 feet (0.3–0.6 m).

Cedrus deodara 'Gold Cone'

A relatively new selection found in Wm. Goodard Nursery of Victoria, British Columbia, Canada, this golden-foliaged form has held up very well in south Georgia for several years. Based on growth rates, it should be a large tree typical of the species. The golden foliage blends well with blue conifers in the garden.

Cedrus deodara 'Patti Faye'

The 'Patti Faye' seedling, found in the nursery of Ralph Rushing in Mobile, Alabama, is named for his wife. This cultivar has the bluest foliage of any deodar cedar we have evaluated, and it displays excellent heat tolerance. A three-year-old plant now growing in Tifton, Georgia, looks great.

Cedrus deodara 'Gold Cone'

Cedrus deodara 'Prostrate Beauty'

Cedrus deodara 'Prostrate Beauty'

In our opinion, this is the best of the low-growing deodar cedars. While the literature says that this plant will eventually produce a central leader, we have yet to observe it. A specimen in Tom's arboretum is 2 feet high × 5 feet wide (0.6 × 1.5 m) after six years. This light green-blue form has numerous landscape applications, from use in rock gardens to mixed planting beds to conifer display gardens. 'Prostrate Beauty' is an introduction from Iseli Nursery.

Cedrus deodara 'Sanders Blue' Blue Velvet™

In north Georgia trials 'Sanders Blue' has proven the most reliable in terms of intensity and retention of blue color and should be a reliable performer in Zones 6 and 7. It is a graceful cedar that stands erect with pendulous form. It has long, brilliant blue needles on arching branches. This selection is especially beautiful in the spring when the new blue growth emerges. It rivals any Colorado blue spruce as a blue exclamation point for southern gardens. We anticipate it will grow to be around 25 feet high × 8 feet wide (7.6 × 2.4 m).

Cedrus deodara 'Snow Sprite'

While some literature treats this cultivar as a "mounding compact grower," we suspect this description is based on growth in other parts of the United States.

As seen in the South, 'Snow Sprite' grows fairly rapidly to a mature height of around 15 feet and a width of 6 feet (4.5 × 1.8 m). Its light color offers a cooling effect to the landscape throughout the year. As an added bonus, the tree will grow well in light shade, and the color is retained well in our heat. The new growth is ivory white. 'Snow Sprite' was introduced by Flora-Vista Gardens, Victoria, BC, in 1981.

Cedrus libani Cedar of Lebanon

Cedar of Lebanon is native to Lebanon and Syria. It is closely related to the Atlas and deodar cedars, and some Cedar of Lebanon specimens are difficult to distinguish from these relatives. As a general rule, *C. libani* has shorter needles than Atlas and deodar cedars and grows in a distinct horizontal plane. In youth it is pyramidal in habit, but as it matures the tree develops a flat-topped profile that is rigid in appearance. The needles are usually a dark green. The species will grow in a number of different soils, from sandy to heavy clay, as long as the soil is well drained. An added plus is that once established, it can tolerate considerable drought. *C. libani* grows quite well in the acid soil of the South and also prospers in neutral and alkaline soils; it should be sited in full sun. In the South, *C. libani* is a faster-growing species than *C. atlantica*. Nice specimens grow at the Knoxville Botanical Garden in Tennessee. It performs best in Zones 6–8a.

Cedrus libani

Cedrus libani 'Glauca Pendula'

There are at least two forms that carry this name. The first is a strongly weeping clone with branches falling almost directly against the trunk. To our knowledge, this type is not grown anywhere in the South but is known from other texts on conifers. The second form has long horizontal branches with a weeping habit at the ends and some branches that fall straight down. Neither clone is particularly glaucous. This is a specimen plant that should be afforded ample, uncrowded room to grow.

Cedrus libani 'Hedgehog'

We consider 'Hedgehog' a highly ornamental plant for any small garden or co-nifer collection and well worth seeking from specialty nurseries. It is blue gray in color and will slowly develop into a low, tight growing mound that will ma-ture at a height of around 1 foot with a width of 3 feet (0.3 × 0.9 m). 'Hedgehog' originated as a chance seedling at Cedar Lodge Nursery, New Plymouth, New Zealand.

Cedrus libani 'Pendula'

In form, this cultivar is very similar to *C. atlantica* 'Glauca Pendula' except with shorter needles and no hint of glaucous color. Also, since it does not tend to exhibit a horizontal branch structure, it will never assume the spread of *C. at-lantica* 'Glauca Pendula'. This cultivar has a certain architectural appeal if one is looking for a weeping cedar that will grow to around 8 feet tall × 5 feet wide (2.4 × 1.5 m). It has been in cultivation since 1850.

Cephalotaxus Plum Yew

The plum yews are among the true unsung heroes of the southern landscape. In fact, aside from their slower growth, the members of this genus have no negative qualities. While the trees seem happiest in a little shade, some forms have also performed well in full sun. Once established, they do not appear to be overly sensitive to stresses such as drought and heat, and they retain a uniform glossy dark green color throughout the year. Unlike *Taxus* (yew), plum yews are not fre-quently browsed by deer, and they are more tolerant of heat than yews. Because they mature to a wide range of growth forms, a selection exists for practically any situation, from mass plantings (where they might be a substitute for junipers) to showcasing as specimen plants. All plum yews are native to Asia, where they range from Japan and Korea in the north to central and southern China and Vietnam in the south. Their east-west distribution spans from the Himalayas and Myanmar to the island of Taiwan. In their native habitat, plum yews are forest understory plants that are happiest in a shade or semishade environment. *C. harringtonia* will grow in full sun in Zones 6–7, but *C. fortunei* should always receive some shade from hot afternoon sun. The *C. harringtonia* in John's former backyard (8b) receive summer sun from sunrise to 2:00 PM and turn yellow in the summer, returning to deep green as the sun gets lower in the sky during the fall and winter months. We have not witnessed this yellowing in full sun in Zones 6 and 7.

Once established, *Cephalotaxus* species compete well with the roots of large deciduous trees. Other worthy attributes include their adaptability to the heavy clay found in many areas of the South as well as their general lack of disease and insect problems. All species produce a plum and olive cone-like fruit that starts out olive green and ripens to purple brown. Plants are dioecious, which results in separate male and female clones. Most clones in the trade are males and therefore will not produce fruit.

As seen in the trade and in collections, there is confusion as to the proper nomenclature for some species. At one nursery, plants sold as *C. oliverii* were actually *C. harringtonia*. This confusion is further complicated by the fact that where different species are planted together, they frequently produce offspring that are an intermediate of the two parents.

In keeping with the intent of this book, we are limiting our discussion to two species, *C. fortunei* and *C. harringtonia*. For those wanting to expand the boundaries and willing to search a bit, both *C. oliverii* and *C. lanceolata* are worth planting; they are perfectly adaptable in Zones 6–8b.

Cephalotaxus fortunei Fortune's Plum Yew

While not that common in the trade, *C. fortunei* demonstrates all there is to love about conifers. The needles, measuring 2–4 inches (5–10 cm) or more, are among the longest in the genus, with a shimmering green that remains consistent throughout the year. The branch tips are slightly pendulous. The color of the stomatal bands on the undersides of the needles varies from bright white to green. After many years, the reddish brown bark peels off in strips. At maturity the plant should not exceed 15 feet (4.5 m) in height. While its normal habit is to form a large multistemmed shrub, it can be effectively grown as a small evergreen tree if all but one central leader is removed. *C. fortunei* is native to China, where it is found planted near shrines and temples. It was introduced into the United States by Robert Fortune around 1858. *C. fortunei* is reliably hardy in Zones 7–9a.

Cephalotaxus harringtonia Japanese Plum Yew

This is a cold-hardy species (Zones 5–9) that ranges in its native habitat across many parts of Japan into Korea and northeastern China. The Japanese plum yew and its forms are the typical plum yew species seen in southern gardens. Its size will vary from a small ground cover form all the way to a 20–30-foot (6–9 m) tree. Because most plants seen in landscapes are derived from lateral cuttings, they tend to form shrubs. When grown from seed they quickly form upright plants. *C. harringtonia*'s 1–2-inch-long (2.5–5 cm) needles are noticeably shorter that those of *C. fortunei*, and its fruit are more rounded and not as long. One frequently sees reference to a var. *drupaceae*, and several nurseries have this species listed as *C. harringtonia* var. *drupaceae*. This variety status is based on the distinct V-shaped (praying hands) foliage. In our observations, most plants labeled as such are actually straight *C. harringtonia* specimens with the var. status added for marketing allure.

Cephalotaxus harringtonia 'Duke Gardens'

This is a very handsome upright spreading selection that develops into a tight plant and will mature to around 6 feet tall × 6 feet wide (1.8 m). Throughout the seasons, 'Duke Gardens' retains its lustrous deep green foliage and can be used effectively as a specimen plant or in mass plantings. It originated as a branch sport of 'Fastigiata' at the Sarah P. Duke Gardens at Duke University in North Carolina. It was discovered in the 1950s and introduced in 1977.

Cephalotaxus harringtonia 'Duke Gardens'

Cephalotaxus harringtonia 'Fastigiata'

For those wanting the look of a columnar Irish yew (*Taxus baccata*), which does not prosper in the South, 'Fastigiata' is a good substitute. This erect-branched shrub, 8–10 feet (2.4–3 m) in height, has the deep green needles of the species, and they radiate in a dense pattern all around its branches. This is a slow-growing selection that will take years to exceed 4 feet (1.2 m). It is best grown in semishade, but too much shade will cause it to lose its tight form. Being a male clone, this plant will be fruitless.

Cephalotaxus harringtonia 'Fastigiata'

Cephalotaxus harringtonia 'Fritz Huber'

Compared to similar forms, this cultivar will tolerate more sun and has brighter green needles. Its habit is stiffer and tends to be more compact. 'Fritz Huber' is a male clone that makes a stunning display with its yellow cones in the spring. Expect the mature tree to reach a height of 4 feet with a width of 12 feet (1.2 × 3.7 m).

Cephalotaxus harringtonia 'Korean Gold'

This selection is similar to 'Fastigiata' in growth habit but may not grow as large. A mature plant growing at the Atlanta Botanical Garden is approximately 5 feet tall × 3 feet wide (1.5 × 0.9 m). It is an exceptional selection for seasonal accent color in the spring garden, where its yellow-gold sprouts of new foliage light up the landscape. It performs best in semishade. Young plants should be vigorously

*Cephalotaxus
harringtonia
'Korean Gold'*

*Cephalotaxus
harringtonia
cones*

pruned to achieve dense growth. 'Korean Gold' was discovered at Shibamichi Hontew Nurseries in Japan and introduced by Barry Yinger through Brookside Gardens, Maryland, in 1977. Not recommended south of Zone 8b.

Cephalotaxus harringtonia 'Mary Fleming'

We like this plant and are left to wonder why it is not more frequently offered. It is similar to 'Fritz Huber' with the main difference being that the needles are markedly recurved, offering a different look. We do not expect the plant to exceed 4–6 feet (1.2–1.8 m) in both height and width. A stunning specimen is located at the J. C. Raulston Arboretum. It was introduced by Yucca Do Nursery of Giddings, Texas, around 1983.

Cephalotaxus harringtonia 'Pedunculata'

This female clone originated from the Arnold Arboretum and became known in the South through the research efforts of Donglin Zhang in connection with his Ph.D. work at the University of Georgia. A plant from Hawksridge Nursery now growing in Tom's arboretum has retained a dark green shrubby form and is quite handsome. Another reason to use this selection is that, being a female plant, it will produce fruit in the presence of male clones. The fact that it is female is significant as most clones in the trade are male. Its ultimate size is estimated to be 5 feet tall × 6 feet wide (1.5 × 1.8 m).

Cephalotaxus harringtonia 'Prostrata'

Will the real *C. harringtonia* 'Prostrata' please identify itself? While there are most certainly plants in the trade that are not true 'Prostrata' and will therefore revert in time, the true cultivar is a highly textural ground-hugging form. The snaking prostrate stems are densely arranged and are ideal as an evergreen, shade-tolerant ground cover. This cultivar would be a good choice for mass plantings or to cascade over a wall, and it is seemingly impervious to full sun, at least in Zones 6 and 7. It is a relatively fast-growing selection that attained a height of 3.5 feet and a width of 12.5 feet (1 × 4 m) in six years in Athens, Georgia. This is the most reliable coniferous ground cover for shady situations we know of. Introduced by Hillier and Sons Nursery in 1923.

Cephalotaxus harringtonia 'Scott Wallace'

This new cultivar has a distinct upright growth pattern that is intermediate between 'Duke Gardens' and 'Fastigiata'. It originated as a branch sport on *C. harringtonia* 'Prostrata' growing in Griffin, Georgia. We anticipate a mature plant will achieve dimensions of 5 feet × 5 feet (1.5 m) with an upright, mounding habit. It was discovered by Scott Wallace of Creekside Nurseries in Hampton, Georgia.

Chamaecyparis False Cypress

With the exception of *Chamaecyparis lawsoniana* (Lawson cypress), which is generally not suitable for the South, all other species in this genus are adaptable to varying degrees and should be used more often in the landscape. The cultivars derived from the two most frequently encountered species could easily fill a small book. In fact, a number of experts would say (and the authors agree) that there are far too many cultivars—in some cases with only miniscule differences in appearance among them. Within this genus there is literally a form for every landscape application, from dwarf to large; for every landscape conditon, from dry to wet, sun to shade; and in every conceivable color combination, with some cultivars even changing color in response to winter temperature. In brief, *Chamaecyparis* is one of the easiest of all conifers to use in the South.

One of the confusing aspects of common names in the trade is that they often conflict with scientific names. When referring to the genus *Chamaecyparis*, the common name is "false cypress"; however, "false cypress" is usually shortened to "cypress" with reference to any number of *Chamaecyparis obtusa* cultivars. One example is *Chamaecyparis obtusa* 'Filicoides', commonly called fernspray cypress. Another example is *Chamaecyparis thyoides*, which is called Atlantic white-cedar. Botanically, cypress belongs in the genus *Cupressus* and cedar belongs in the genus *Cedrus*. Here we have elected to use the name that you will most likely find in the trade. When in doubt, refer to the genus name for accuracy.

With the exception of *Chamaecyparis thyoides* (Atlantic white-cedar), all are native to regions that border the Pacific Ocean. Two are native to the United States, and three are native to Asia. Cultivars are generally reproduced from vegetative cuttings. A number of interesting selections have been made by planting seed from existing cultivars.

Optimal performance is derived by planting them in full sun (especially selections of *C. pisifera*) in a well-drained acidic soil. They prefer moist soil during the summer months and dislike extremely dry conditions. While they are accepting of some dryness, they should not be classified as drought tolerant. Repeated moisture starvation will definitely produce plants with a ratty appearance and hasten their death. This is especially true of plants that are newly planted. All respond well to pruning, and although they accept pruning at any time of the year, the best time is in the spring. All species listed are adaptable in Zones 6–8.

Chamaecyparis obtusa Hinoki Cypress

At present count, there are more than 200 named selections comprising almost every imaginable size, shape, and color. Of the numerous ones on which trials have been conducted at Tom's arboretum, all have done well once established. A note of caution: many nursery retail centers sell small specimens in 4-inch pots. While this is a cheap way to get started, such plants lack well-established root systems, so it is easy to lose them during the hot summer months unless one can regularly water them. For the average homeowner, a #1 container (sometimes referred to as a one-gallon container) may be preferable. The species and all cultivars perform best in full sun but are accepting of light shade.

Unless one knows what to look for, *C. obtusa* is sometimes difficult to differentiate from *Thuja occidentalis* and some of the *Chamaecyparis pisifera* forms. The first key in differentiating *C. obtusa* from *Thuja* is the presence of white, X-shaped stomatal markings on the underside of *C. obtusa* foliage. The foliage tips on *C. pisifera* are generally sharper (acute) and the cones are very small. The needles on *C. obtusa* are more bluntly rounded (obtuse) at the tips. The seed cones on both species are globose, with those on *obtusa* being larger than those of *pisifera*. Also, the foliage on *obtusa* develops in flattened sprays with pronounced stomatal markings, whereas on some *pisifera* forms it is ropelike, with less-pronounced stomatal markings. *C. obtusa* bark is a rich brown that with age becomes grayish brown; it is furrowed and peels in long vertical strips.

Chamaecyparis obtusa 'Chabo-yadori'

This import from Japan is one of the better-performing cultivars in Zones 6 and 7. It does not grow as well in Zone 8. Having an unstable growth pattern, it produces soft-textured juvenile and adult foliage on the same plant, creating subtle and interesting color variations. Unlike some cultivars that seem to grow in nearly symmetrical form, the unpredictable growth habit of 'Chabo-yadori' offers a certain contrasting charm in the garden. This compact conifer should mature to around 4 feet × 4 feet (1.2 m) in five years. This plant will perform well in full sun or partial shade. It was first described in 1971.

Chamaecyparis obtusa 'Confucius'

Of all the yellow forms of *Chamaecyparis* we have observed, 'Confucius' exceeds them all for consistent, all-season bright yellow color and for tight form and vigor. Also adding interest is its light green interior foliage, which offers a nice contrast to its yellow exterior. Unlike some two-toned plants that can seem

Chamaecyparis obtusa 'Confucius'

unharmonious in the landscape, the color shift in 'Confucius' is so subtle that the eye does not immediately notice it. Simply put, this is the gold standard for yellow upright selections. While the more commonly available 'Crippsii' is generally considered the standard for upright, yellow *C. obtusa* cultivars, 'Confucius' has superior form and holds its color better. Although the plant will prosper in light shade, full sun is best for realizing its color potential, which is certain to enhance the landscape year round. Expect a height of 10 feet and a width of 5 feet (3 × 1.5 m) in six years. This selection was introduced into cultivation in 1984 by Duncan and Davies Nursery in New Zealand as a sport from the cultivar 'Nana Aurea'.

Chamaecyparis obtusa 'Crippsii'

While 'Confucius' may be superior in form and color to other yellow *Chamaecyparis* cultivars, this in no way should diminish the garden worthiness of 'Crippsii', an old standby. It is one of the garden stalwarts one should seek when looking for a taller-growing yellow-leaved evergreen that is pyramidal in shape. It appears to have no serious pests and once established is very drought tolerant. A light clipping of the foliage in late spring will produce a plant with tighter form and more refined appearance. A superior selection marketed as 'Crippsii' is floating around the South. It has been a standout yellow conifer in John's trials, suggesting that it is a more heat-tolerant clone. This selection reached a height of 16 feet with a spread of 11 feet (5 × 3.4 m) in 10 years. Conifer producers in the South should propagate from a known southern plant. 'Crippsii' originated in Tunbridge Wells, England, before 1899 and was first described in 1901.

Chamaecyparis obtusa 'Crippsii'

Chamaecyparis obtusa 'Fernspray Gold'

The bright gold fernlike foliage of this cultivar is similar to that of 'Filicoides' and is now being produced by a number of southern growers in preference to the green form. We agree that 'Fernspray Gold' is a highly desirable form, with its long sweeping branches that grow almost horizontally and droop at the tips. The foliage often appears not as a flat frond but with four distinct faces. 'Fernspray Gold' was introduced by Duncan and Davies Nursery of New Zealand in 1975.

Chamaecyparis obtusa 'Filicoides'

This cultivar often surprises gardeners with its eventual height, which in 10 years seems to top out at around 12 feet with a width of 5 feet (3.7 × 1.5 m). Its common name is fernspray cypress, which is no doubt derived from the fernlike appearance of its foliage. During the warmer months, the plant is clothed in a lush green color that gradually turns a darker, rather dull green as the temperature drops below around 20°F (-6°C). 'Filicoides' takes well to pruning; if left un-pruned, it can assume a rather gaunt habit with open areas devoid of foliage. In terms of size, the earlier pruning is done, the better the plant will look. This selection was first described in 1867 and was introduced by Dr. von Siebold to Leiden, Netherlands, from plants growing in Japan.

Chamaecyparis obtusa 'Gimborn Beauty'

This cultivar is quite similar to the more common cultivar 'Split Rock' but in our opinion is a superior selection. In the landscape, 'Gimborn Beauty' appears to grow faster and has a better form as it matures. Its foliage is a pleasing aqua green with silvery undersides—a coloration enhanced when the tree is grown in full sun. The blue color is derived from the juvenile-type foliage that is always coated in glaucous waxy deposits. This color remains throughout the year on the juvenile foliage but is less prominent on the adult parts. Paired with *C. obtusa* 'Confucius', the two plants make a stunning color combination for all four seasons. This is one of the faster-growing cultivars, growing to 10 feet tall × 5 feet wide (3 × 1.5 m) in 10 years. It was introduced by the world-famous Dutch conifer expert J.R.P. (Dick) van Hoey Smith, who found it in the von Gimborn Arboretum in the Netherlands.

Chamaecyparis obtusa 'Golden Fern'

This is one of the better *Chamaecyparis* cultivars released in the past several years and, in light shade, a perfect companion to almost any combination of other plants. 'Golden Fern' (also known in the trade as 'Gold Fern') possesses all the attributes of a landscape plant where space is a concern and where stun-ning color is sought. Also, because the plant displays different shades of yellow, it produces a kaleidoscopic mossy effect that makes it easy to combine with plants having different foliage colors. Its beautiful yellow foliage remains juve-nile, retaining a tight fernlike habit. Unlike some of the juvenile foliage forms of *Chamaecyparis*, it does not seem bothered by fungal pathogens. It is very slow growing at approximately 1 inch (2.5 cm) per year and will eventually mature to a height of around 4 feet (1.2 m). 'Golden Fern' was found as a branch sport from *C. obtusa* 'Fernspray Gold' in 1980.

Chamaecyparis obtusa 'Golden Whorl'

Among the *C. obtusa* cultivars, 'Golden Whorl' should perhaps carry the moni-ker "most unusual." With its abundant flattened fasciations (cockscombs), it is reminiscent of *Cryptomeria japonica* 'Cristata', but the fasciated growth appears only on the ends of branches. Sporting bright gold ropelike foliage, it also bears a strong resemblance to *C. obtusa* 'Torulosa'. Owing to its stiff habit and heavily

contorted branches that can appear artificial, we have found the plant more curious than beautiful, and it may be difficult to incorporate into some landscapes.
For the collector, this plant is a must-have. It is slow growing, with a twisted,
pyramidal habit to around 4 × 4 feet (1.2 m).

Chamaecyparis obtusa 'Graciosa'

This elegant old cultivar has stood the test of time. With its ascendant fernlike
sprays of dense medium-green foliage, 'Graciosa' is easy to incorporate into the
landscape, where it has a softening effect. Taller than wide and slow growing, it
will not overpower its surroundings. Its final size is around 10 feet high × 5 feet
wide (3 × 1.5 m). 'Graciosa' is a 1965 plant introduction from the Netherlands
that originated as a branch sport of 'Nana Gracilis'.

Chamaecyparis obtusa 'Lutea Nova'

Along with *C. obtusa* 'Confucius' and 'Crippsii', this cultivar is third in the preferred Big Three of larger growing treelike forms of *C. obtusa* cultivars with
yellow foliage. The habit of 'Lutea Nova' is similar to that of the other two, but it
can easily be distinguished by its lacier foliage.

It is best to purchase as large a plant as possible, because young plants often
scorch in the hot summer sun. Older plants grow out of this tendency. 'Lutea
Nova' takes well to pruning; if left unpruned, it can assume a rather gaunt habit
with open areas devoid of foliage. An annual, light tip pruning in early spring
ensures a well-grown specimen that will be a focal point in the landscape. Its ultimate size is 15 feet tall × 6 feet wide (4.6 × 1.8 m). 'Lutea Nova' was introduced
into the trade from Germany in 1904.

Chamaecyparis obtusa 'Moonlight Lace'

How plants sometimes arrive in commerce is fascinating to consider. 'Moonlight Lace' is a branch sport from *C. obtusa* 'Graciosa', and 'Graciosa' is a branch
sport of 'Nana Gracilis'. Does that make them second or third cousins? Of the
numerous variegated *Chamaecyparis* cultivars we have evaluated, 'Moonlight
Lace' is one of the better forms in terms of stability in and adaptability to southern growing conditions. The variegation is subtle and thus not difficult to site.
In its catalog, Iseli Nursery of Boring, Oregon, describes the foliage as "a light
dusting of creamy white variegation" with "beautiful texture and restrained variegation." Both descriptions are on target with what we have observed. This selection works well in full sun and also in light shade. We like it best in light shade
as a plant that adds contrast to the landscape. Its mature height is 10 feet with a
width of 5 feet (3 × 1.5 m).

Chamaecyparis obtusa 'Nana Gracilis'

This is one of the most common cultivars encountered in the trade and in gardens. The sprays of its shiny dark green foliage have a cuplike or scalloped appearance, presenting a wavy effect when viewed from a distance. To understand the appropriateness of certain cultivar names, it is of interest to note those of the following three *C. obtusa* cultivars: 'Nana', 'Gracilis', and 'Nana Gracilis', with the last being intermediate in form (mainly height) between the other two. As with too many plants in the trade (especially conifers and Japanese maples), the three are often mixed up. The true 'Nana Gracilis' is broad and conical, growing slowly to approximately 6 feet (1.8 m). It was first described in 1891.

Chamaecyparis obtusa 'Nana Lutea'

As the world of conifers turns, 'Nana Lutea' is a sport from 'Nana Gracilis'. Are you confused yet? Aside from its gold color, it bears the same cupped foliage as its parent. It too is slow growing to a height of 3 feet (0.9 m) and is accepting of full sun once established. Do not plant it in full sun if the plant comes in a container smaller than a #1. Introduced from the Netherlands and first described in 1966.

Chamaecyparis obtusa 'Nana Lutea'

Chamaecyparis obtusa var. *formosana*

Chamaecyparis obtusa var. *formosana*

Native to north and central Taiwan, where it grows in the mountains at elevations of 4000–9000 feet (1200–2700 m), often forming pure stands at higher elevations, var. *formosana* grows in a wetter climate than its Japanese relative and thus will tolerate wetter soils. This variety appears to be a much better plant for the South than *C. formosensis* (not covered in this book), which grows at lower elevations in Taiwan. While reaching heights of 130 feet (40 m) in the wild, it will likely grow no taller than 50 feet (15 m) in cultivation. A plant in John's trial reached a height of 22 feet with a spread of 15 feet (6.7 × 4.6 m) in 10 years. The leaves are dark green above, with white markings beneath and with obtuse (blunt) leaf tips. We like this variety for its more delicate lacy sprays and graceful form than var. *obtusa*. We recommend its use as a specimen tree where space permits. The bark is fibrous, brown, and fissured into small strips. The tree is very attractive and full as a young plant, the canopy opening with age as true of many conifers. Its foliage turns brown in the winter, often regreening by late February in Zone 8b. Breeding work is ongoing to make selections that remain green through the winter. So far no pest problems have been noted, and seedlings adapt well to container production. First described in 1914 as originating in Taiwan and reported to be thriving as far north as Philadelphia, Pennsylvania.

Chamaecyparis pisifera Sawara Cypress

In its native habitat of Japan, where it grows on the islands of Honshu and Kyushu at elevations from 2300 to 5000 feet (700–1500 m), the typical species form of Sawara cypress can obtain enormous heights: 150 feet (45 m), with a trunk up to 7 feet (2 m) in diameter. While the straight species form is rarely offered, there are some imposing trees in the range of 60 feet tall with trunk diameters of 7 feet (18 × 2 m) scattered throughout various arboreta and public parks. Most if not all the immense specimens are located outside the South. Old specimens can be seen in places such as Old Westbury in Long Island, New York, and in the Pacific Northwest. Occasionally, in undisturbed locations such as a cemetery, one will stumble upon an old tree that has survived in the South, but we have never seen one larger than around 30 feet (9 m), and all look ratty with age. The reddish brown bark is smooth and peels in thin strips. Leaves of juvenile plants are needle-like, whereas those of older plants are scalelike and overlapping on the twigs. In Japan, the Sawara cypress is considered to have a high degree of adaptability to humid areas with unproductive soils and is thought to be cold hardier and easier to root from cuttings than the Hinoki cypress.

As with the Hinoki cypress, what one commonly sees with Sawara cypress are the numerous cultivars, which are all much smaller than the species. Many of these are quite colorful and available in various forms and textures. As a group, they can contribute a practically limitless variety to the landscape. They generally are considered to have three distinct foliage types:

Filifera form (threadleaf cypress) includes cultivars with stringy, ropelike branches, having pendulous combinations of awl-like or scalelike leaves closely pressed to the twigs; some can appear quite bizarre.

Plumosa form (plume cypress) includes cultivars with foliage that is soft and airy and more like feathery plumes than flat sprays.

Squarrosa form (moss cypress) includes cultivars with soft, needle-like leaves that stand far out from the twigs and create a mossy appearance. They never develop adult scalelike leaves, and the foliage is soft and fluffy to the touch. Their color is usually blue silver and they tend to make upright shrubs with a central leader.

As a general rule, the plumosa form is the least adaptable to the South as it has a susceptibility to fungal pathogens such as *Passalora* and *Phomopsis* that cause unsightly dieback in parts of the plant. For this reason, popular cultivars such as 'Boulevard' have been omitted from the list of recommended plants. Many yellow-foliaged forms performed very poorly in Zone 8 during the record summer heat in Georgia and surrounding states in 2010 and 2011.

If ever there was a grouping of cultivars that are mixed up in the trade, with different cultivar names for the same plant, the listing of *C. pisifera* selections fits that bill. Misinformation about these cultivars is rampant, and many nursery catalogs appear to copy the same incorrect information from one another. Unfortunately, even with this book as a guide, we are all subject to purchasing a plant that is not true to its label. *C. pisifera* was introduced into cultivation in 1861 by the nursery firm J. G. Vietch in England.

Chamaecyparis pisifera 'Bright Gold'

Rare in the trade, this bright gold form is appropriately named. It is sometimes listed as 'Bright Gold Form', which is incorrect. Based on personal observation, the plant is slow growing and remains dense, even in some high shade. The most spectacular feature is the intensity of the gold color on new growth. This plant deserves to be better known, and it is a mystery as to why more nurseries don't offer it. We expect it to reach a maximum height of 4 feet with a width of 3 feet (1.2 × 0.9 m).

Chamaecyparis pisifera 'Filifera Aurea Nana'

Probably the same plant as 'Golden Mop', which is also sometimes incorrectly listed as 'Mops'. Almost as common in the southern landscape as Leyland cypress (*Cupressus* ×*leylandii*), this selection has proven time and again that conifers will prosper in the South. We have seen this plant thriving in some of the most horrific conditions, and it just keeps on ticking. It works well in mass plantings as well as in mixed plantings where one desires bright color. While it is amenable to light shade, the best color is achieved in full sun. While it is sometimes listed as a dwarf form, it is not and will eventually attain a height of approximately 8 feet (2.4 m).

Chamaecyparis pisifera 'Gekko'

As one of the purposes of this book is to introduce the reader to great yet sometimes obscure plants, we include 'Gekko'. Tom received a rooted cutting from the J. C. Raulston Arboretum a number of years ago, and it has become one of the best performers in his arboretum and a favorite of all who see it. A number of nurseries have begun propagating it, and a plant was just sent to the U.S. National Arboretum for inclusion in the Gotelli collection. Two-year-old cuttings from the Atlanta Botanical Garden have made saleable plants in #2 containers. In appearance, 'Gekko' is somewhat similar to 'Snow'. New growth in the spring boasts white-tipped (frosted) foliage that never quite disappears as the season progresses. The form remains full and has shown no signs of dieback after 10 years in the ground. The reported final height of this plant is 15 feet with a spread of 10 feet (4.6 × 3 m). Tom's plant has reached a height of 4 feet

(1.2 m) in approximately 10 years. The Japanese name for this plant translates to "moonlight."

Chamaecyparis pisifera 'Golden Sands'

After evaluating a number of the variegated forms where white or gold specks mix with the green, we have determined that most are not good for the long haul in the South. 'Golden Sands' is an exception. Like the previously mentioned *C. obtusa* 'Golden Fern', it meets all the requirements for a great landscape plant where one has limited space and light shade. That's why the renowned Cedar Lodge Nurseries in New Zealand describes it as "A dwarf plant of merit." Its color is a light green suffused with faint yellow and white specks that occur throughout the foliage. It is very slow growing at less than 1 inch (2.5 cm) per year and should mature at around 5 feet tall, with a width of 3 feet (1.5 × 0.9 m).

Chamaecyparis pisifera 'Juniperoides Aurea'

For some unknown reason this beautiful cultivar is not commonly found in nurseries. It has a number of attributes that make it a good choice for the South. For starters, it is trouble free and will not overpower an area. The color, a light green, is soft and easy to work with. It remains tight, and the new spring growth is an even brighter color (more white than yellow). This finely textured selection will max out at around 4 feet × 4 feet (1.2 m). This cultivar is also known as 'Plumosa Juniperoides' and was introduced into cultivation in 1965.

Chamaecyparis pisifera 'King's Gold'

'King's Gold', a newer introduction, shows real promise because of the intensity of its golden yellow foliage that takes the heat and never misses a beat. More southern nurseries are beginning to offer this selection, which has shown itself to be much more compact and spreading in growth habit than 'Golden Mop'. In a four-year trial in Zone 7b, it has retained its brilliant golden yellow color exceptionally well in the heat and humidity. 'King's Gold' will make an excellent foreground or accent plant and provides a beautiful color contrast when planted against darker green or purple foundation plantings. A similar selection making the rounds in southern nurseries is 'Paul's Gold', which we also recommend. 'King's Gold' reaches a mature height of 3–5 feet, with a spread of 3–6 feet (1–1.5 × 1–2 m), and is best when grown in full sun.

Chamaecyparis pisifera 'Lemon Thread'

Evaluation of this selection against the more frequently offered 'Filifera Aurea' has shown it to be a better selection for intensity of color. Displaying both juvenile and adult foliage, this sport of 'Squarrosa Lutea' (that is, 'Squarrosa Aurea') is slower growing than 'Filifera Aurea' but more upright and larger growing, with a mature height of 14 feet and a spread of 6 feet (4.3 × 1.8 m). 'Lemon Thread' was introduced in 1988 from Mitsch Nursery in Oregon.

Chamaecyparis pisifera 'Mini Variegated'

'Mini Variegated' is another of those great little plants that is seldom offered. The foliage is a pleasing green with creamy white splashes throughout. It performs best in Zones 6 and 7 and is happiest in light shade. Requiring no pruning, it will form a perfect bun with a height of less than 1 foot (0.3 m). In a shaded portion of the garden, 'Mini Variegated' will add light, and it is a great companion to hosta, ferns, and a host of other woodland plants. The further south one gardens, the more shade it should receive. Not recommended for Zone 8a and higher.

Chamaecyparis pisifera 'Mini Variegated'

Chamaecyparis pisifera 'Snow'

While many of the reference books list this as a "dwarf bun-shaped plant," it is anything but. Specimens seen growing in north Georgia and around Asheville, North Carolina, are well over 10 feet tall (3 m) and still growing. Nevertheless, it is one of the truly great selections for use in shade and does not seem to conflict with other colors. The plant lends itself to any number of pruning methods. In its natural form it will become pyramidal to around 12 feet high × 5 feet wide (3.7 × 1.5 m). Another effective way to grow the plant is to prune it at the desired height to a rounded form. One may further allow the foliage to grow from the ground up or prune off the bottom foliage completely to form a lollipop. The color of this cultivar is gray green, with new growth in the spring tipped a creamy white. It holds this light coloration longer in the South than many of the other *C. pisifera* forms. To maximize coloration, prune lightly in late winter. Not a plant for full sun or windy conditions in the South. 'Snow' was introduced to the trade by Hillier Nursery in England in 1971.

Chamaecyparis pisifera 'Vintage Gold'

Discovered as a fern-leafed sport found on 'Golden Mop', cultivar 'Vintage Gold' maintains its bright yellow color throughout the seasons. The flattened ferny gold fronds make an interesting plant, and it should be considered one of the better bright yellow conifers. Easy to grow and trouble free, reaching a height of 4 feet with a width of 3 feet (1.2 × 0.9 m).

Chamaecyparis pisifera 'Yadkin Gold'

This introduction from Rob Means of Yadkin Valley Nursery in North Carolina is another of the better gold forms. According to Rob, the plant was purchased from an unknown source in Connecticut and

Chamaecyparis pisifera 'Yadkin Gold'

touted as a plant that in full sun does not sunscald. After a number of years of evaluation, he determined that 'Yadkin Gold' was the best performer among five other named cultivars of like color and form. Like similar cultivars in the trade, it does eventually get pretty big. One needs to remember to remove all the apical limbs and to take cuttings only from the sides. Reaches 15 feet tall × 6–7 feet wide (4.6 × 2 m).

Chamaecyparis thyoides Atlantic White-cedar

Atlantic white-cedar is a large tree reaching heights of 75 feet (23 m) or more in its native range from Maine southward to Florida and westward to Mississippi. In its native habitat, this tree is commonly found growing in bogs, along streams, or in freshwater swamps. Atlantic white-cedar performs well in garden situations where adequate irrigation is available. It performs very poorly under drought conditions. Dr. Michael Dirr at the University of Georgia evaluated more than 50 selections, and most died within 15 years primarily because of drought. Plants grown in containers do not tolerate even one missed irrigation event! When adequate moisture is available, trees perform well even in partial shade. In general, selections from the northern part of the natural range are one to two zones cold hardier compared with southern germplasm. Numerous dwarf selections have been made, while the old selection known as 'Ericoides' can often be found growing at old home sites and cemeteries. All do well when planted at the water's edge near a stream or pond.

Chamaecyparis thyoides 'Rachel'

This round-headed form reached a height and width of about 15 feet (4.6 m) in 10 years in trials in Tifton. The foliage is a nice dark green. 'Rachel' tends to lose its lower foliage but can be trained as a multistemmed small tree.

Chamaecyparis thyoides 'Red Velvet'

This cultivar was chosen by 3 Rivers Nursery of Ft. White, Florida, as a selected seedling. Differing from 'Rachel' in that its foliage remains more juvenile and is not as tight, its winter color—a vivid rose purple—makes 'Red Velvet' a real standout in the landscape. It would contrast well with the dark green of several *Chamaecyparis obtusa* selections as well as with the yellow winter color of pines such as *Pinus sylvestris* 'Gold Coin'. Though production numbers are being ramped up, this selection is not yet commercially available. As one of our purposes is to make you aware both of newer introductions and those in the pipeline, we include it here. Thus far in our trials, 'Red Velvet' has shown good

Chamaecyparis thyoides 'Red Velvet'

disease resistance and better drought tolerance than other juvenile foliage selections. The mature size of this plant is around 12 feet tall × 3 feet wide (3.7 × 0.9 m).

Chamaecyparis thyoides 'Rubicon'

This plant is often seen in the trade as 'Red Star'. Growth is columnar, sometimes reaching heights of 15 feet (4.6 m) or more in the landscape. The soft, juvenile foliage is bluish green in the summer and often turns an attractive purplish color in the winter. Similar clones to consider would be 'Heatherbun', 'Little Jamie', 'Meth Dwarf', and 'Top Point'.

Larger selections that have performed well at Tom's arboretum in light shade near a stream are 'Webb's Gold' and 'Emily'. Both are worthy additions where one can provide moisture. Two excellent blue forms worth searching for are 'Tom's Blue' and 'Yankee Blue'.

Cryptomeria japonica Japanese Cedar

This evergreen of Japan is one of the stateliest of all trees. In its native land, it is accorded the honor of national tree and is highly valued for its aesthetic appeal and as a fine source of timber. Growing to heights in excess of 125 feet (38 m), it is also one of the tallest and longest-lived trees in Japan. One tree growing there is reported to be 213 feet (65 m) tall. Since the Japanese have been growing *Cryptomeria* for so long, a number of distinct and isolated forms have been propagated. Also, there are differences between populations originating around the Sea of Japan, where snowfall is abundant, and those growing on the Pacific side. Some researchers suggest that there is a Chinese species, *Cryptomeria fortunei*, though others afford it a varietal rank, *Cryptomeria japonica* var. *sinensis*. Because this taxonomic classification is in dispute and there is no documented evidence to prove that trees growing in China were not planted there, we have decided to treat *Cryptomeria* as a monotypic genus. In addition to the different natural forms, the genus has produced a prodigious number of cultivars—well over 100, in fact. These are derived from witch's brooms and seedling variations. Many of the cultivars have the word "sugi" in their names: for example, *Cryptomeria japonica* 'Sekkan Sugi'. Since *sugi* is the Japanese word for cedar, we have treated the word as redundant and elected to omit it from the cultivar name.

Cryptomeria is found mostly in mountainous areas of Japan that receive upwards of 100 inches (250 cm) of rainfall per year. Considering the less than 60 inches (152 cm) of annual rainfall customary across our southeastern states, this difference in precipitation does not appear to have a negative impact on trees grown in the South, as the genus is right at home here. In fact, once established, tree form cultivars such as 'Yoshino' and 'Sekkan' prove to be quite drought tolerant. Our evaluation has shown that while the cultivars will not tolerate wet feet, best performance and overall plant health are realized through regular irrigation. We conclude that the key to success in growing *Cryptomeria* in the South is moisture management. Supplemental irrigation in the winter seems to lessen winter browning as well.

Plants grow best in acidic soils and do very well in the Piedmont region. Additional fertilizer makes for a better-looking plant on the sandy soils of the Coastal Plain. Winter browning is caused by the production of rhodoxanthin, a carotenoid pigment produced to prevent damage by the sun when temperatures are low in the winter. Light pruning on new growth works well to alleviate this problem. Cutting plants back into old wood with no foliage below the cut will result in a dead branch back to the main trunk. Many homeowners become alarmed when they see a dead branch on the tree form. This is a normal occurrance, and dead limbs can easily be snapped off by hand. *Cryptomeria* is perfectly adaptable in Zones 6–8, whereas dwarf forms are best grown in Zones 6–8a.

Cryptomeria japonica 'Araucarioides'

This cultivar takes its name from another conifer genus, *Araucaria*, which it somewhat resembles. Unlike many of the named cultivars that have only minor differences, 'Araucarioides' is totally unlike any other *Cryptomeria*. What sets it apart is its branch structure. It exhibits long whiplike branches that form octopus-like terminal whorls at the ends. The foliage is dark green during the warmer months and exhibits winter bronzing during the colder periods. It will perform equally well in full sun or moderate shade, either as a specimen plant or in a grouping where its bizarre habit is further accentuated. Because there are no known older specimens growing in the South by which reasonably to predict its final height, we estimate a maximum around 30 feet (9 m). A plant growing in John's trials in Tifton, Georgia, reached a height of 12.2 feet with a spread of 10 feet (3.8 × 3 m) in 10 years. Some authorities give 35–50 feet (11–15 m) as the ultimate height. First described from Japan in 1844, 'Araucarioides' was later introduced into cultivation in the Netherlands in 1859. This cultivar may also be known as 'Athrotaxoides' or 'Viminalis'. Another cultivar sometimes seen in nursery catalogs is 'Dacrydioides'. We have been unable to determine whether this is the same plant as 'Araucarioides'.

Cryptomeria japonica 'Beaumont's Dwarf'

This is one of several good-looking selections growing at the Atlanta Botanical Garden. Planted in 1994, the specimen is now about 18 feet (5.5 m) tall. As used here, the name "dwarf" indicates its size relative to that of a full-grown *Cryptomeria*. All branches are finely textured, and the needles are shorter than those on the species, giving it the appearance of a *Dacrydium*. It will grow into a pyramidal form that should ultimately reach a height of about 20 feet (6 m). 'Beaumont's Dwarf' has demonstrated excellent adaptability throughout the Southeast. Described in 1972 from New Zealand, it was introduced to England in 1984.

Cryptomeria japonica 'Black Dragon'

This compact form has extremely dark green foliage and an irregular pyramidal shape. While not uncommon in southern landscapes, it is still considered a connoisseur's plant. 'Black Dragon' produces some of the darkest green foliage of any of the *Cryptomeria* selections, and no evidence of the characteristic winter bronzing has been discovered. In youth the plant can look a bit irregular and stiff, but as it matures it takes on a dense upright habit that offers unusual texture in the landscape. This selection should be adaptable to full sun throughout the South and is a good choice for containerized trees in the landscape. Its chief negative is a predisposition to foliage dieback. Regularly prune out dead branches to keep the plant looking its best. A plant in the Tifton, Georgia, trials reached a height of 10 feet and a width of 4.5 feet (3 × 1.5 m) in 10 years. The cultivar sports readily, and many "forms" of 'Black Dragon' are unfortunately being sold. It was introduced by Iseli Nursery around 1985.

Cryptomeria japonica 'Buckiscope'

This sport arising from 'Jindai' is one of the better selections when one is looking for an upright, dense evergreen accent. While some of the literature indicates that the foliage bronzes in the winter, this has not been observed in Zone 7 or higher. Several North Carolina nurseries such as Mountain Meadows and Hawksridge Farms are now offering this excellent cultivar. Expect a mature size of 12 feet, with a width of 4 feet (3.7 × 1.2 m). 'Buckiscope' was introduced by Koemans Nursery of Boskoop, Netherlands, in 1987.

Cryptomeria japonica 'Cristata'

Several years ago the authors had the thrill of seeing a mature 'Cristata' specimen growing at the Iseli Nursery display garden in Boring, Oregon. At approximately 30 feet tall (9 m), this plant makes you grab both the camera and the credit card. Owing to its bizarre fasciated, cockscomb-like growth, this plant is certain to elicit "wows" from all who see it. 'Cristata' is probably best suited for Zones 6 and 7, where it retains its dark green color through all seasons. In Zone

Cryptomeria japonica 'Cristata'

8 its cockscombs often become necrotic, and it has shown evidence of interior dieback. 'Cristata' was first described in 1901 after being imported from Yokohama Nursery in Japan around 1900.

Cryptomeria japonica 'Giokumo'

This plant is new on the scene, and we predict it will become one of the top-tier *Cryptomeria* cultivars in the southern landscape. Similar in form and size to the more widely known 'Gyokuryu', this selection produces more refined foliage and a perfect pyramidal form. Its best attribute emerges in the winter when the outer foliage turns a pinkish orange that is certain to brighten any day. 'Giokumo' is a 1968 introduction from Alpenglow Gardens in British Columbia, Canada.

Cryptomeria japonica 'Globosa Nana'

This is yet another trouble-free conifer that is perfectly adaptable throughout Zones 6 and 7. (A 'Globosa Nana' specimen in Zone 8b reached healthy size after seven years but was dead by year eight.) When all its attributes are summed, 'Globosa Nana' should rank among the top five dwarf *Cryptomeria* selections. While many references list the cultivar as growing to 2–3 feet tall with a similar spread, in the South it will mature to at least 6 feet tall with a spread of 4 feet (1.8 × 1.2 m). Its bright green, slightly twisted foliage shows only slight winter bronzing, and its dome-like form and slightly drooping habit create architectural interest in the landscape. 'Globosa Nana' is ideal for mass plantings in full sun and would look especially striking interplanted with day lilies. Varietal status was given to this plant in 1923, but it later received cultivar status in 1965.

Cryptomeria japonica 'Gracilis'

This is another of those hidden gems that deserves wider attention. Its light green foliage is considerably shorter than that of the species, and in most of the South it should display only minor winter bronzing. Unlike many of the shorter-leafed forms that tend to be stiff and dense, 'Gracilis' is an upright plant with an airy, soft, graceful appearance. 'Gracilis' was introduced in the Netherlands in 1854 and was first described in 1861.

Cryptomeria japonica 'Gyokuryu'

'Gyokuryu' has become one of the more commonly available Japanese cedar cultivars in southern nurseries. Its popularity is no doubt due in part to ease of propagation, satisfactory growth rate, and wide acceptance by consumers. It also

Cryptomeria japonica 'Gyokuryu'

performs well under nursery conditions when grown in containers. We agree that 'Gyokuryu' is a great choice for the South. Densely pyramidal in form, its needles—some of the darkest of any cultivar—hold their color well in the winter. We consider 'Gyokuryu' the best compact form for the Coastal Plain region. It holds its interior foliage better than most other *Cryptomeria* cultivars and appears to be resistant to leaf diseases that plague some Japanese cedars.

There is contradictory information in the trade as to its ultimate size. A plant in Tifton, Georgia, reached a height of 11.8 feet with a width of 9 feet (3.6 × 2.7 m) after 10 years in the field, and we estimate a mature height of 20–25 feet with an 8–10-foot spread (7.6 × 3 m). Don Howse, longtime American Conifer Society member and owner of Porterhouse Farms in Boring, Oregon, relates in a personal communication that a plant he purchased from the late Jean Iseli in the 1980s is now a multitrunked tree at least 40 feet (12.2 m) tall. He explains, "when I pruned the lower limbs in order to keep it from blocking a pathway, I found several trunks that were beautiful to see. People comment on the beauty of the tree from some distance, and then praise it for the beauty of the trunks when close by." Since there are likely no specimens in the South the age of Howse's tree, time will be the final decider.

Rouse et al. (2000) argues that 'Gyokuryu' is the same cultivar as 'Giokumo'. A study of plants recently received for evaluation and labeled as 'Giokumo' suggests that they are not the same at all. A newer, still unreleased selection from Moon's Tree Farm in Loganville, Georgia, may turn out to be the best of the three. The parent tree is approximately 18 feet tall × 9 feet wide (5.5 × 2.7 m) and features the brightest green color of any *Cryptomeria* we have observed to date. In trials at Tom's arboretum, it has retained its color throughout winter.

Cryptomeria japonica 'Jindai'

'Jindai' fills a niche in the 10–12-foot height (3–3.7 m) range for gardeners and landscapers seeking irregular vertical growth with less formality than other Japanese cedar cultivars. Its light green needles that project from numerous branchlets create a handsome, broadly pyramidal look. Even though the branches are stiff, this cultivar never looks rigid. It may be the same as 'Monstrosa'.

Cryptomeria japonica 'Kilmacurragh'

This dwarf cultivar of Irish origin deserves a place in the garden. 'Kilmacurragh' is unusual in that the tips of the branchlets are often fasciated and irregular, resembling a small version of 'Cristata'. Do not expect to find these crests on young plants, as it will take several years before they start to develop. 'Kilmacurragh' is a low-mounding plant that will probably not exceed 4 feet (1.2 m). It is light green most of the year, but you can expect some off-color foliage during the colder parts of winter. A plant in Tifton, Georgia, has been growing in 55 percent shade for several years and is doing fine. It has also performed well in Mobile, Alabama. This cultivar was first described from Ireland in 1966.

Cryptomeria japonica 'Knaptonensis'

Of the numerous Japanese cedar cultivars we have evaluated, 'Knaptonensis' is the best for consistent variegation. Its only negative is that parts of the plant tend to revert to uniform green in Zone 8. The new growth is an almost pure white that can enliven a shady nook, especially in the winter garden. Give it the light shade it prefers so that the new growth doesn't burn, but be sure it gets plenty of reflected light to keep it bright and showing to its best advantage.

Cryptomeria japonica
'Komodo Dragon'
(photo by Courtenay
Vanderbilt)

This is another cultivar typically described as "dwarf." Considering observation of a 12-year-old specimen growing at Tom's arboretum, we estimate the mature height to be approximately 12 feet (3.7 m) with an upright irregular spread. First described in the 1930s, this cultivar was discovered in Italy as a witch's broom.

Cryptomeria japonica
'Komodo Dragon'

'Komodo Dragon' is an exciting new plant introduction from Rick Crowder at Hawksridge Nursery in Hickory, North Carolina. Chief

Cryptomeria japonica 'Knaptonensis'

among its attributes are its retention of green color in winter, its mounded form, and its compact growth reminiscent of broccoli. We estimate its mature size to be in the 5–6-foot (2 m) range. While it may be difficult to find, it is worth searching for.

Cryptomeria japonica 'Little Champion'

This selection from Europe has been floating around for several years and is now beginning to show up in U.S. nurseries and collections. Among its attributes are bright green color, dwarf size, and dense, compact, rounded form. The tiny needles overlap each other in a handsome chevron pattern along the densely clustered curvy branchlets, with the thickness and interesting appearance of woven cord. Unlike some selections that turn an unattractive brown in the winter, 'Little Champion' turns a pleasing bronzy color at the onset of cold weather, particularly at the tips of the branches. Expect the mature plant size to be 3 feet × 3 feet (0.9 m).

Cryptomeria japonica 'Little Diamond'

This cultivar is new to us, but after seeing several, we are certain that 'Little Diamond' has a place in the southern landscape. What sets it apart from other dwarf Japanese cedar cultivars is its foliage, which resembles the cultivar 'Araucarioides' but with shorter needles and dwarf habit. Dense, multibranched, and neat in appearance, the foliage at the branchlet ends resembles pearly green starbursts that will be noteworthy in the garden. We anticipate a mature height of 3 feet with a spread of 4 feet (0.9 × 1.2 m). This selection is reportedly a branch sport from 'Bloomers Witch's Broom'.

Cryptomeria japonica 'Pom Pom'

'Pom Pom' is certainly one of the better dwarf forms. Sometimes compared to a dwarf 'Yellow Twig', which it does resemble strongly, the cultivar has a rounded habit, with short, fine, light green needles that form airy plume-like sprays or tufts at the branch ends. Sadly, only a few nurseries specializing in conifers offer this little gem. Visitors to Tom's arboretum all admire its beauty. The plant grows very slowly to 8 feet × 3 feet (2.4 × 0.9 m).

Cryptomeria japonica 'Radicans'

Along with 'Yoshino', the cultivar 'Radicans' has become the industry mainstay for large-growing *Cryptomeria*. The two are similar in their tall, pyramidal growth habit. 'Radicans' has a slightly denser form than 'Yoshino' and its summer foliage tends to blue green rather than simple green. It is also reportedly less susceptible to winter bronzing than 'Yoshino'. Field tests reveal that 'Radicans' is better suited for Zones 6 through 8a. Some dieback has occurred on plants growing in Tifton, Georgia, and Monrovia Nursery Company in Cairo, Georgia, has dropped it from container production because of leaf spot problems. It has now become a mainstay for many nurseries in Zones 6 and 7.

Cryptomeria japonica 'Rasen'

As a conversation piece for collectors of bizarre plants, 'Rasen' may be in the top 5. What sets 'Rasen' apart from other spiral-form cultivars is its eventual height and the exceptional degree of twist in its irregular branches. The needles coil so closely around the branchlets and branches that they resemble springs or helixes. Moreover, every branch is completely encircled in foliage from top to bottom, even the main trunk. Despite its unusual form, 'Rasen' can grow a surprisingly upright 20 feet tall (6 m). The bright green foliage does not fade or turn color in the winter and, once established, 'Rasen' is a fast grower. A plant in John's trials reached a height of 20 feet with a spread of 10 feet (6 × 3 m) in 10 years.

Cryptomeria japonica 'Rasen'

Cryptomeria japonica 'Rein's Dense Jade'

To many conifer lovers, this is the Rolls Royce of upright Japanese cedars. In our opinion, it unquestionably possesses all the attributes of a great landscape plant for Zones 6–8a. For starters, it is not particularly fast growing and therefore will not soon outgrow its space. Also, because it readily accepts pruning, it can be maintained at a smaller size. The rich, dark green color does not appear to vary during any month, and the foliage is the densest of any of the tall-growing

Japanese cedars. Over many years it can grow to a height of about 20 feet, with a spread of 12 feet (6.1 × 3.6 m). Where patience and space allow, this is a highly recommended selection. Introduced by Vermeulen Nursery in 1977 from a witch's broom growing on 'Lobbii'.

Cryptomeria japonica 'Sekkan'

If you're seeking a visually dominant tree for spring fireworks, this cultivar should be on your list. 'Sekkan' is a vigorous grower with whitish yellow-green new growth that fades to a light yellowish green in the heat of summer. Its spring display lasts from two to three weeks. The fireworks begin in May, normally after the peak spring bloom of many flowering shrubs and trees such as dogwoods, redbuds, and azaleas. As its flush rivals that of most flowering plants, this cultivar's late display extends the season of vivid color. The color of new growth is brightest in Zones 6 and 7, which don't warm up as quickly as zones further south. This

fast-growing tree will form a pyramidal shape that should top out at around 25 feet (7.6 m). A specimen attained a height of 18.5 feet with a spread of 12.7 feet (5.6 × 3.9 m) after 10 years in John's trials. Given adequate moisture, 'Sekkan' accepts full sun without suffering sunburn, and once established it has proven fairly drought tolerant. This would be a great selection to interplant among some of the purple-leaved deciduous trees, such as *Cercis canadensis* 'Forest Pansy' (forest pansy redbud) or *Prunus cerasifera* 'Krauter Vesuvius' (purple leaf plum). Most nursery catalogs call this cultivar 'Sekkan Sugi', but since *sugi* is the Japanese word for cedar, we find its use redundant in the cultivar name.

Cryptomeria japonica 'Sekkan'

Cryptomeria japonica 'Spiraliter Falcata'

Several years ago at a plant show, Jody Karlin, owner of Just Add Water Rare Plant Nursery in Conyers, Georgia, put together a conifer display. He later reported that of all the "cool" plants in his booth, 'Spiraliter Falcata' garnered the most excitement. It seems that everyone wanted to touch it. With its spiraled foliage, it bears some resemblance to 'Spiralis' and 'Rasen' but is distinctive in branches that twist and curve in all directions like hydras. From an early age, 'Spiraliter Falcata' is an upright plant with a thinner branch structure and smaller stature than other spiral forms. It reaches a mature height of around 5 feet (1.5 m).

Cryptomeria japonica 'Tansu'

'Tansu' is one of the commoner cultivars in the trade. In Zones 6 and 7, it is a medium grower in the 5-foot (1.5 m) range and one of the denser forms with an irregular habit. This irregularity makes it ideal as a complement to some of the more perfectly rounded forms. 'Tansu' will occasionally send up a sport that usually has no garden merit; you can easily remove it without damaging the plant. 'Tansu' will perform in full sun but needs some shade to look its best. In Zone 8b the plant may grow quite large: John's plant is 16 feet (4.9 m) tall after seven years in the ground. This is an excellent selection with nice winter color for Zone 8. It was introduced by Iseli Nursery in 1981.

Cryptomeria japonica 'Yellow Twig'

'Yellow Twig' derives its name from the bright yellow color of the stems of its new growth rather than the color of its foliage. While the plant will prosper in full sun or light shade, it will display its best color in full sun. This selection will benefit from annual pruning for the first several years after planting to make it denser. 'Yellow Twig' is a trouble-free selection that should grow about 7 feet high and 4 feet wide (2.1 × 1.2 m).

Cryptomeria japonica 'Yoshino'

For good reason, this is one of the most widely planted conifers in the South. Along with *Thuja* 'Green Giant', it has largely taken the place of Leyland cypress (*Cupressus* ×*leylandii*) as the preferred evergreen screen. It is a stallion. Significant among its many attributes are its fast growth rate, uniform pyramidal form, and bright green color. Once established, the tree has excellent drought tolerance. In the Atlanta drought of 2007, all specimens at Tom's arboretum, which he planted as a screen, survived with no supplemental watering.

Different forms of this cultivar are circulating in the trade. The cultivar growing in the Mobile, Alabama, area appears to be different from the cultivar growing in many nurseries. The plant growing in John's trials reached a height of 27 feet with a spread of 18 feet (8.2 × 5.5 m) after 10 years.

Cryptomeria japonica 'Yoshino'

Cunninghamia China Fir

Depending on the authority, this is a genus of either two or three species that are all indigenous to central and south China, Taiwan, and Vietnam. In the South, *Cunninghamia* are commonly called monkey puzzle tree (*Araucaria araucana*), which they are not. In their native range, they can grow to heights of 80 feet (24 m) and are used extensively for timber. Because of their resistance to rot, they are frequently used in the manufacture of coffins. Like coast redwood (*Sequoia sempervirens*), *Cunninghamia* is one of the few conifers that will regenerate after being cut to the base of the trunk. The species *C. lanceolata* is commonly seen around old home sites in the South, many with multiple trunks. It is believed that a freeze in the 1950s took them back to the ground and that is why so many are multitrunked trees. While we generally discourage the practice of allowing taller growing conifers to develop multiple leaders, this does not seem to have a negative impact as the tree matures. Among the best specimens in the South, one grows in the town of Norman Park, Georgia, just off Highway 319, and another in the town of Aiken, South Carolina. China fir likes evenly moist soils, although established plants are highly tolerant of short-term drought. Prune sucker shoots from the base at any time as needed. Cutting limbs back to bare wood usually results in branch dieback to the trunk. China firs are at their best when grown in full sun to light shade. Discovered in China in 1702 and introduced into England in 1804.

Cunninghamia konishii Taiwan Fir

Like many of the conifers from Taiwan, *C. konishii* is perfectly at home in the South. While less hardy than the more common *C. lanceolata*, it should be perfectly adaptable in Zones 6–9a. It differs from *C. lanceolata* in its shorter leaves and smaller cones and is less prickly to the touch. Because of its lack of availability in local nurseries, this species rarely appears in southern landscapes. It must be ordered from specialty nurseries and even then can be hard to locate. This is unfortunate for the species; it makes a beautiful tree in the landscape and has a different visual appeal than that of the more commonly encountered *C. lanceolata*.

Some authorities report that *C. konishii* has stomatal marking on both sides of its needles. We have not found this to be consistent across the species and in some cases see it only on the tops of young foliage. There is a superb specimen planted at Steven F. Austin University's Mast Arboretum in Nacogdoches, Texas, as well as a nice specimen at the University of Tennessee Arboretum in Knoxville. A splendid glaucous form is growing at the Atlanta Botanical Garden. First described from Taiwan in 1908.

Cunninghamia konishii 'Coolwyn Compact'

This cultivar offers an appealing variation on the normally large growing forms of Taiwan fir. At first glance, one might easily confuse it with one of the many *Cryptomeria* cultivars. In fact a true miniature variety, it grows about 1 inch (2.5 cm) per year and remains a tight green ball. In the winter, it takes on a haunting purplish cast. This is a plant for collectors looking to incorporate the rare and unusual into their landscapes. 'Coolwyn Compact' can be a bit tricky to grow in the South. Without adequate water, it readily suffers dieback in its interior. Found by Leo Coolwyn in his native Australia.

Cunninghamia konishii 'Little Leo'

This selection grows a bit faster than 'Coolwyn Compact' and will eventually become slightly larger. While 'Little Leo' is less well behaved and can become a bit irregular in form, it makes a nice conversation piece, especially when planted in sight of tall-growing straight species. In side-by-side comparisons of 'Little Leo' and 'Coolwyn Compact' over a three-year period at Tom's arboretum, 'Little Leo' is the better performer. All the dwarf selections of *C. konishii* have garnered mixed reviews from conifer collectors who have tried growing them, and we suspect they may perform best in Zones 6–7 in light shade. If interior dieback occurs, cut the plant all the way back to all-green foliage and new growth will reemerge. Be sure to wear gloves! Because both 'Little Leo' and 'Coolwyn Compact' mature to less than 3 feet (0.9 m), they function well as container plants or as accents in rock gardens. 'Little Leo' is an introduction from Australia.

Cunninghamia lanceolata China Fir

In travels throughout the South, you will frequently encounter *C. lanceolata*—a testament to its formerly widespread popularity and use. Despite its common name, China fir is not a "true" fir of the genus *Abies*. A tall-growing tree, it can attain heights of 125 feet (38 m) in its native habitat. Here in the South, a large tree tops out at around 40 feet (12 m) and can assume both single- and multi-trunk forms. Both forms appear to survive equally well. China fir is adaptable to Zones 6b–8 in the South, with the glaucous form (see cultivar 'Glauca' below) being perhaps a half-zone more cold hardy.

The tree's main negative is the tendency of its lower branches and limbs to abscise, creating a bit of a litter nuisance. On the plus side, the bark peels back to expose rich brown strips that present a rugged look. Owing to its decay-resistance, the Chinese have traditionally used *C. lanceolata* to make caskets, and recently a new industry has sprung up where the roots are polished and shaped to produce fine bowls. China fir prefers evenly moist soils, although established trees are highly tolerant of short-term drought. It will perform well either in full sun or part shade and seldom needs pruning. (If you must prune, you will get best results by pruning only young growth.) China fir is one of only a few conifers with the ability to resprout after being cut down to ground level (coppiced). British physician Dr. James Cunningham first collected this tree in China at the turn of the eighteenth century.

Cunninghamia lanceolata
'Chason's Gift'

Simply put, this plant is one of the best tall-growing conifers for the South. Unlike the species, cuttings from this cultivar are orthotropic: that is, they soon grow in a vertical direction to develop a central leader. In contrast, cuttings from other cultivars sometimes take years to produce orthotropic growth. This is especially true of cuttings taken from side branches, as if the plant had a memory of the direction in which its limbs and branches were growing. 'Chason's Gift' needs to be more available in the trade. A plant in John's trials attracts attention and has grown to more than 12 feet (4 m) in four years. David Johnson, owner of Johnson Nursery in Willard, North Carolina, donated this cultivar to the late Dr. J. C. Raulston. This particular plant came from a cutting Mr. Johnson propagated from a plant in his mother's Chapel Hill garden. It is named for Margaret Chason Richie, Mr. Johnson's grandmother.

Cunninghamia lanceolata 'Chason's Gift'

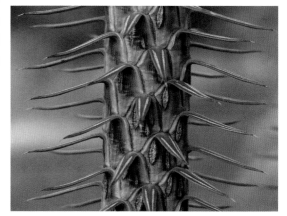

Cunninghamia lanceolata 'Chason's Gift,' stem

Cunninghamia lanceolata 'Glauca'

This cultivar's striking blue needles create a cool ambiance in the landscape. Once established, the tree grows rather quickly and can add at least 2 feet (0.6 m) per year. Where there is adequate space to accommodate it, 'Glauca' is one of the top trees for architectural interest. It retains its soft blue color throughout the seasons, and its form is upright with horizontal branching that is somewhat pendulous at the tips. As an added bonus, the bark peels in rich brown strips. In the spring, all parts of the reproductive structure are interesting to observe. It is considered hardier than the species and was described as early as 1850.

Cunninghamia lanceolata 'Greer's Dwarf'

If one is looking for a dwarf *Cunninghamia*, this might well be the ticket. Unlike the dwarf forms of *C. konishii* that tend to suffer dieback, 'Greer's Dwarf' is a clean plant. It is similar to the species except smaller in all parts. The ¾-inch (1.9 cm) foliage remains a vibrant green throughout the year. The plants we have observed thus far tend to sprawl rather than produce upright growth. Because these were produced no doubt from cuttings, upright growth may come with time and maturity. Based on its slow growth—4 inches (10 cm) per year—this plant is not expected to get much larger than 3 feet × 3 feet (1.0 m).

Cunninghamia lanceolata 'Samurai'

This cultivar originated at the University of Tennessee. John's major professor, Hendrik van de Werken, told him that the winter of 1983 damaged a

Cunninghamia lanceolata 'Samurai'

Cunninghamia lanceolata growing on campus back to the ground and that it resprouted with glaucous foliage the following spring. After the plant sprouted blue, Dr. Will Witte propagated it and first distributed it as 'Samurai' at the Southern Plant Conference in 1993. The original plant John received in 1993 reached a height of 35 feet (10.8 m) in 10 years. By contrast, after three years in Tom's arboretum a specimen made from a cutting has yet to develop a central leader. At present, 'Samurai' doesn't look any bluer than 'Glauca', and a comparison of 'Samurai' with a large form of 'Glauca' growing in a public garden in Hickory, North Carolina, reveals no discernible differences. That said, the acquisition of a plant with either name will reward the purchaser with a spectacular plant.

Cunninghamia unicanaliculata Sichuan China fir

Although of questionable identity as a distinct species, this plant is briefly mentioned here because of its pleasing color, soft foliage, and graceful form. In 1996, the famous British plantsman Roy Lancaster gave the plant to J. C. Raulston Arboretum, which went on to distribute it. While the arboretum described Sichuan China fir as a shrubby form, a plant growing at Tom's arboretum is treelike. All who see it remark on its delicate beauty and blue-tinged foliage, which turns shades of purple in winter. We like this plant and expect it to be hardy throughout most of the South. While hardy in Zone 7b (Cox Arboretum) and Zone 8b (Steven F. Austin Arboretum), the plant has suffered from spring frosts in Savannah, Georgia, and Gainesville, Florida.

Cupressus Cypress

Cupressus have a wide distribution range: from the United States and Mexico to Honduras; across the Mediterranean region, from southern Europe around the Middle East into northern Africa; and across the Himalayas and southern China. The genus comprises some 16 evergreen species and approximately eight varieties and subspecies.

Depending on which taxonomist one goes with, the exact number of species and varieties can be a moving target. Much of the disagreement appears to stem from variation in and among relictual populations that have been historically subject to an array of naming and classification schemes. Probably no conifer genus has engendered more taxonomic disagreement.

Most resembling the genus *Chamaecyparis*, cypresses have proven a mixed bag in the South, with different cultivars doing well in some areas and poorly in others. Generally, cypresses native to the Pacific coastal regions of the United

States, such as Monterrey cypress (*Cupressus macrocarpa*), do not adapt well to the South and should not be considered long-lived.

Most cypresses become tall trees of imposing beauty, though a few remain shrubby. Where site conditions are to their liking, *Cupressus* make some of the most beautiful conifers we can grow. They are versatile, providing a wide range of colors to choose from, and there are enough dwarf forms to suit smaller spaces.

One common problem for cypresses in the South is that their top growth tends to outpace their roots, making them susceptible to blowing over in high winds. Some species are more prone to toppling than others, and we cover this aspect in more detail in the species descriptions. All cypresses resent being transplanted, so carefully choose a site for permanent establishment. If you must relocate a tree, carefully root prune it at least a year before digging. In a personal communication with the authors, the owners of the world-famous Cedar Lodge Nursery in New Plymouth, New Zealand, observe the following: "We take the cuttings and set them in propagation for three months and then take them out and re-wound them. Then they root well even if it takes two years. We have speeded that up now I think. Also, when repotting we trim the roots, as they almost always have just one root that sends out smaller roots from the base of the cutting instead of a mass of roots. Cupressus for this very reason do not like being transplanted and usually die."

With a few exceptions, the majority of cypress species come from arid areas where they grow on rocky outcrops, on coastal cliffs and ridges, in canyons, and on sunny slopes of dry hills in chaparrals. Accordingly, they require sites with good drainage. Full sun is best for strong growth, color intensity, and overall quality of foliage. Also, all cypresses prefer good air movement and do not like to be planted where they are crowded, as is frequently done with Leyland cypress to create screens. Most are quite drought tolerant once established. Propagation is by rooting and grafting: *Cupressus* ×*leylandii* has proved to be a strong rootstock. As with all other large-growing conifers except for *Cunninghamia*, multiple leaders should be removed at an early stage to prevent the plant from breaking apart as it ages. On a final note, however tempting it might be to purchase a large plant, the smaller the specimen at planting, the greater its likelihood of survival.

Cupressus arizonica var. *glabra* Smooth Barked Arizona Cypress

As mentioned in the *Cupressus* overview, there is disagreement over the taxonomic identification of cypress, and this species is no exception. Many plants labeled *C. arizonica* are actually *Cupressus arizonica* var. *glabra*, and some authorities call them *Cupressus glabra*. There are approximately 30 named selections in the trade, and all appear to be from this variety. A significant number of these originated in Australia and New Zealand.

Most cultivars tend to be straight growing with a uniform taper. Because of this form, some commercial growers in the South sell them as Christmas trees. When brushed or touched, they emit a pleasing aroma. The cones are spherical in shape, take two years to mature, and remain on the tree for an extended period. The thin reddish brown bark exfoliates in long sinuous strips, revealing smooth bark underneath. By contrast, var. *arizonica* shows an underlying bark characterized by interconnected fibrous ridges. As a whole, var. *glabra*

Bark of *Cupressus arizonica* var. *glabra*

tolerates heat and dry soil (both clay and sand) and is cold tolerant in the South. All cultivars need full sun and are adaptable in Zones 6b–9a.

Cupressus arizonica var. *glabra* 'Blue Ice'

'Blue Ice' has become a popular introduction. Its form is symmetrical with an upright habit to around 20 feet (6 m). It is a more compact grower than 'Blue Pyramid', and the foliage is a lighter powdery silver blue. It was found as a chance seedling in New Zealand and introduced in 1984 by Duncan and Davies Nursery.

Cupressus arizonica var. *glabra* 'Blue Pyramid'

This striking selection of Arizona cypress should mature to around 30 feet (9 m). It is fast growing: a specimen planted as an 8-foot (2.4 m) tree at Tom's arboretum (Zone 7b) in 2001 is now 20 feet tall and 6 feet wide (6 × 1.8 m) and completely insect and disease free. After 10 years, a specimen grew to 24 feet × 12 feet (8 × 4 m) in John's trials (Zone 8b). Despite its rapid growth, it has shown

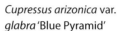

Cupressus arizonica var.
glabra 'Blue Pyramid'

no propensity for leaning or blowing over in high winds. This cultivar was introduced by Duncan and Davies Nursery of New Zealand in 1972.

Cupressus arizonica var. *glabra* 'Carolina Sapphire'

Growers like this plant: it roots well from cuttings and grows vigorously. It is therefore not uncommon to see 'Carolina Sapphire' used in various landscape applications throughout the South. What sets it apart from some of the other tighter-growing cultivars such as 'Blue Pyramid' is its openness. 'Carolina Sapphire' is slightly airier. It is silver blue in color and should mature to a height of 30 feet and a width of 15 feet (9.2 × 4.6 m). This cultivar was selected in 1968 from wild seed and developed by Clemson University in cooperation with the South Carolina Forestry Commission.

Cupressus arizonica var. *glabra* 'Chaparral'

With its creamy white foliage, 'Chaparral' brings originality and freshness to the garden palette. At its best in the winter and spring, 'Chaparral' undergoes a slight color change during the hotter months when its color is slightly less intense. A beautiful cultivar year round, it blends well with some of the bluer selections and, as a plus, it does not burn in full sun. Everyone who sees this plant seems to love it, so we are puzzled as to why it is so seldom commercially available. A specimen in John's trials grew to 17 feet × 10 feet (5.2 × 3 m) in 10 years. Discovered in 1989 as a seedling by John Emery of Drue Nursery in Berry, New

Cupressus arizonica var.
glabra 'Chaparral'

Cupressus arizonica var. *glabra* 'Limelight'

South Wales, Australia, 'Chaparral' was introduced to the United States by Coenosium Gardens.

Cupressus arizonica var. *glabra* 'Limelight'

Like 'Chaparral', this cultivar adds unusual color to the mix, except this time, instead of cream, the foliage color is lime green to yellow. 'Limelight' does not appear to be as prone to the disease problems that limit the use of the gold forms of *Cupressus macrocarpa* in the South. It is reportedly hardy in Zones 7–9 and tolerant of heat, sun, drought, wind, frost, and soils ranging from acidic to alkaline. A handsome narrow form, 'Limelight' deserves much more frequent use.

Cupressus arizonica var. *glabra* 'Raywood's Weeping'

Where proper site conditions are met, there is no finer weeping tree. All the secondary branches hang straight down. An upright variety with light gray foliage, 'Raywood's Weeping' grows to around 20 feet tall and 3 feet wide (6.1 × 0.9 m). A combination of root pruning and staking can mitigate this selection's tendency to fall over. 'Raywood's Weeping' was introduced by Raywood Nursery in Australia around 1989.

Cupressus arizonica var. *glabra* 'Raywood's Weeping'

Cupressus arizonica var. *glabra* 'Sapphire Sky'

As blue conifers go, no cultivar—including some of the outstanding selections of *Picea pungens* (Colorado blue spruce) and *Cedrus atlantica* (Blue Atlas cedar)—are more intensely blue. The growth rate and mature size of this cultivar are typical for *C. arizonica* var. *glabra* in the South. Gardeners can create arresting color contrasts by planting 'Sapphire Sky' with 'Chaparral' or 'Limelight'. This new introduction was found by Dr. Michael Dirr as he and his wife, Bonnie, were driving past an abandoned farmhouse in Madison, Georgia.

Cupressus arizonica var. *glabra* 'Silver Smoke'

This pyramidal silver gray selection maintains its beautiful form and fine texture through all seasons. It is the perfect choice where one is looking for a narrow specimen. Its growth habit is more columnar than 'Blue Pyramid' and its color more silvery or whitish. This plant was a Duncan and Davies introduction from New Zealand in 1984.

Cupressus funebris

Cupressus funebris Chinese Mourning Cypress

At one time, Chinese mourning cypress was classified as *Chamaecyparis funebris*, and some reference books still list it that way. Reminiscent of a well-presented specimen of *Cupressus cashmeriana* (sans silver foliage), this is another of the more beautiful weeping conifers. Its common name derives from the evocatively forlorn appearance of its foliage. *Cupressus funebris* is native to China, where it is often planted around temples, cemeteries, and monasteries. There is apparently more than one selection within this group, as some plants labeled Chinese mourning cypress are moderately pendulous while others are extremely so. The foliage is light green in color. A mature specimen should attain a height of around 30 feet and a spread of 10 feet (9 × 3 m).

Cupressus ×leylandii Leyland Cypress (*Cupressus macrocarpa* × *Cupressus nootkatensis*)

Leyland is one of several naturally occurring *Cupressus* hybrids that originated in the United Kingdom. It would be practically impossible to have lived in the South for the past 15 years and not heard of Leyland cypress. For years, it has served as the mainstay in large screening projects in subdivisions, office parks, and private residences. It is capable of growing to immense proportions—100 feet (30 m) or higher—and in England its use has been banned in some locales because of the amount of shade it casts on neighboring properties. Although it is common as a screen, perhaps its most effective use is as a single specimen or planted in groups of three or five with sufficient space between the plants to allow the entire plant to be seen. Allow a minimum spacing of 20 feet (6 m) between trees.

While the tree has received some unjustifiably bad press and has been knocked from the top spot by *Thuja* 'Green Giant' and *Cryptomeria*, it is still being sold by the thousands for its fast-growing properties. When given suitable growing conditions, Leyland cypress is a noble tree with dense growth and a near-perfect form for a Christmas tree. It prefers evenly moist soils, although once established it is highly tolerant of short-term drought. The major problems associated with Leyland cypress are a result of spacing them too close together, thus restricting air flow, and planting them in a hot, dry, clay soil with no supplemental water during the hottest summer periods. It is amazing to come across healthy plantings in some of the most inhospitable growing conditions. It performs well in full sun to part shade and seldom needs pruning. If pruning is necessary, cut back only young growth for best results.

Cupressus ×leylandii 'Castlewellan'

While this tree is marketed as one of the yellow types, most of the yellow foliage occurs on new spring growth that by June has turned green. If you desire a true yellow cultivar in your landscape, there are better selections. A dense form, 'Castlewellan' is slower growing than some of the other yellow selections. But slow growth—an asset when one is looking to create a tall hedge—is its main attraction. This cultivar was discovered growing at the Castlewellan Arboretum in the United Kingdom.

Cupressus ×leylandii 'Gold Rider'

Owing to its uniform yellow color, 'Gold Rider' is the best of the available yellow forms of Leyland cypress for the South. Its richest, brightest color occurs in the

late spring and early fall. Because of *Phomopsis* tip blight, this selection becomes unsightly in the warmer parts of Zone 8, so it is better suited to Zones 6b through 8a and probably performs best in Zone 7. This cultivar reached a height of 24 feet with a spread of 12 feet (7.3 × 3.7 m) in 10 years in Tifton, Georgia, but had to be removed after 13 years in the ground. 'Gold Rider' was discovered as a mutation in a Boskoop, Netherlands, nursery before 1985. A similar form with greater disease resistance is 'Gold Nugget'.

Cupressus ×*leylandii* 'Gold Rider'

Cupressus ×*leylandii* 'Moncal' Emerald Isle®

Slower growing than most cultivars, this selection will likely not get much larger than 30 feet tall and 8 feet wide (9 × 2.4 m). The foliage is dark green, and no pruning is required to maintain its density.

Cupressus ×*leylandii* 'Naylor's Blue'

This blue-green cultivar is perhaps the most graceful among the Leyland cypress selections for the South. Contributing to its grace is an open branch habit with pendulous branch tips. While not as blue as some of the cultivars of Colorado blue spruce (*Picea pungens*), 'Naylor's Blue' is more versatile in terms of its ability to adapt to all regions of the South and presents a fresh and unexpected look. It is moderately fast growing to 40 feet tall × 15 feet wide (12 × 4 m). A specimen in Tifton, Georgia, grew in the test plots to 27 feet × 20 feet (8.2 × 6 m) in 10 years. It is sometimes grown effectively as a Christmas tree. 'Naylor's Blue' has

Cupressus ×leylandii 'Naylor's Blue'

not shown the severe disease problems that send other cultivars to the burn pile in south Georgia. This is an old cultivar with origins tracing back to 1911.

Cupressus lusitanica Cedar of Goa or Mexican Cypress

Cedar of Goa is a very popular ornamental tree throughout much of Mexico and the tropics. Reaching 100 feet (30 m) in its native habitat, one can expect heights of 30–40 feet (9–12 m) in the southeastern United States. Originating from areas that receive summer rainfall, this species appears to be well adapted to the lower south. Very few cultivars are commercially available at this time, but growers are beginning to select for form and color. Seed of *Cupressus torulosa* ordered from commercial seed vendors often turns out to be this species. Cuttings from a limited number of clones have proven difficult to root, so grafting is probably the best option for propagation. This species performs best in Zones 7 and 8.

Cupressus lusitanica 'Glauca Pendula'

'Glauca Pendula' is a powder blue, weeping form of Mexican cypress released by Hillier Nurseries in the 1920s. A beautiful specimen grows at the Atlanta Botanical Garden. This cultivar is worth the search.

Cupressus lusitanica 'Glauca Pendula'

Cupressus nootkatensis Alaska-cedar, Yellow-cypress

Formerly classified as *Chamaecyparis nootkatensis*, this gem from the west coast of North America has proven quite adaptable to the South. Alaska-cedar inhabits a long coastal range, stretching from the Kenai Peninsula in Alaska all the way into northern California. This tall tree with drooping branches and flat sprays of dark green scalelike leaves has been the source of several great conifer introductions. Most have been selected for their narrow form and weeping, graceful appearance. Some are quite similar, and we suspect there is some identity confusion in the trade. Alaska-cedars make strong focal points in the landscape and can also be used effectively for screening. Where space permits, they are spectacular in mixed plantings with larger form deodar cedars and *Cryptomeria*. Alaska-cedar's growth rate is slow to moderately fast to a height of about 40 feet (12 m). It is fairly maintenance free, with little to no pruning ever required. Well-drained soil is a prerequisite for its long-term survival. It performs best in semishade to full sun in Zones 6–7b.

Cupressus nootkatensis 'Green Arrow'

This narrow form will grow to 30 feet tall but only 5 feet wide (9 × 1.5 m), making 'Green Arrow' a perfect name. It is a great choice for small gardens or tight spaces. This outstanding selection was made at a forestry research station in British Columbia.

Cupressus nootkatensis 'Jubilee'

'Jubilee' is a stately tree that is also distinctly weeping. What gives it an interesting character and sets it apart from the other weeping cultivars described here is its wider habit, the result of its natural tendency to produce secondary subleaders. Its foliage is a rich dark green.

Cupressus nootkatensis 'Strict Weeping'

Of all the *Cupressus* forms we have observed, this one is possibly the narrowest, because it produces (or appears to produce) fewer secondary subleaders. The draping foliage hangs down against the main telephone pole–like trunk. As the subbranching is not uniform, this cultivar is also the most irregular of the weeping forms. This irregularity is not a negative but lends its own unusual charm.

Cupressus nootkatensis 'Green Arrow'

Cupressus ×*notabilis* Noble Cypress (*Cupressus arizonica* var. *glabra* × *Cupressus nootkatensis*)

This is an attractive tree and a fast grower here in the South. It has shown good drought tolerance once established. Displaying glaucous green foliage, it reveals its *Cupressus arizonica* var. *glabra* parentage. It also resembles its other parent, *Cupressus nootkatensis*, featuring large, flattened sprays of drooping foliage. Noble cypress forms a more open crown than Leyland but may not get as large. We estimate a mature height of 40 feet with a width of 15 feet (12.2 × 4.6 m). This hybrid dates back to 1956, when seed was collected from a *Cupressus arizonica* var. *glabra* growing at Leighton Hall in Lancashire, England.

Cupressus ×ovensii Ovens Cypress (*Cupressus lusitanica* × *Cupressus nootkatensis*)

This represents the third spontaneous hybrid with *Cupressus nootkatensis* as one of the parents. A tree currently gaining popularity in the South called Murray X is described as a "finer textured" and "faster growing" Leyland cypress. Murray X appears to be a marketing name, as we have determined that it is actually Ovens cypress. It is the fastest growing of the three hybrids and has the potential to become popular among Christmas tree growers. Because fast growth can produce weak wood, Ovens cypress may become prone to limb breakage, but to date we have not observed this tendency. We anticipate it will grow taller than 40 feet (12.2 m) as a seven-year-old tree in Tifton, Georgia, reached a height of 37 feet (11.4 m). In the lower south, this tree does not appear to be as susceptible to *Cercosporidium* leaf blight as some of the Leyland cypress cultivars. Ovens cypress originated from seed collected from a *Cupressus lusitanica* growing at Westonbirt Arboretum in Gloucestershire, England.

Cupressus sempervirens Italian Cypress

Italian cypress, the classic Mediterranean conifer, adorns many southeastern landscapes. When the landscape calls for stately vertical accents, Italian cypress is the ideal plant. It is definitely *not* the tree to site under house rooflines as a foundation plant! Trees in the 30–50-foot (9–15 m) range can be found in old home and garden plantings and in cemeteries. The species performs well in Zones 7b–8b and, because of salt tolerance, is useful in coastal settings. Plants are propagated from cuttings, as seedlings can be quite variable. Cultivars grown for the landscape trade are part of the 'Stricta' group, selected for columnar growth and vertical branching. The cultivar 'Glauca' has been selected for blue-green foliage and dense, columnar growth.

Cupressus sempervirens 'Monshel' (PP12933 Tiny Tower®)

This is a compact Italian cypress that in 10 years reaches a height of 8 feet with a spread of 2 feet (2.4 × 0.6 m). It is an ideal selection for smaller gardens or topiary work. A Monrovia Nursery introduction, Tiny Tower® is reportedly cold hardy to 0°F (-17.8°C) and well suited to Zone 7a.

Cupressus sempervirens 'Swane's Gold' (PP3839)

'Swane's Gold' can be found for sale in many southern retail nurseries. While it produces bright gold new growth and looks good in a container, we do not

consider it a top-tier conifer for the South. Its color quickly fades as summer unfolds, especially in more southerly regions, and unless provided optimal site conditions, it can quickly turn ratty. Originated at Swane Brothers Nursery near Sydney, Australia, in 1944, it was introduced by the company in 1956.

Cupressus sempervirens 'Swane's Gold'

Fokienia hodginsii Fujian Cypress

This monotypic genus from southeast China, northern Laos, and northern Vietnam is only rarely seen in cultivation. Evergreen with leaves that form flattened branchlets, the pronounced stomatal markings on the undersides of its leaves—one of its most alluring features—are even more striking than those on the genus *Thujopsis*.

In its native habitat, Fujian Cypress grows in mixed broadleaf and coniferous forests on ridges and slopes where annual rainfall exceeds 65 inches (154 cm). When properly grown, this tree makes a beautiful specimen. Unfortunately, because of poor training at an early age, most plants observed in cultivation appear misshapen. Care should be taken when the plant is young to stake it properly and to prune it lightly for denser form. *Fokienia* has the appearance

Fokienia hodginsii

Foliage of *Fokienia hodginsii*

of an ancient relic—which it is. In its native environment, it can attain treelike proportions to 100 feet (30 m) and is a valuable timber tree. In the South, it probably won't grow any taller than 20 feet (6 m).

Owing to the fact that it grows in light shade and does not overpower a space, Fujian Cypress is a valuable addition to the landscape where one is looking for something unusual. Regrettably, it is an underrepresented conifer species in southern nurseries and should be made more readily available. It will blend well with both broadleaf evergreen plants such as tea olives (*Osmanthus*) and with smaller deciduous trees such as dogwoods (*Cornus*), *Acer japonicum* cultivars, and *Cercis* (redbuds). Based on its native habitat, it should grow well in the Coastal Plain area of the South, especially where rainfall or supplemental moisture is abundant. *Fokienia* is cold hardy as far north as Zone 7a and may tolerate colder zones as well. It will not survive long where the soil is not well drained, performing best in light shade with evenly moist, slightly acidic soil.

Fokienia is now listed as a vulnerable species and, as such, is receiving some measure of protection. New germplasm is now being received from plants growing in northern Vietnam, presenting an opportunity to select a clone with improved natural form. Plants root readily from cuttings.

Ginkgo biloba Maidenhair Tree

This Chinese native is sometimes called a living fossil, because *Ginkgo biloba* is one of the oldest plants on earth. Based on fossil remains, the tree has been around for at least 100 million years, and its ancestors once inhabited North America. While Ginkgo is not a true conifer, it is a *gymnosperm* (a plant that bears naked seed) and is included here because it is frequently incorporated into conifer collections and nursery catalogs tend to list it in the conifer section. While the fruits appear fleshy, like those of certain *angiosperms* such as plums and cherries, Ginkgo seeds are not embedded in fleshy fruit. In other words, once the naked ovules are pollinated, the seed itself turns fleshy.

Because Ginkgo is neither a conifer nor a broadleaf deciduous tree, it holds a unique position in the plant kingdom. No other tree in the world is like it. Its

Ginkgo biloba fall color

common name, Maidenhair Tree, refers to the similarity of its fan-shaped leaves to the Maidenhair fern (*Adiantum*), and its species name, *biloba*, derives from its distinctive bilobed leaf. *Ginkgo biloba* is dioecious, meaning that some trees are female and others male. The males produce small pollen cones while the females produce ovules. Because female trees produce fruit that emits a rank, fetid odor when it falls to the ground, most gardeners should opt for a male clone, purchasing a named selection produced from a male tree.

The tree is slow growing until well established and then grows at a moderate pace to become eventually a very large tree. In youth it is open and of little ornamental merit, but as it matures, it develops into one of the great landscape trees. Aside from its unique leaf, the Ginkgo tree's main attraction is its usually reliable bright yellow fall color. Moreover, it is long lived, seemingly impervious to insects, and produces minimal leaf litter. A well-formed specimen in its fall cloak is an object of breathtaking beauty. The tree is well adapted to upper portions of the South, and there are some very large specimens. One particularly large tree (approximately 60 feet [18.5 m]) can be found on the grounds of the High Museum of Art in Atlanta, Georgia. It bears a plaque commemorating its status as the largest Ginkgo in the city. Homeowners with limited space should purchase one of the many named smaller-growing cultivars.

There is considerable debate as to whether the Ginkgo tree still exists in the wild or is now extinct. Considered sacred in China, where it is often planted around Buddhist temples, Ginkgo trees are heavily planted in Seoul, South Korea, as street trees. The Ginkgo tree is also the source of a very popular over-the-counter medicinal extract made from its dried leaves and touted to increase memory function and blood circulation. The largest plantation of Ginkgo trees in the world is located in Sumter, South Carolina (Garnay, Inc.), where millions of trees are planted for production of the herb *Ginkgo biloba*.

Over the past 10 years, a plethora of cultivars seem to have arrived on the scene. Many of these are quite distinct from one another in form, leaf shape, and pattern of variegation. Owing to their adaptability and ability to mix well with true conifers, Ginkgos make some of the best landscape plants for the South. All cultivars are reproduced by grafting onto Ginkgo understock.

Ginkgos seem to prefer the summer heat in the South as well as our acid soil. Chill hours appear to limit its southern distribution, as it is rarely seen south of Tallahassee, Florida. This observation aligns with research conducted on container-grown trees at Auburn University in Alabama, where 600 chill hours in a cooler were required for good budbreak. Trees that received 1100

Ginkgo biloba variegated form

chill hours showed the best growth. (On average, Athens and Atlanta, Georgia, receive about 1200 chill hours per year, with Tifton, Georgia, receiving 750.)

For optimum growth, plant your Ginkgo in a well-drained but not extremely dry location. It will grow faster with supplemental watering during the summer and with periodic fertilization (in March, April, and October). While Ginkgo trees are relatively easy to transplant, they can be rather slow to recover. Transplant only during the winter months and do not mulch around the trunk: the plants will perform much better where the soil gets air. Pruning is best done in spring.

The first *Ginkgo bilobas* were brought from England to the United States around 1786. As previously mentioned, new selections are fast becoming available from specialty growers. One the best of the smaller forms is 'Buddy' (so named because of its large buds), which was introduced by long-term American Conifer Society member Bill Barger. Among other smaller-growing forms we have observed and recommend are 'Barabit's Nana', 'Beijing Gold', 'Elmwood', 'Gnome', and 'Mariken' (selected by the American Conifer Society as a Collectors Conifer of the Year).

Ginkgo biloba 'Autumn Gold'

This is a male clone and one of the better selections when one desires of a large tree (50 feet × 30 feet [15 × 9 m]). Its primary feature is a regular and broadly conical symmetrical form with reliable golden yellow fall color. The original cultivar was selected from San Jose, California, in 1957.

Ginkgo biloba 'Blagon' Gold Spire™

This new introduction from France has been brought to market and trade-marked by Commercial Nursery Company of Decherd, Tennessee. Of all the fastigiate forms we have seen, this one, in our view, is the best. The foliage on this narrow, pyramidal form remains quite dense from top to bottom.

Ginkgo biloba 'Chase Manhattan'

This particular cultivar is a slow-growing dwarf form that will likely reach only 6 feet (1.8 m) at maturity. The leaves resemble the species but are much smaller and more compact. The fall display is an outstanding bright yellow. It is ideal for bonsai and rock garden plantings. This cultivar is also listed occasionally as 'Bon's Dwarf'.

Ginkgo biloba 'Chi-Chi'

'Chi-Chi' is a multistemmed, slow-growing, dense selection that becomes a mounding shrub to around 4 feet (1.2 m) tall. It can be left as a natural form or lightly pruned each spring to make a perfectly round ball. Either way, it is highly effective in a mixed landscape. Its leaves are the typical two-lobed fan-shaped type of the species but somewhat smaller. As with the species, this male clone shows off bright yellow fall foliage. We rate this selection "highly recommended."

'Chi-Chi' is often incorrectly listed in catalogs and collections as 'Tschi-Tschi' or 'Tit'—a larger growing form that is rarely offered in the trade. 'Tschi-Tschi' translates to "breast" and is so named because of its tendency to produce breast-shaped protuberances—unusual swellings or clusters of dormant buds that appear on the bark of plants as they mature. A plant so labeled at the J. C. Raulston Arboretum is a tall-growing tree that displays this remarkable feature.

Ginkgo biloba 'Munchkin'

There is some debate as to who actually introduced this cultivar, and this debate drives discussion as to which name is correct: 'Munchkin' or 'Chris's Dwarf'.

Under either name, this is a spectacular little plant that supposedly originated from seed. Arguably the standard by which any small-leaved form should be measured, it has an upright habit and numerous slender branches that are closely attached. The branches grow from the stem in a circular fashion, making it a very dense plant, and its leaves do not exceed the size of a nickel. 'Munchkin' tends to be more regular in shape than some of the other small selections. It may eventually reach 6 feet (1.8 m), but its growth rate is slow at only about 4 inches (10 cm) per year.

Ginkgo biloba 'Golden Globe' (PP12675)

This is an unusually densely branched form that produces a full crown at a young age and matures into a broad, round-headed tree with spectacular yellow fall color. In addition, it is reportedly a fast grower. This male selection arose from a seedling discovered by the Cleveland Tree Company in Fort Valley, Georgia.

Ginkgo biloba 'Jade Butterfly'

'Jade Butterfly' is a dense, dark green plant with foliage that clumps to form a vase-shaped shrubby outline. This semidwarf form reaches a height of about 10 feet (3 m). By using your imagination, you can envision how the plant shape resembles a butterfly with open wings. This is an introduction from Duncan and Davies Nursery in New Zealand.

Ginkgo biloba 'Jehosaphat'
(or 'Jehoshaphat')

This selection is quite striking—even in winter when one can appreciate the interesting sculptural effect of its branch habit. While we have yet to observe a mature specimen, 'Jehosaphat' supposedly develops into a dwarf or semidwarf plant with an extremely dense, symmetrical overall form and a somewhat pyramidal habit. This cultivar was discovered as a witch's broom at Spring Grove Cemetery in Cincinnati, Ohio.

Ginkgo biloba 'Jehosaphat'

Ginkgo biloba 'Magyar'

This cultivar develops into a nicely formed specimen with uniform symmetrical branching and an upright narrow pyramidal form, measuring 60 feet × 30 feet (18.5 × 9 m). Several southern nurseries offer it, as it is well suited to urban planting as a street tree. 'Magyar' is a male form discovered growing in front of Magyar Bank in New Brunswick, New Jersey.

Ginkgo biloba 'Majestic Butterfly'

In our opinion, this is simply the best of the variegated forms we have observed. The leaf variegation on plants we evaluated has proven extremely stable, displaying spectacular yellow and green streaking that lasts the entire growing season. Once established, 'Majestic Butterfly' appears to adapt well to full sun but performs best with light afternoon shade. We don't yet know the final height of this cultivar but anticipate no more than 10 feet (3 m). Crispin Silva of Crispin's Creations Nursery in Molalla, Oregon, discovered this variegated Ginkgo tree. It reportedly arose as a sport from *Ginkgo biloba* 'Jade Butterflies'.

Ginkgo biloba 'Princeton Sentry' (PP2720)

A very popular male form, 'Princeton Sentry' assumes an upright habit that tapers to a point. Reaching a height of 60 feet, with a spread of 25 (18.5 × 7.6 m), this well-known cultivar is slow growing with big decorative leaves. We consider it an improvement over the cultivar 'Fastigiata'. Named for a tree growing in Princeton Cemetery in Princeton, New Jersey.

Ginkgo biloba 'The President'

This selection introduced by Dr. Michael Dirr was found growing in front of the University of Georgia presidential residence. It develops a dense upright crown and a broadly pyramidal to oval shape. Despite strongly ascending branches, it is not an erect narrow form or "fastigiate." It grows to a height of 50 feet (15 m).

Ginkgo biloba 'Saratoga'

Slow growing to approximately 35 feet (10.5 m), this male cultivar has a distinct central leader with an upright compact habit that widens with age to form a dense pyramidal outline far superior to the irregular, unpredictable form of the species. It produces dense ascending branches, with leaves that are relatively long and narrow and more deeply lobed than the species. Despite its slow growth rate, over time 'Saratoga' becomes one of the best selections among all the *Ginkgo biloba* cultivars. (It is Tom's favorite.) Fall color is typical of the species, and leaf drop is sudden, leaving an interesting pattern of golden leaves under the naked tree. 'Saratoga' is a 1975 selection from the Saratoga Horticultural Research Foundation in San Martin, California.

Ginkgo biloba 'Shangri-la' (PP5221)

One of the better male Ginkgo selections for those seeking a plant slightly smaller than the species. 'Shangri-la' is fast growing and produces a compact pyramidal form with dense branching to 40 feet (12 m).

Ginkgo biloba 'Troll'

This somewhat new introduction is our personal favorite among the dwarf, bushy, compact forms. Its leaves vary from typical to rounded at varying heights. Combined, these attributes make for a real conversation piece. At least one southern nursery—Commercial Nursery of Dechard, Tennessee—is growing this selection. It was discovered by Johann Wieting as a witch's broom on a tree in Krefeld, Germany. 'Mariken' is similar in form to 'Troll', with very tight growth.

Ginkgo biloba 'Troll'

Ginkgo biloba 'Mariken'

Ginkgo biloba 'Weeping Wonder'

This is one Ginkgo that, in our opinion, should not be mixed up in the trade as it is too unlike any cultivar on the market. This bizarre form's leaves vary in size and shape to the point of appearing malformed. Some leaves are strap-like, some spatulate, some spoon-like, some spindly, all randomly mixed and varying from full to small size. During the American Conifer Society's international trip to the Czech Republic in 2008, we noted that several gardens had labeled this plant 'Mutant Weeper'. The correct name is 'Weeping Wonder'. Though its side branches are reportedly either horizontal or pendulous, judging by the appearance of the specimens we have observed, it is difficult to envision this cultivar's being truly pendulous. Purportedly found by Rich Eyre at Oak Ridge Cemetery in Springfield, Illinois, near the burial place of President Abraham Lincoln, it was propagated from a witch's broom that was hanging down from the parent.

Glyptostrobus Canton Water Pine/Chinese Swamp Cypress

This bald cypress look-alike is one of only five conifer genera that are deciduous in winter. It differs in appearance from bald cypress mainly in its slightly glaucous foliage and pear-shaped (rather than round) cones—up to ¾-inch (1.9 cm) long and broadest near the apex—which are borne on short stalks. While at one time it enjoyed a much wider distribution, its native range is now subtropical southeastern China, from the province of Fujian west to southeast Yunnan and into portions of southern Vietnam. Despite its native habitat, the plant is hardy throughout Zones 7 and 8 and, depending on seed source, probably Zone 6.

Like bald cypress, it grows around streams and riverbanks; the Chinese sometimes plant it to stabilize soil from erosion. While it is said to produce knees, the authors have yet to observe any. Two specimens growing at Tom's arboretum in or near water have shown no signs of knees in nine years. In the South no trees have ever been observed that were larger than 30 feet (9 m). A tree in John's trials in Tifton, Georgia, grew 17 feet (5 m) in 10 years. Though a specimen reportedly growing at the University of California–Davis is 65 feet tall with a 4.6-foot girth (19.8 × 1.4 m), don't anticipate a tree's growing to nearly that size in the South. *Glyptostrobus* can be propagated from seed or cuttings.

The chief attributes of *Glyptostrobus* are its rarity, its ability to withstand wet conditions, and its rich rusty red fall color. Best growth rate and form are achieved when the plant is grown on the edge of permanently shallow water in full sun. When planted on dry land, the plant fails to impress and, over time, will take on a ragged appearance. It is inferior in form to either *Taxodium* or *Metasequoia* and is apt, therefore, to remain in the domain of the collector or the gardener in search of a conversation piece. In an interesting note, the species name *glyptostroboides* (as in *Metasequoia glyptostroboides*) was derived from the genus *Glyptostrobus*. This plant is reportedly extinct in the wild in China with the only remaining known wild populations occurring in central Vietnam and eastern Laos.

Glyptostrobus pensilis 'Woolly Mammoth'

Introduced by Rob Means of Yadkin Valley Nursery in Yadkinville, North Carolina, this cultivar's new growth has a slightly bluer color than the species. Likewise, its form is slightly better. A tree growing at Rob's nursery is approximately 30 feet (9 m) tall. He tells us he selected 'Woolly Mammoth' from a batch of seed he received.

Glyptostrobus pensilis bark

Glyptostrobus pensilis cones

Juniperus Junipers

Along with pines, junipers are among the most maligned plants in the South. This is unfortunate as the vast number of selections in the trade offers a wide spectrum of colors, sizes, textures, and forms from which to choose. The genesis of this "bad rap" traces, we think, to the trade itself. Garden centers and landscapers for so long offered the same selections that, over time, they took on a dull and dreary uniformity. While the number of landscape-worthy species adapted to the South is limited to about a dozen, there are some excellent selections within this group if one is willing to search for them on the Internet or at nurseries specializing in conifers.

Depending on which taxonomist one chooses to follow, there are approximately 60 juniper species worldwide. With the exception of *Juniperus procera* (a disjunct species from the lake-mountain area of eastern equatorial Africa), all are native to the Northern Hemisphere, ranging from the Arctic Circle to the tropics. They are adapted to habitats in exposed areas with poor and often dry soils. Owing to their toughness, they are often found naturally on rocky, barren land where dramatic seasonal fluctuations are common. They differ from other members of the Cupressaceae family in that their fleshy reproductive cones resemble berries. (The female cones are composed of coalescing scales that fuse together, giving the appearance of a berry.) Depending on the species, seed can take between 6 and 18 months after pollination to germinate. Junipers are a highly variable group. On most species, leaves have one of two forms: needle-like and standing out from the twig or scalelike and pressed close to the twig. Some species bear both types of leaves, though most young plants bear needle-like foliage. This may be nature's way of protecting plants at the juvenile stage from animals. Some species are monoecious and others dioecious. They can vary in size from small trees to small shrubs to ground-hugging plants. Propagation is by seed, cuttings, and occasionally grafting.

Junipers are some of the most adaptable of all plants. They will survive in just about any site as long as it is well drained. Best results, irrespective of species, are obtained in full sun: heavy shade will result in plants that are thin and look unkempt. For the first year after planting, we recommend periodic watering during the hotter dry months in order to establish a deep, extensive root system. After that, no supplemental watering is usually necessary. Some of the species that frequently appear in retail centers, such as *Juniperus scopulorum* (Rocky Mountain Juniper), have been omitted from discussion, as they have proven to do poorly in the heat and humidity of the South.

Juniperus cedrus Canary Islands Juniper

Given the fact that this juniper is native only to the Canary Islands (Tenerife, Palma, and Madeira), its adaptability in the South has been a total surprise. Several plants have been growing extremely well for the past four years in the Atlanta area. Classified by most authors as a Zone 9 plant, it has proven cold hardy throughout Zone 7; its "sweet spot" appears to be Zone 8.

While there may be variations in wild populations, plants seen in the trade have short, glaucous green leaves and permanent juvenile foliage that is soft to the touch. The glaucous appearance is most pronounced on new growth, where the branchlet tips appear silvery white. The new foliage will retain this color for several months, thereby extending the nice green-and-white color contrast. Combined with the weeping nature of its branchlets, the Canary Islands juniper has much to offer in the landscape. Based on our observations, after 10 years one can expect a small tree in the vicinity of 15 feet tall and 5 feet wide (4.6 × 1.5 m). Judicious pruning can keep the plant at a much smaller size. *Juniperus cedrus* is endangered in its native range because of overharvesting for its wood and overgrazing by goats. This species was introduced into cultivation in 1847.

Juniperus chinensis

This native of China and Japan is perhaps the best of the non-native junipers for the South. All specimens seem to do well, whether planted in heavy clay or dry soil or situated in partial shade. As a species, *Juniperus chinensis* is highly variable in the wild and has produced a number of outstanding cultivars. There is some disagreement among plantsmen as to which selections are pure *J. chinensis* rather than natural hybrids with *J. sabina* that are often labeled *Juniperus ×media* or *J. ×pfitzeriana*. *Juniperus ×media* is considered an illegitimate name and has been replaced by the rather daunting *Juniperus × pfitzeriana* (Spath) Schmidt [Pfitzer Group]. We have omitted these classifications here in favor of straight species designations until further agreement is reached.

J. chinensis is dioecious, with female trees bearing glaucous green fruit that turn brown at maturity. The fruit is rounded and irregular in shape and contains two to five seeds. The only downside to this species is that most selections grow larger than expected and, over time, may become too crowded. The reader will note that there are numerous cultivars within this species. We have listed what we believe are some of the best.

Juniperus chinensis 'Angelica Blue'

Juniperus chinensis 'Angelica Blue'

Prized for its glaucous, bright blue-green needles that cast a beautiful light, this introduction is becoming increasingly popular in newer landscapes. Densely branched and wide spreading, 'Angelica Blue' shows to best advantage when used as a specimen plant rather than in mass plantings. In our view, this is a bet-

ter landscape selection than the more common Blue Pfitzer ('Pfitzeriana Glauca'). This cultivar should attain a mature height of 4 feet with a spread of 6 feet (1.2 × 1.8 m). 'Angelica Blue' was introduced by Angelica Nurseries in Maryland.

Juniperus chinensis 'Blue Point'

This Chinese juniper is a slower growing upright form with grayish blue adult foliage. While most often observed at heights of less than 10 feet (3 m) tall, this selection can grow larger with a spread at the base of 3–5 feet (0.9–1.5 m). 'Blue Point' is an excellent choice when a vertical accent is needed for large containers or in small yards. Monrovia Nursery introduced this selection in 1973.

Juniperus chinensis 'Blue Point'

Juniperus chinensis 'Blue Vase'

'Blue Vase' is a moderately slow-growing form of Chinese juniper that is wider at the top than at the bottom. Its teal blue foliage is softer to the touch than that of most junipers. A fairly common plant in Coastal Plain landscapes, it ranges in height from 5 to 10 feet (1.5 m × 3 m). This medium-sized juniper looks good year round, makes a nice hedge, and is an excellent choice for use in tight spaces.

Juniperus chinensis 'Daub's Frosted'

This cultivar's bluish foliage is suffused with golden yellow–frosted sprays that create a striking contrast. In addition, the foliage tips are somewhat pendulous. This combination makes 'Daub's Frosted' one of the more interesting color forms for low-spreading growth. A fast grower that matures at around 15 inches tall with a spread of 5 feet (0.4 × 1.5 m), 'Daub's Frosted' is a good candidate for mass plantings as well as for mixed beds. Care should be taken in late fall to remove fallen leaves and leaf litter from the top of the plant in order to prevent dead spots.

Juniperus chinensis 'Gold Lace' (PP8202)

Attaining a height and spread of 4 × 6 feet (1.2 × 1.8 m), 'Gold Lace' is one of the best yellow forms for small spaces or where a shrubby but not overpowering plant is desired. The yellow of this cultivar paints the entire plant, old growth and new, and is not confined to new growth as in many other gold forms. 'Gold Lace' works equally well in mass plantings or in mixed beds. Tom has used it

Juniperus chinensis 'Gold Lace'

with 'Angelica Blue' and *Thuja occidentalis* 'Rheingold'. The blue and yellow hues of the two junipers combined with the orange of 'Rheingold' never fail to offer cheer on a winter day. 'Gold Lace' was discovered in Ontario, Canada, in 1983 as a branch mutation of *J. chinensis* 'Aurea'. A similarly landscape-worthy form we have come across is 'Gold Star'.

Juniperus chinensis 'Hetzii Columnaris'

Having both adult and juvenile leaves, 'Hetzii Columnaris' is an upright-growing, green-foliaged juniper that produces regular crops of greenish gray cones. It makes a good substitute for Leyland cypress, though not quite as dense or as large, and it can be used instead of Hollywood juniper ('Kaizuka') next to a building where a smoothly conical rather than a convoluted form is preferred. In sandy soils, 'Hetzii Columnaris' performs best with regular fertilization. Plants can reach 15 feet (4.6 m) in 10 years.

Juniperus chinensis 'Hetzii Columnaris

Juniperus chinensis 'Iowa'

As one would expect of a tree from Iowa, this is a tough plant. Erect with coarse, blue-green foliage, it is slower growing than some of the other selections of *J. chinensis* and has a more formal appearance. It will likely grow 15 feet tall × 4 feet wide (4.6 × 1.2 m). Left natural, it forms a loose pyramid that can be tightened up by judicious pruning of wayward side branches. Leaves are awl-shaped and scalelike, and the fruit is a highly ornamental silvery blue. May Nursery in northern Florida is offering this selection. This 1948 introduction came from Professor F. J. Maney of Iowa State University and was named after the state.

Juniperus chinensis 'Kaizuka'

The Hollywood juniper is a favorite with some gardeners and appears virtually bulletproof in terms of survivability, even in the most inhospitable of conditions. As they say, "beauty is in the eye of the beholder," and this selection is one that gardeners either love or hate. Undoubtedly, though, it has a form that should not be confined to restricted spaces as it can attain heights and widths of at least 15 feet × 5 feet (4.6 × 1.5 m). Seen growing everywhere in southern California, where it is a popular landscape plant, and sporadically throughout the South, its

Juniperus chinensis 'Kaizuka'

dark green branches grow upright in multiple directions to form a large shrub of irregular habit. Native to Japan, it is also sold under the name *J. chinensis* 'Torulosa'. This popular cultivar was first described in 1939.

Juniperus chinensis 'Kaizuka Variegata'

This relatively small-growing variegated form exhibits creamy yellow patches of foliage intermingled with green. It is often used against brick walls, where its color stands out. Unless situated as a background plant in light shade or otherwise subdued, 'Kaizuka Variegata' always appears too bold. Plants usually mature at less than 10 feet (3 m).

Juniperus chinensis 'Plumosa Aurea'

Certainly this cultivar is one of the best golden-foliaged, upright forms of Chinese juniper we have observed. The yellow green of the foliage intensifies through the seasons, culminating in golden bronze in winter. With a V-shaped habit, this juniper's long branches become quite dense, even without pruning. Also found listed as *Juniperus ×media* 'Plumosa Aurea', this older cultivar was first introduced in 1923.

Juniperus chinensis 'Saybrook Gold' (PP5014)

For spring color in junipers, this cultivar may be The Best. The new flush is a refreshing bright gold that announces spring's arrival. Combined in the landscape with the blue of a dwarf form of Colorado blue spruce or the red of a Loropetalum, 'Saybrook Gold' gives a star performance among early spring conifer displays in the South in a show that lasts for about one month. After this, the plant blends into the landscape for the remainder of the year with no remarkable attributes. Aside from primary needle-like foliage, which for some people might be off-putting, the plant's one negative feature is that it turns a bronzy yellow in winter. We like this juniper both for its seasonal color and for its horizontal lines that show well in prominent places, such as on a bank. Expect a height of 4 feet and a width of 6 feet (1.2 × 1.8 m). For best color, grow this cultivar in full sun. It was discovered as a branch sport at Girard Nurseries in Geneva, Ohio, in 1965.

Juniperus chinensis var. *sargentii*

Indigenous to northern Japan from sea level to altitudes of 7500 feet (2300 m), this variety is generally low growing, reaching a height and width of less than 2 feet (0.6 m). Several cultivars are available, including 'Compacta', 'Glauca', and 'Viridis'. This variety was originally discovered in Japan in 1892 by Professor C. S. Sargent of the Arnold Arboretum.

Juniperus communis Common Juniper

The common juniper has the distinction of being the most widespread of all conifers, spanning much of North America and extending throughout Europe, Iran, Afghanistan, and the western Himalayas. It is also one of only three conifers native to the United Kingdom, and a native population has even been reported in the vicinity of Anniston, Alabama. The seed cones of common juniper are used for flavoring gin. With a size variability that ranges from small trees to small shrubs, including prostrate forms, four subspecies are recognized. The foliage is silvery underneath, awl shaped, and prickly to the touch. Whorls of three leaves comprise the leaf pattern. Common juniper has a single stomatal band on the adaxial (upper) leaf surface, separating it from *J. formosana*, which has two stomatal bands. Because it is typically overlooked in favor of more garden-worthy cultivars, the species is rarely ever seen in cultivation. Many selections have the undesirable trait of turning an off-brown color during the colder months. It should be noted that not all selections are suitable for Zone 7b and above. In the southeastern United States (North Carolina and Virginia), the plant is found naturally at higher elevations (>2000 feet or 600 m). The selections listed below have demonstrated adaptability.

Juniperus communis 'Depressa Aurea'

An old cultivar that has been around since 1939, this semidwarf form grows to a height of 4 feet and a width of 6 feet (1.2 × 1.8 m) in about 10 years. At the onset of warm weather, this conifer comes alive with bright golden color on its branch tips and is one of the more stunning plants of spring. The show lasts for about three weeks. After that, 'Depressa Aurea' turns a dull green and fades into the background. As winter approaches, it turns a purplish hue. Given the right placement among nearby golden or bright blue winter forms, this can be an effective plant.

Juniperus communis 'Gold Cone'

Where tight form and vertical accent are desired, 'Gold Cone' is a good candidate. The term "gold" is a bit misleading in the South, where the plants observed display merely a shade's lighter green on the newer growth. Growing to a moderate size of 5 feet tall × 2 feet wide (1.5 × 0.6 m), this conifer makes a good selection for display in large pots. Its major deficiency is a tendency to fall apart with age, though periodic pruning can minimize this. Introduced by Kordes Nursery of Bilsen, Germany, in 1980, 'Gold Cone' performs best in Zones 6 and 7.

Juniperus communis
'Gold Cone'

Juniperus communis 'Horstmann'

Simply stated, this is one of the best of the weeping junipers that can be successfully cultivated in the South. Its form is slightly irregular, which adds to its allure. Each branch grows outward and then sweeps up in an arc with the foliage hanging down. Nighttime visitors to Tom's arboretum frequently engage in a game of "what does it remind you of." Some have said they expect to see the literary character Ichabod Crane emerging from behind the mournful foliage. When young, the plant can be weak rooted, and for the first year staking is advisable. Despite being a *J. communis* type, 'Horstmann' foliage is not as prickly as some of the other selections and is much softer than that of *J. rigida*. Since Tom's 'Horstmann" has never produced fruit, we suspect the plant is dioecious. It is not likely to exceed a height of 20 feet or a spread of 6 feet (6 × 1.8 m). This clone is a nice selection that came from the famous Horstmann Nursery in Germany around 1982.

Juniperus communis 'Oblonga Pendula'

'Oblonga Pendula' is another weeping form of common juniper that retains its bright blue-green color all year. While not as graceful as some weeping forms, it makes a good selection when one wants something a bit unusual: the twisting and turning branches have been likened to pigs' tails. In circulation since 1838, this cultivar is for some reason rarely found in landscapes. This is odd, because apart from its quite sharp needles (which some growers may find undesirable), in our view it has no truly negative features. Where we have observed it, 'Oblonga Pendula' grows slowly to reach a height of 12 feet (3.7 m).

Juniperus conferta Shore Juniper

Some well-respected taxonomists such as Aljos Farjon now classify this plant as *Juniperus rigida* subspecies *conferta*, but since the preponderance of garden books and nursery catalogs still list it as *J. conferta*, we have elected to treat *J. conferta* as a distinct species for ease of reference.

This well-known juniper from coastal Japan is no stranger to the South, where it is used (too often as some would argue) for ground cover. In its native habitat, it forms dense, low-growing plants with a spreading habit. The slender stems bear aromatic blue-green awl-shaped needles that are half an inch (1.3 cm) long and borne in fascicles of three. Each needle has a single white band along its length.

The first clue to its success in the landscape is that it grows naturally in sand, which suggests the need for good drainage. We have seen numerous cultivars planted in heavy clay; they seem to survive well as long as there is adequate

Juniperus conferta

drainage. It is also salt tolerant, which makes it suitable for planting in coastal areas. There are some interesting cultivars that, with a bit of searching, can be readily obtained.

Juniperus conferta 'All Gold'

We highly recommend this newcomer to the mix of ground cover junipers. 'All Gold' brings a completely new dimension to ground cover junipers, because all of its foliage stays gold year round. This makes it a real standout in winter when color is a welcome attribute. In three years of evaluation at Tom's arboretum, it has proven to be a vigorous plant that seems perfectly at home in the South. It forms a flat carpet with a spread of at least 6 feet (1.8 m). We have observed this plant for sale in several nurseries in Tennessee, North Carolina, and Georgia.

Juniperus conferta 'All Gold'

Juniperus conferta 'Blue Lagoon'

This selection was discovered in Japan in 1976 by John Creech and Sylvester March of the U.S. National Arboretum and introduced to the nursery trade in 1997. 'Blue Lagoon' is shorter and more mat-like than the rest of the species, reaching a height of only 6 inches (15 cm).

Juniperus conferta 'Blue Pacific'

Introduced in the 1970s, this selection is reportedly cold hardier in Zone 6 than other selections. 'Blue Pacific' has bluer foliage and is more compact than the rest of the species, reaching an ultimate height in the landscape of 10–12 inches (30 cm). This is the most common form of Shore juniper right now produced by southern growers. As with all selections, good nutrition during container production is essential for making quality plants.

Juniperus conferta 'Brookside Variegated'

'Brookside Variegated' is to variegated ground cover junipers what 'All Gold' is to golden forms: The Best. A dense, low growing plant, this cultivar forms a flat carpet with a spread of at least 4 feet (1.2 m), and its bluish green foliage is randomly splashed with yellow. A well-behaved cultivar, 'Brookside Variegated' seems equally at home in full sun and light shade. Mitsch Nursery introduced this clone in 1988.

Juniperus conferta 'Silver Mist'

Growing to a height of 16 inches (40 cm), this exceptionally dense, compact form rounds out the color spectrum with its silvery blue-green foliage that

Juniperus conferta 'Silver Mist'

develops a slight purple cast in winter. 'Silver Mist' performs well in Zones 6–8 and thrives in either full sun or light shade. In shady landscapes, it makes a handsome companion to perennial plants such as *Asarum* (wild ginger), *Epimedium* (Bishop's Hat), and *Hosta*. 'Silver Mist' was introduced to the United States as 'Shiro Toshio' in 1983 by Barry Yinger of Brookside Gardens.

Juniperus conferta 'Sunsplash'

This cultivar is similar to and often confused with 'Brookside Variegated', but instead of the variegated foliage of the latter, 'Sunsplash' has golden yellow branchlets set off by bluish green foliage. This variegation appears stable and remains fresh all year. 'Sunsplash' forms a flat carpet with a spread of at least 4 feet (1.2 m). It performs best in Zone 8 in partial shade. Sometimes listed as 'Variegata', 'Sunsplash' is a highly recommended selection.

Juniperus conferta 'Sunsplash'

Juniperus davurica Dahurian Juniper

This spreading shrub is very popular in the southeastern United States. The fact that Dahurian Juniper performs so well even down into northern Florida is interesting, given that it is native to areas that include eastern Russia and northern Mongolia as well as the Austrian Alps. The plant grows in a variety of acidic soils (including the sandy soil of the Coastal Plain), and this may explain its adaptability. On adult foliage, leaves are usually grayish green and scalelike. Cones are purple to brown and covered with a whitish or gray bloom. Some experts currently regard the species as *J. sabina* var. *davurica*, though in the early 1990s the cultivars were considered forms of *J. chinensis*.

Juniperus davurica 'Parsonii'

Hardy in Zones 6–9a, 'Parsonii' is one of the most popular ground cover junipers of the Gulf Coast region, where it is often found in both residential and commercial landscapes. This is a female form, often decked with glaucous blue-green cones. It prefers well-drained soils, and we have seen it die a slow death in landscapes with heavy soils where the lawn is overwatered. During the growing season, southern lawns need only about one inch of water every seven days—and that's in the absence of supplementary rainfall. When rain is regular, lawn irrigation should occur less frequently. This plant has been listed in the literature as 'Expansa'. Two variegated forms are known: 'Expansa Aureospicata', with yellow variegation, and 'Expansa Variegata', with splashes of cream or white.

Juniperus deppeana Alligator Juniper

The alligator juniper, named for the checkered bark characteristic of older specimens, is native to the southwestern United States and northern Mexico. The bark, unique among junipers, is reminiscent of that on old persimmon trees. In its native range, the species is known to hybridize with other species (such as *J. monosperma)* where they overlap geographically. A number of varieties and forms have been described, but not all authorities accept them.

Alligator juniper is remarkably drought tolerant, and growers have selected several interesting forms with this useful characteristic. Particularly noteworthy are the blue selections. Among them, one can find blues to rival those of any conifer alive. The species is mostly dioecious with juvenile foliage on young plants that later becomes scaly.

This is a good selection for the middle South, where the number of conifers with intense blue foliage is limited. In Zone 8 regions, where hot, humid summers are the rule, alligator juniper is prone to interior dieback. All selections prefer full sun and well-drained soil.

Juniperus deppeana 'McFetters'

Reaching dimensions of around 15 feet × 5 feet (4.6 × 1.5 m), slow-growing 'McFetters' is a dense alligator juniper with permanent silver-blue foliage. If

Juniperus deppeana 'McFetters'

Juniperus deppeana
'McFetters' bark

you get a chance to see the beautiful specimen at the Virginia House in Richmond, Virginia, you'll want to grab a shovel and immediately add one to your own landscape. At least one southern nursery now produces this plant for sale. Discovered by Ralf McFetters in Arizona, the cultivar was introduced by Catalina Heights Nursery of Tucson around 1982.

Juniperus formosana
Formosan Juniper

Because this graceful upright weeping conifer is nowhere to be found in the South, except in a few specialty nurseries, it exemplifies the general underuse of conifers in southern landscapes. Native to the mountains of Taiwan, it grows in the high, wild regions of the Sheipa, Taroko, and Yushan national parks as well as in the mountain forests of China and Tibet. In the wild it can grow to heights of 40 feet (12 m), but in the South it should mature to no taller than 25 feet (7.6 m). Eckenwalder classifies the Formosan juniper as a Zone 9 plant, but we have seen it perform just fine in Zone 7. A very nice specimen can be viewed at the J. C. Raulston Arboretum in Raleigh, North Carolina. The plant was first described from Taiwan in 1908 (then known as Formosa), and its species name *formosana* means "beautiful" in Latin.

Juniperus formosana

A multistemmed species, Formosan juniper's spreading branches and pendulous branchlets create a fountain effect in the landscape. It is a top-tier plant and one of the best forms of any weeping juniper. Adding to its allure, the bark is deep brown and shaggy and exfoliates in long thin strips. It can be easily confused with *J. rigida*, but its needles are softer and its habit is notably more columnar. It also appears to be dioecious, whereas the clone of *J. rigida* in the trade freely produces fruit without the presence of a male.

Juniperus horizontalis Creeping Juniper

This prostrate juniper is native to the boreal regions of North America (as far east as Maine and westward to Montana up into portions of Alaska). Given its provenance and the fact that it occurs naturally in open, dry, sandy and rocky, as well as prairie, habitats, its adaptability in the Southeast is surprising. It is probably the most frequently used of all junipers in the South, especially on slopes and banks in mass plantings. The branches are creeping, and the species never seems to grow taller than 18 inches (0.5 m), though it can attain widths of 20 feet (6 m). Keys to its identification include dark brown bark that exfoliates in thin strips; flat leaves that overlap in a scalelike pattern (on juvenile plants the leaves are needle-like); and mature fruit of a blue-black to brownish blue color. Creeping juniper is a dioecious species. It spreads via vegetative reproduction when the natural layering of branches produces new roots. The species was first described in 1794 and introduced into cultivation in 1836.

Juniperus horizontalis 'Andorra Compact'

Considered the best form of the Andorra juniper, this cultivar is also identified in the older literature as 'Plumosa Compacta'. For landscapers and gardeners seeking winter interest, this is a good selection, with a very dense branch form and a pleasing cold-weather color of bronze purple. It attains heights of less than 2 feet with a spread of roughly 5 feet (0.6 × 1.5 m). The famous German taxonomist G. Krussmann first described Andorra juniper in 1972.

Juniperus horizontalis 'Bar Harbor'

This popular selection is a low-growing, wide-spreading form. Its bluish green leaves turn a deeper reddish purple in the winter than those of the similar cultivar, 'Wiltonii'. An older cultivar than 'Wiltonii', 'Bar Harbor' can spread to 10 feet, but will remain only about 1 foot high (3 × 0.3 m). It was found on Mount Desert Island in the state of Maine during the 1930s and first described in 1939.

Juniperus horizontalis 'Blue Chip'

A handsome juniper with silvery blue foliage, 'Blue Chip' often holds its color very well through the winter. While it performs admirably in the upper southern regions, *Phomopsis* tip blight can trouble this cultivar in the Deep South. Introduced from Denmark around 1940 and first described in 1984, 'Blue Chip' grows 2 feet high with a spread of 6 feet (0.6 × 1.8 m).

Juniperus horizontalis 'Golden Carpet'

This relatively new addition to the prostrate ground covers merits prominent introduction. When summer's high temperatures and humidity subside and the fresh muted gold of its summer foliage fades, get ready for a surprise. This cultivar's color is never uniform. Especially in the cooler months, 'Gold Carpet' is a many-hued patchwork ranging from light purple to orange to various shades of pale yellow. Even in the dead of winter, its color brings interest to the landscape. It is very popular in Europe, where some growers plant it in mass around a central group, which they stake up to give the illusion of a forest with mountains. The effect is quite dramatic when used in a wide, open area. We much prefer 'Golden Carpet' to the better-known cultivar 'Mother Lode', which isn't a great performer in the South. Also, 'Golden Carpet' grows faster, with no tip burn in full sun. Some nursery catalogs list this as 'Gold Carpet', which is incorrect. 'Golden Carpet' originated from H. Kruse in Bad Zwischenahn, Germany, and was introduced by a Dutch nursery in 1992.

Juniperus horizontalis 'Maiden Gold'

A 'Mother Lode' look-alike but better suited to the South, this virtually unknown cultivar arose as a sport from 'Wiltonii' and was introduced by Maiden Nursery in Newton, North Carolina. A plant growing at Tom's arboretum seems right at home: after four years, it has spread to 4 feet (1.2 m) without missing a beat. It grows in full sun with no discoloration, and the creamy yellow summer color becomes coppery orange in cold weather.

Juniperus horizontalis 'Maiden Gold'

Juniperus horizontalis 'Monber' Icee Blue®

Juniperus horizontalis 'Monber' (PP9639 Icee Blue®)

A good-looking silvery blue selection from Monrovia Nursery, and our favorite of the blue ground covers, Icee Blue® is a recommended juniper that grows well in much of the Southeast. The foliage has short internodes and thus maintains a dense crown. A moderate grower, attaining heights of 4 inches and spreads of 8 feet (0.1 × 2.4 m), this cultivar is reportedly a sport from 'Wiltonii'.

Juniperus horizontalis 'Pancake'

Appropriately named, this dwarf creeping juniper grows as flat as a pancake. The feathery, scalelike bluish green foliage typically grows to only 2 inches (5 cm) tall, making it the lowest-growing form we have observed. Though some literature claims a 6-foot spread (1.8 m), we estimate a spread no greater than 2 feet (0.6 m). The foliage remains attractive all year. In winter, it turns a medium shade of purple.

Juniperus horizontalis 'Wiltonii'

This is a very popular ground cover juniper that does well in heavy clay soils. The silvery blue foliage of summer turns purple with the onset of cold weather. 'Wiltonii', also known incorrectly as 'Blue Rug', is a female form that was found off the coast of Maine and introduced by South Wilton Nursery of Connecticut in 1914.

In addition to the *Juniperus horizontalis* cultivars listed above, two newer selections, 'Gold Strike' and 'Gold Fever', will soon be available. Islei Nursery of

Boring, Oregon, reports that they tend to burn in full sun, so both appear to be great selections for dappled shade.

Juniperus pingii Ping Juniper

This obscure Asian species deserves to be offered to the landscaping public. Native to the high, forested slopes of southwest Sichuan, northwest Yunnan, and Xizang (Tibet), Ping juniper grows slowly over many years into a dense upright tree of 20 feet high × 8 feet wide (6 × 2.4 m). Resembling *J. formosana*, though much wider, it develops a broadly pyramidal, semiweeping form with slender, pendulous branchlets. Plant Ping juniper in full sun and use it to its best advantage as a specimen or accent plant. It would work well planted next to a big rock or beside a water feature.

Juniperus pingii

Juniperus procumbens Japanese Garden Juniper

Classified by some authorities as *Juniperus chinensis* var. *procumbens*, this species is native to the island of Kyushu in southwestern Japan. While the species itself seldom shows up in the South, its two cultivars are commonly grown here and always seem happy. These are 'Nana' (see below) and 'Greenmound', an introduction from Hines Nursery of Irvine, California, which differs little from the former. In its native habitat, this prostrate juniper will grow 1 to 2 feet tall and can spread 15 feet (0.3–0.6 × 4.6 m). The foliage forms a dense mat with a pleasing texture (soft to the touch) and a bluish green color. It works well in light shade and is one of the better species for the South.

Juniperus procumbens 'Nana'

Juniperus procumbens 'Nana'

The selection typically found in garden centers, 'Nana' resembles the species but is smaller, growing 1 foot tall × 10 feet wide (0.3 × 3 m). The branches mound over each other to form a neat mat that develops a slight purple cast in winter. A great selection for training over walls or massing, it also works well planted beneath taller-growing plants such as maples, dogwoods, and redbuds, as well as other conifers—particularly those of contrasting color. We have seen it used effectively as a small weeping shrub by the staking of a leader. 'Nana' is also popular for use in bonsai. The cultivar was first described around 1922.

Juniperus rigida Temple Juniper

Where space allows, this shrub or small tree makes a beautiful weeping specimen. *Juniperus rigida* often adorns temple grounds in Japan because of its signal attribute: those graceful, weeping branches. Its limbs project downward from the tree at approximately 45-degree angles, creating a ghostly appearance. Leaves are awl shaped and sharp to the touch.

The foliage bronzes slightly in winter and then turns a luscious bright green in spring. It is free fruiting (even at a young age) and does not appear to require a male pollinator, though the species is classified as dioecious. The green fruit

Juniperus rigida

matures to dark purple. Both young and mature fruits are present simultaneously, which makes for a splendid show of color, especially in winter.

Most catalogs list 'Pendula' as a cultivar of *Juniperus rigida*. After much evaluation, we have chosen to describe the species as pendulous, as this is its usual form in nature. *J. rigida* is native to China, Japan, Russia, and Korea. It will grow about 20 feet tall and 10 feet wide (6 × 3 m). Temple juniper is best suited to Zones 6 and 7, as the species is very prone to damage from spider mites in Zone 8.

Tom received a selection from Arrowhead Alpines in Fowlerville, Michigan, under the name of *J. rigida* Purnett Form. It has a slender form along the lines of some of the newer selections of Nootka cypress, and all its branches are decisively pendulous. We expect that, in time, demand for this plant will increase.

Juniperus rigida
fruit

Juniperus virginiana Eastern Red-cedar

This North American native occupies a wide swath east of the Rocky Mountains, making it the most widespread of conifers in the United States. It, too, is one of the most variable of all conifers in the world. It is fascinating to observe the numerous, varied forms one sees driving north on I-75/I-24 from Georgia to Nashville, Tennessee. Here among the ubiquitous limestone outcroppings are selections that would fit almost any landscape requirement, save one with swampy conditions. Red cedars can also be seen growing in straight rows beneath utility lines where birds have deposited seed while perched on the wires.

While there are more than 50 known cultivars, only a few ever seem to be offered by nurseries. We can only speculate as to why this is the case, but one reason may lie in their being found everywhere in the native landscape, where they come up wild from seed. For those seeking to utilize more native plants, the excellent cultivars that are in trade make wonderful additions.

While red cedar cultivars seem to thrive in limestone-based soils, *J. virginiana* has proven adaptable elsewhere. Size can range from 50-foot (15.2 m) specimens to low spreading forms. The species is closely related to *Juniperus scopulorum*, which is not particularly suited to the South. Owing to its dense growth, Eastern Red-cedar is a favorite for windbreaks and screens. On the other hand, because of its coarse root system, it is not a good candidate for transplanting. If you have to move your plants, do it when they're small. All cultivars are adaptable to light conditions from full sun to moderate shade.

Juniperus virginiana

Juniperus virginiana var. *silicicola* 'Brodie'

Variety *silicicola* is a southern form that differs little from the species (if it is indeed distinct). A comparison of 'Brodie' to straight *Juniperus virginiana* reveals that the needles of 'Brodie' are shorter. Its color is a consistent green in winter, and it has a dense, pyramidal habit to 25 feet (7.6 m) that makes it useful for screening. 'Brodie' has performed very well in Zones 6–8 and always receives positive comments. Nursery grown plants can sometimes be weak rooted and blow over in a strong wind. If you decide to purchase larger sizes, plan to stake them for the first year or two to allow for adequate root establishment. 'Brodie' was first described in 1963.

Juniperus virginiana 'Burkii'

'Burkii' is a full-size selection of red cedar with rich blue foliage that turns slightly purple in winter. For about the first 10 years it forms a dense plant with ascending branches that over time will open up if not pruned. Needles are mostly scalelike on mature plants, but awl-shaped juvenile foliage is always present—especially in the interior. Needles are not sharp to the touch. 'Burkii' will grow equally well in full sun or light shade, reaching a height of 25 feet (7.6 m). This is an older cultivar first introduced in 1932. 'Staver Blue' is a similar selection that also performs well in the South.

Juniperus virginiana 'Staver Blue'

Juniperus virginiana 'Glauca Compacta'

Whether or not this selection is indeed a cultivar of *Juniperus virginiana* remains open to question, as the plant so closely resembles *Juniperus scopulorum*.

Juniperus virginiana 'Glauca Compacta'

What we do know is that this tree performs admirably in the South and displays beautiful silver blue color year-round. We don't believe any *J. scopulorum* would perform so well. A favorite of all who see it, 'Glauca Compacta' is definitely a plant for the future in southern landscapes. This cultivar is a 1958 introduction from Monrovia Nursery of Azusa, California.

Juniperus virginiana 'Grey Owl'

As with several other cultivars within this species, the true identity of this plant remains in question: some authorities classify it as a hybrid between *J. virginiana* 'Glauca' and *J. chinensis* 'Pfitzeriana' (the latter of which it resembles in habit). The bottom line, though, is that 'Grey Owl' is a very good selection for southern gardens. Its silvery gray foliage is consistently beautiful year-round, and it will get larger than one might imagine seeing it in a one-gallon container at a nursery center: 6 feet tall with an equal spread (1.8 m). 'Grey Owl' is amenable to heavy pruning and can be shaped to fit any desired application. Introduced to the trade from the Netherlands in 1949, it reportedly derives from a seedling of *J. virginiana* 'Glauca'.

Juniperus virginiana 'Reptans'

Juniperus virginiana 'Reptans'

This low-growing form with stiff arching branches can easily be trained to weep. It is reportedly difficult to propagate, which might explain its rarity in the trade. At one time, a beautiful specimen grew in the display garden at Iseli Nursery in Boring, Oregon. During our last visit, the plant was no longer there and, sadly, had not been propagated. Fortunately, a plant is growing at Tom's arboretum, and he has shared many cuttings in hopes of getting this plant into production. 'Reptans' is a top-tier native juniper that works especially well in rock gardens. This older cultivar was first described in 1896.

Juniperus virginiana 'Royo'

A favorite of Tom's wife, Evelyn, and also of John, 'Royo' merits attention for its low-spreading habit, silver blue color, and heavy set of cobalt blue fruit. It is

Juniperus virginiana 'Royo'

particularly striking when grown on a low 1- to 2-foot (0.3–0.6 m) standard, which accentuates its flat top. The exact spread is unknown, but it should reach at least 5 feet (1.5 m). We consider 'Royo' another top-tier juniper for growing in full sun.

Juniperus virginiana 'Silver Spreader'

This excellent, trouble-free spreading juniper with silver blue foliage is appropriately named. It offers the color of 'Grey Owl' in a low-growing form. It is more arching than 'Royo' and lacks its intense blue color. California's Monrovia Nursery made this introduction in 1955.

Juniperus virginiana 'Silver Spreader'

Juniperus virginiana 'Taylor'

The best of the narrow forms we have seen, this upright grower makes a wonderful vertical statement in the landscape. The one drawback is the brownish color of its winter foliage, but 'Taylor' is otherwise a wonderful conifer to have in the garden. Introduced by the Nebraska Statewide Arboretum, 'Taylor' has proven a tough plant even for the Great Plains states.

Juniperus virginiana 'Taylor'

Keteleeria

The keteleerias are almost never mentioned in garden books, and one seldom sees reference to them in books dedicated to conifers. This may be due to the fact that almost all books on conifers tend to focus on colder climates. This is a shame, because in those locations where keteleerias can be grown, they make wonderful specimens. In fact, for gardeners with *Abies* envy, the keteleerias are quite similar. Both have cones that grow straight up, and the leaf structure is similar. Whereas the cones of *Abies* disintegrate on the tree, those of *Keteleeria* fall intact. One distinct bonus is that keteleerias tend to be better adapted to heat and drought than any of the true firs. They are moderate growers in the South and over time develop into large trees in the range of 25–30 feet (7.6–9 m). Since keteleerias show great variability in the wild, some authorities identify 10 species while others identify only two, with the rest being subspecies.

Keteleerias are best planted in full sun; they will not tolerate heavy shade or wet feet. Water them weekly during the first growing season and then only when conditions are extremely dry. Once they are well established, leave them alone. They tend not to be the happiest of plants when moved, so plan their placement in advance. Keteleerias take well to pruning, which generally should be done in early spring. A light annual haircut will result in a fuller plant. The genus was first described in 1866.

Keteleeria davidiana

While nowhere common in the South, this is the most frequently encountered species and one that has proven happy here. It is the hardiest of the keteleerias

Keteleeria davidiana

Keteleeria davidiana cones

and the best species for Zone 6 parts of the South. There are three varieties: var. *davidiana* and var. *calcarea* from southeastern and south central China and var. *formosana* from Taiwan. Where left to its own devices, it forms a pyramidal tree with two-ranked shiny dark green leaves. (A two-ranked leaf arrangement is one where leaves or needles emerge from opposite sides of the twig, with all needles on a single horizontal plane.) Beautiful specimens are located in the conifer garden at the Atlanta Botanical Garden, as well as at the J. C. Raulston Arboretum in Raleigh, North Carolina. As with many conifers, cuttings taken from side shoots will result in plagiotropic—that is, horizontal rather than vertical—growth. In John's trials, seedlings have been slow to grow in containers (possibly because of inbreeding depression resulting from self-pollination), but they take off once established in the landscape, reaching a height of 21 feet (6.4 m) in 10 years. John's tree has also been producing cones with some viable seed for several years. This species makes a fine specimen tree in the landscape. It was introduced into cultivation around 1888.

Keteleeria evelyniana

As a native to southern China, Laos, and Vietnam, this species is not as cold hardy as *K. davidiana* and may not be as drought tolerant. An exquisite specimen, which John manages, grows on the University of Georgia–Tifton campus. The leaves of K. *evelyniana* aren't as shiny as those of *K. davidiana* but are instead glaucous and more linear in shape and more upswept like those of a true fir. No cone production has been noticed on trees growing in the Southeast. Nice specimens grow at the North Florida Research and Extension Center in Quincy, Florida, and at the Lovett Pinetum in Lufkin, Texas. Trees at the Steven F. Austin State University Arboretum in east Texas were damaged by 10°F (-12.2°C)

Keteleeria evelyniana

Keteleeria evelyniana bark

temperatures in 2010. This species reportedly does not grow as large as *K. davidiana*, but this information may not be accurate. Like all keteleerias, *K. evelyniana* requires well-drained soil. It performs best in Zone 8, but plants are doing well at the Atlanta Botanical Garden site in Gainesville, Georgia (Zone 7b).

Metasequoia glyptostroboides Dawn Redwood

No conifer has a more storied history than the Dawn redwood. Along with Ginkgo, it is a living fossil that, until its discovery in 1941, was believed extinct. At one time, it was native to North America. As the story goes, in 1941 a Japanese scientist named Shigeru Miki, professor of botany at Osaka City University, published a study of certain fossils believed to be in the genus *Sequoia*. Remains of a fossil named *Sequoia disticha* had been found in rocks up to 60 million years old. In his examination of fossil fragments, Dr. Miki observed that the needles of the *Sequoia disticha* are opposite while those of *Sequoia sempervirens* are arranged in alternating pairs. Given the distinction in needle arrangement, he proposed a new genus and species, *Metasequoia glyptostroboides*—the prefix *meta-* denoting something "like" a sequoia and *glyptostroboides* denoting something like a Canton Water Pine (*Glyptostrobus pensilis*). The story almost ended there.

In 1944, a Chinese forester named Wang came upon an unfamiliar tree near the village of Mo-tao-chi, in the province of Szechwan in west central China. Collections of needles and cones were sent to the National Central University in Nanking. Realizing that the tree was one they had never seen before, Chinese botanists called in other experts. Somewhere along the way it was determined that the tree looked exactly like the fossil previously described by Professor Miki as *Metasequoia*. This event was akin to what it would be like to find a living dinosaur.

This tree—thought to be extinct for more than five million years and known only by fossil remains from Japan, North America, and Manchuria—miraculously was still growing in a remote part of China. Happily, too, because of the efforts of Dr. E.

Metasequoia glyptostroboides

D. Merrill at Harvard's Arnold Arboretum, seeds were collected in 1947 and subsequently distributed to botanical gardens throughout the world.

Interestingly, the temperature and total precipitation in eastern Szechwan where the Dawn redwood was discovered are similar to those in Atlanta, Georgia. A natural population was later discovered growing in Hupeh Province, whose climatic conditions somewhat resemble those of Georgia's Coastal Plain. As in the Coastal Plain, rainfall in the Hupeh Province is fairly heavy, about 50 inches (127 cm) a year. In contrast to the Coastal Plain, however, the winters where Dawn redwood naturally occurs are relatively dry, while the summers are wet, with most precipitation falling during the months of June, July, and August.

Like several other deciduous conifers, namely *Glyptostrobus* and *Pseudolarix*, *Metasequoia* is a monotypic genus. It also shares their trait of foliage that turns a beautiful fall color (copper brown) before needle drop in late autumn. *Metasequoia* is most closely related to *Taxodium*, from which it differs by virtue of its opposite leaves. A quick way to tell the difference is to employ the ABC rule: Alternate = Bald Cypress.

Occurring naturally at low and middle latitudes, it is well suited for almost all parts of the South. It is fast growing and performs well in dry or wet soil in full sun or light shade. It can become quite large, growing to 100 feet (30 m) over many years. Large specimens can be seen at the Atlanta Botanical Garden in Georgia, and at the Birmingham Botanical Gardens in Alabama. One of the largest specimens growing in the Coastal Plain region is on the campus of the Baptist facility in Norman Park, Georgia. To date, several gardenworthy selections of the species have been made, and new ones continue to surface. Selection work continues at the Dawes Arboretum in Ohio and at Rutgers University in New Jersey. Dawn redwood is propagated by cuttings, seed, or grafting. Pruning is rarely required as all selections are well behaved. If necessary, though, prune in late winter. Once established, *Metasequoia* is very forgiving of abuse. The species has a propensity to grow large surface roots, which is problematic in lawn areas and near or under sidewalks. We have not observed this tendency in any of the cultivars.

Several newer selections of note are a small globose form named 'Schirrmann's Nordlicht', marketed in the United States as 'Northern Light', and 'Snow Flurry', an excellent variegated selection that holds its color well, even in full sun. For a distinctive look, 'All Bronze' is a larger selection with bronzy-green foliage that turns a pleasing full bronze in the fall.

Metasequoia glyptostroboides 'Golden Dawn'

Metasequoia glyptostroboides 'Golden Dawn' (PP11848)

This patented selection is a smaller growing 'Ogon', with a brighter, crisper gold foliage that contrasts handsomely with its cinnamon-colored bark. It does not appear to be as dense as 'Ogon' and has a slower rate of growth, reaching a height of about 5 feet in 10 years with a 4-foot spread (1.5 × 1.2 m). Discovered by Kenneth W. Murray in Wilmington, Delaware, 'Golden Dawn' is the result of a seedling mutation from seeds of the species sown in 1986. A similar form from Kools Nursery in Deurne, Netherlands, and called 'Kool's Gold', reportedly has better yellow color.

Metasequoia glyptostroboides 'Ogon'

This golden-needled form is one of the best plant releases in recent history. Dutch horticulturalist Peter Zweinburg brought it to Europe, where he changed its name to 'Gold Rush'—probably because 'Gold Rush' is a catchier name for marketing purposes. The American Conifer Society recently selected it as Collectors Conifer of the Year, and it has been selected as a Georgia Gold Medal plant as well. 'Ogon' is a large-growing cultivar that holds its color well in the heat of the South. The growth rate is a bit slower than that of the species. We have seen the plant utilized in a number of handsome applications. At Plant Delights Nursery in Raleigh, North Carolina, Tony Avent has used multiple plants to form an

allée (a straight tree- or shrub-lined avenue). Japanese beetles have shown an appetite for this cultivar but nothing really serious. This cultivar was selected in 1974 from 28,000 seedlings that were irradiated with X-rays in Japan. 'Ogon' is likely the same plant as 'Golden Oji' (PP9346) before it was renamed.

Metasequoia glyptostroboides 'Ogon'

Metasequoia glyptostroboides 'Ogon, branchlet

Metasequoia glyptostroboides 'Sheridan Spire'

This cultivar is similar in all respects to the species but narrower in form. The distinctly upright branch angle should produce a slender habit as the plant ages. Discovered by Sheridan Nurseries of Canada in 1968, it was introduced in 1976.

Metasequoia glyptostroboides 'Silhouette'

This newer selection is certain to become popular once it is better known. The creamy white variegation of its spring foliage slowly fades with the heat of summer. In terms of size, it fits a niche that previously had not been filled—a narrow upright form of Dawn redwood that grows to only around 8 feet tall (2.4 m).

Metasequoia glyptostroboides 'White Spot'

In spring, faint white markings are visible in the centers of the leaves. At the onset of summer, the white fades and the foliage then differs little from that of the species. Compared to *Metasequoia glyptostroboides*, the bark of 'White Spot' is much darker and shaggier—so much so, in fact, that going by bark alone, one wouldn't believe 'White Spot' belongs to the species. We like the cultivar's dense form and distinctive dark, shaggy bark that brings winter interest to the landscape. The observed growth rate on tested plants has been slower than that of the species.

Microbiota decussata   Russian Arborvitae

This evergreen ground cover for full sun and semishady areas does reasonably well in Zone 7 and performs even better in Zone 6. It survives in Zone 8, where it

Microbiota decussata

prefers light shade, though it still turns brown in the winter, even that far south. In Zones 6 and 7, *Microbiota* will benefit from sunnier conditions and will even grow well in full sun as long as adequate moisture is provided during summer. To avoid the root rot that will kill it, do not plant *Microbiota* on poorly drained or compacted sites with heavy soils. Where this monotypic genus can be cultivated, it makes a respectable ground cover, but it will never be a mainline plant. Several West Coast and European nurseries are producing plants on standard stem that range in height from 1 to 4 feet (0.3–1.2 m). There are only two attractive cultivars with ornamental merit.

Microbiota decussata 'Jacobsen'

Derived as a sport, 'Jacobsen' is an unusual upright form that is billowy and soft to the touch. Despite being introduced in 1990, it is rarely seen in collections in the United States. To prevent its contact with the ground and rain splash, which can invite pathogens, this cultivar is best grown on a standard. Discovered by Arne Vagn Jakobsen of Denmark, this plant was introduced by Germany's Horstman Nursery.

Microbiota decussata 'Variegata'

This rarely seen green and yellow variegated form (also sold as 'Carnival') makes a beautiful plant when grown on a standard. The only nursery we know that produces it is Boyko in Boring, Oregon. Several nurseries sell a Microbiota decussata by the name 'Carnival'. Plants we have observed under this name are weakly variegated and, therefore, an inferior choice.

Nageia

This is a group of monoecious evergreen trees with five recognized species that occur naturally in southeastern Asia and Malaysia. The often densely foliated crowns produce a narrowly columnar canopy. In general, experts distinguish the genus *Nageia* from the genus *Podocarpus* because of the absence of a central midrib on its foliage and the lack of a fleshy podocarpium below its seed cone. Plants can be propagated from seed or cuttings. Cuttings root easily, but plants are slow to produce finished containers under production conditions, thus limiting commercial availability.

Nageia nagi Nagi

This tall tree or large shrub reaches heights of 75 feet (23 m) under ideal growing conditions, with 20–30 feet (6–9 m) being typical. The 3-inch (7.6 cm) leaves

Nageia nagi

are dark green and occasionally glaucous, with numerous parallel veins that converge at the tip of each leaf. In our coverage area, Nagi appears to be marginally cold hardy in Zone 8b, while larger landscape specimens grow in Zone 9a. Plants can be grown in full sun or partial shade. There are several nice specimens growing on the University of Florida campus in Gainesville. The best specimens we have seen grow at Leu Gardens in Orlando, Florida (Zone 9b). Nageias are highly susceptible to magnesium deficiency in the landscape, expressed as marginal yellowing on older foliage. This can be corrected with the application of magnesium sulfate (Epsom salts). We are not aware of any cultivar selections for this species grown in the Southeast, but John does have a selection that is cold hardy as far north as Augusta, Georgia (the border of Zones 8a and 8b).

Picea Spruces

As with some of the rarer conifers we introduce in this book, many of the spruces we discuss here have received little evaluation to date beyond trials in a few locations that include our own. In fact, we treat here only those species about which we have actual data from specific locations where they have been growing for more than five years. Given the absence of data elsewhere, we have made educated guesses about their general adaptability across the South. Based on our observations, all species listed below should perform well in Zones 6 and 7. With noted exceptions, further evaluation is required in Zone 8.

Picea chihuahuana

Typically considered plants for northern gardens, spruces are among the most underrepresented plants in southern landscapes. Nevertheless, climate adaptive species are available to match many a southern garden zone. It is a given, of course, that the further north one gardens, the more choices of spruce are available. In general, spruces are absent from Zone 8, though John is trying several species (*P. morrisonicola*, *P. orientalis*, and *P. smithiana*) and has had success with *P. chihuahuana* from Mexico for 13 years.

As a group, the spruces make an interesting study. They are an important source for the manufacture of pulp and paper, building materials, and musical instruments, and they form much of the garden backbone throughout the northern tier of the United States. At the species rank, spruces grow to be medium-sized or large trees. As with pines, it is not uncommon to find stunted spruces where growing conditions are severe—at mountain tree lines, for example, or along blustery coastal bluffs. Depending on the particular view of the taxonomist, they comprise some 35 species, and all are native to the Northern Hemisphere. They concentrate most densely in the boreal regions of the north.

Much confusion surrounds the differentiation of a spruce from a fir (*Abies*). There are a number of keys to their identities, with the most obvious one being the cones. On true firs, the cones grow upright and, upon ripening, disintegrate rather than fall to the ground intact. On spruces, the cones hang downward near the end of year-old branchlets and fall intact. With most species, the cones usually fall after the first year. The second key is found in the needles. On spruces, each needle radiates singly from a tiny peg-like projection that grows along and around the twig. When the needles fall or are removed, the pegs remain, making the twig rough to the touch. No such leaf pegs are found on firs; instead, a scar is left behind when needles fall. True to their name, fir trees are normally softer to the touch than spruces. Also, in the South, in favorable years with abundant moisture, it is not uncommon for spruces to continue growing from spring until fall.

Propagation of the species is best from seed, but selected cultivars are usually grafted. Some success has been obtained grafting *P. pungens* and other species cultivars onto *P. abies* understock. Plants grown in containers are very susceptible to root rot in Zone 8, whether grafted or on their own roots. Spruces grow best in full sun but will grow in light shade. They prefer acidic, well-drained soil that is evenly moist. All transplant well.

Picea abies Norway Spruce

Norway Spruce is perhaps the most widely planted spruce in the world and in some areas of the United States, overplanted. Such is not the case in the South. Up until 10 years ago, we would not have believed that this, or any other spruce, would be suitable for southern regions, except the higher elevations of North Carolina, Tennessee, and Kentucky. As with many other plants, we need to be willing to conduct trials of different selections to determine scientifically which ones will adapt and which ones will not. If people based their landscaping decisions solely on where a plant grows naturally, bald cypresses never would have been planted on permanently dry land nor azaleas brought to the United States.

At the species rank, Norway spruce grows to be a large tree, 40–60 feet tall × 30–35 feet wide (18 × 10.7 m). In the southern United States, this European species is rarely encountered in gardens, except in cultivar form. Several nice specimens grow in the north Georgia town of Suches and an 87-foot (26 m) specimen grows in Rabun Gap, Georgia. We recently visited the property of collector Johnny Withrow in Ellijay, Georgia, and saw numerous Norway spruce as tall as 30 feet (9 m). All were perfectly healthy. The species has naturalized in portions of the northern United States but is not reported as invasive. It is also popular as a Christmas tree. As a result of numerous witch's brooms, seedling variants, and sports, there is a *Picea abies* selection for almost every landscape application.

The species name is likely derived from the fact that, at one time, Norway spruce was commonly called Spruce fir, hence *abies*. This species grows best in Zone 7b and throughout Zone 6.

Picea abies 'Acrocona' (photo by George Bradfield)

Picea abies 'Acrocona'

Picea abies 'Acrocona'

Discovered around 1890 in a forest in Uppsala, Sweden, this popular species, still produced in large numbers, has stood the test of time and the whims of gardeners. Its most noteworthy feature is its propensity to produce an abundance of cones, even at a young age. (The name Acrocona means "with terminal cones on the ends of branches.") A five-year-old plant growing at Tom's arboretum cones heavily each year, showing off in spring its immature, purple-red cones that keep their bold color for about three weeks. 'Acrocona' grows slowly into a broadly pyramidal form around 8 feet tall and 6 feet wide (2.4 × 1.8 m). A nice specimen can be seen at the Sarah P. Duke Gardens in North Carolina.

Picea abies 'Cincinnata'

This medium-sized tree has dense branches and long, bright green needles. Its shape and habit are intermediate between snakelike forms, such as 'Virgata', and pendulous forms, such as 'Pendula'. Particularly pendulous and full, the lower branches create a draping effect. 'Cincinnata' is a good selection and a strong grower that was first described in 1897.

Picea abies 'Clanbrassiliana'

Interesting as a structural accent in the landscape, 'Clanbrassiliana' is a mounding form that grows to 5 feet tall × 5 feet wide (1.5 × 1.5 m). It retains its tight, dark green form as it matures. For those with special interest in conifer history, 'Clanbrassiliana' is reportedly the first dwarf spruce grown from a witch's broom and also the first named *Picea abies* cultivar. A choice selection that originated on the Moria estate near Belfast, Ireland, it was introduced by Lord Clanbrassil in the early 1800s—hence its name.

Picea abies 'Cobra'

Another selection from Oregon's Iseli nursery, 'Cobra' is relatively new on the scene. Intermediate between 'Pendula' and 'Virgata', this selection features a bizarre weeping form and long snakelike branches that we like. Over time, it can grow to at least 20 feet (6 m). Be sure to stake 'Cobra' when it is young, taking care to select only one terminal branch to form the central leader.

Picea abies 'Cupressina'

Another of the interesting Norway spruce cultivars, moderately fast growth and narrow habit make 'Cupressina' very popular. It is one of the narrowest forms of Norway

Picea abies 'Cupressina'

spruce known and, as its name suggests, has an upright, cypress-like habit. These features make it an excellent accent point or screening plant in the landscape. In parts of the South that receive snow, tie supports around the branches during the winter to prevent their breaking under the weight. 'Cupressina' grows about 10 feet tall and 2 feet wide (3 × 0.6 m). It was discovered growing in the wild in Germany in 1904.

Picea abies 'Formanek'

First described in 1908, 'Formanek' is the lowest-growing form we have observed. Left to its own devices over time, it will form a densely matted carpet. Its leaves are light green, and its branches radiate outward, much like those of some of the more prostrate junipers. It may occasionally produce a branch that wants to grow upward. Instead of removing the branch, we have found it easy simply to pin the branch down for a year or so, at which point it lies flat again. A U-shaped sod staple works well for this purpose and is unobtrusive. An excellent selection, 'Formanek' looks especially handsome in groupings of varied conifers and shows to its best advantage near a large rock over and around which its branches can cascade. The selection grows to a height of 1 foot with a spread of 6 feet (0.3 × 1.8 m). A taller-growing form we like is 'Reflexa'.

Picea abies 'Reflexa'

Picea abies 'Gold Drift'

'Gold Drift' is a clonal selection destined for greatness. On first seeing it at the Farwest National Nursery and Greenhouse Trade Show in 2010, we were astounded by its pendulous form and striking gold coloration. It was discovered by Bob Fincham of Coenosium Gardens in Washington State as a branch sport on *P. abies* 'Reflexa'. On Coenosium's Web site, Fincham states that 'Gold Drift' is "unlike anything else presently available anywhere." We agree. Tom has been evaluating this plant since fall 2010. The plant is bright gold in the fall and winter, and it holds its color well into May when the needles turn a light green with yellow tips. If you're looking to lighten up an area in spring with a dwarf conifer, 'Gold Drift' will do you proud. Also consider 'Perry's Gold', which has bright yellow new growth that turns lime green in the summer.

Picea abies 'Inversa'

If you're in the market for something unusual, 'Inversa' is a great choice. With creative staking, it can assume many shapes, from large and shrubby with weeping branches to any number of elegant or extravagant pendulous forms. Further adding to its allure, the main and secondary branches sweep downward in an irregular, layered fashion. For upright form, this selection must be trained. Otherwise, it will remain a sprawling plant, with a spread of around 10 feet (3 m). In its prostrate form, 'Inversa' is not as graceful as 'Formanek'. This clone was first described in 1862.

Picea abies 'Pendula'

As far as we can discern, any number of forms with pendulous branches receive the name 'Pendula'. This tendency provides a good example how plants and plant names get mixed up in the trade, and in our opinion the name should be dropped. The really good 'Pendula' selections have been trained with a main central leader and branches that cascade down. Occasionally a

Picea abies 'Pendula'

wayward branch will want to grow outward, which can disturb the plant's symmetry. By attaching a weight to a small rope and tying it to the end of the branch for about eight months, you can easily correct this. Like 'Inversa', this cultivar makes a dramatic statement in the landscape. It can be maintained in symmetrical, pyramidal form to create formal but eerie screens or allées, or it can be trained and staked to produce eccentric forms, reminiscent of topiary but shaggy. After many years, this cultivar will likely reach a height of 20 feet with a spread of 10 feet (6 × 3 m).

Picea abies 'Pusch'

Surprisingly, this dwarf cultivar is rarely mentioned in conifer literature. While not the easiest plant to grow and sometimes difficult to obtain, 'Pusch' is a worthy addition to the landscape. Its main attraction is profuse production of perfect miniature cones, even at a young age. In the continuum of cone maturation, the cones first appear at the ends of the branch tips as a bright magenta red that eventually fades to light brown. In the spring, this cone set is one of the best shows in town. This great asset, however, is also the cultivar's greatest liability: all the energy put into cone production makes for a weaker growing plant in the South. As difficult as it might be at first, the pruning of cones from young plants for the first few years might make 'Pusch' a stronger plant. This selection received the American Conifer Society's Dwarf Collector's Conifer of the Year honor in 2008. It arose from a witch's broom growing on 'Acrocona', the original of which was found by Mr. Pusch in Berlin, Germany, around 1987.

Picea abies 'Tompa'

Slow-growing at 1–6 inches (2.5–15 cm) per year, this compact form works well in large containers and where space is limited. Please, garden centers, 'Tompa' should be one of the only plants offered when customers are seeking the common Alberta spruce look. The shape is conical, and the color is a clean, bright green. Maturing to a height 5 feet with a 6-foot spread (1.5 × 1.8 m), this plant can be maintained to be shorter with annual light pruning. 'Tompa' originated at the famous Barabit's Nursery in Hungary and was described in 1987.

Picea abies 'Virgata'

Because of its bizarre form, you will either immediately take to 'Virgata' or, just as quickly, dislike it. An older cultivar described in 1853, it is commonly called the "snake branch spruce" because of its very long main branches, which have few or no lateral branches. The needles are long and dark green in color. When properly sited, 'Virgata' provides an eye-catching focal point. Other forms with open and long, whorled branches include 'Cranstonii' and the hard-to-find 'Aarburg'. Seeing a full-grown 'Aarburg' specimen at Arrowhead Alpines nursery in Fowlerville, Michigan, is as good as it gets.

Picea alcoquiana Alcock Spruce

This Japanese species seldom shows up in southern gardens, and where it does appear, it is almost certainly the cultivar 'Howell's Dwarf', which may also be listed as *Picea bicolor* 'Howell's Dwarf Tigertail'. Found mainly on the Pacific side of central Honshu, it is accustomed to a cooler climate than occurs throughout much of the South. Typically, plants from this part of Asia do well in Zones 6–7. Plants growing in partially shaded sites in Zone 7b show no signs of stress. To our knowledge, Alcock spruce's adaptability to growing conditions further south has not yet been tested. This species performs well in western Kentucky at Yew Dell Gardens, and a small specimen can be seen growing at the J. C. Raulston Arboretum in North Carolina.

Picea alcoquiana 'Howell's Dwarf'

This Alcock spruce cultivar is normally grown as a semidwarf, flat-topped shrub. This, we believe, offers the best form, allowing it to grow wide enough to make a stunning plant. Over time, it may develop a central leader and want to become an irregular-looking tree. If one desires the tree form, judicious pruning may be required to give it shape. Otherwise, allow the plant to grow to the desired height and simply remove any errant leaders. The principal reason to grow 'Howell's

Picea alcoquiana 'Howell's Dwarf'

Dwarf' is its needles—silver blue beneath and light green above. Viewed at eye level, the needles' bicoloration is clearly evident, and the silvery undersides are visible from a distance. 'Howell's Dwarf' produces pendant cones—purple when young, maturing to brown—and unlike some spruces we have evaluated, it does not tend to heavy cone production at a young age. A clone first introduced in 1985 by Vermeulen Nursery of New Jersey, 'Howell's Dwarf' typically grows 1 foot or more per year to mature at a height and width of around 6 feet (1.8 m).

Picea brachytyla Sargent Spruce

To see a well-grown, mature Sargent Spruce is to experience all that is beautiful about this genus. Sargent spruce produces a dominant central leader from which all the side branches grow horizontally long and pendulous. The needles are closely held along a midrib and curve downward. Somewhat reminiscent of *Picea alcoquiana* described above, its needles are a rich dark green and snowy white beneath.

Picea brachytyla

As with many other species, this spruce is largely untested in the South. A specimen at Tom's arboretum has been growing for several years as though it were on steroids, making us think that it may be adaptable throughout Zones 6 and 7. Based on careful observation, Sargent spruce performs well in heavy (clay) soil but probably prefers a lighter soil as long as it is kept moist. Avoid siting it in locations where it may go for long periods without water. It doesn't tolerate drought, and it will not prosper long in the shade. Give this spruce a prominent location with lots of room, as it can grow to at least 40 feet (12 m).

Picea morrisonicola Taiwan Spruce

We were first introduced to this spruce during a tour of the Mobile Botanical Garden in Mobile, Alabama, and were surprised to find such a good-looking spruce so far south. Taiwan may well prove the workhorse spruce in terms of adaptability across a wide range of growing conditions. Considered the tallest tree in Taiwan, this tree will need plenty of room to grow. We estimate a height of 20 feet (6 m) in 10 years—a growth rate much slower in Zone 8 than in Taiwan. Its light green needles are very short and densely packed. Where you want a spruce and have space to grow a big one, this choice is your best bet as far south as Zone 9a.

Picea morrisonicola

Picea omorika Serbian Spruce

This graceful spruce is one of the better conifers for the South. Its two-toned needles are green on top and bluish white underneath. One of the best features of Serbian spruce is its straight central leader, which—like all the straight species of this plant in the trade—displays some degree of pendulous branching. A number of plants are sold as 'Pendula', and owing to the variability of the species, all look different. While it grows on limestone soils in its native home on the upper Drina River in Bosnia and Serbia, it has proven perfectly adaptable to the soil types of the South. Serbian spruce also tolerates dry conditions better than most spruce species. It will grow faster, however, if you give it periodic watering during dry spells. This straight species and its cultivars are among the top-tier conifers for the South. When used as a specimen tree, any of the larger-growing Serbian spruces can bring instant "wow factor" to any landscape.

Picea omorika 'Berliner's Weeper'

Named by the late Dr. Berliner of New York State, this is our favorite of the full-size selections. It grows as straight as an arrow, with all side branches being pendulous. Intermediate in form, it is narrower than most selections sold as 'Pendula' but more open than 'Pendula Bruns'. In addition to its perfect shape, its bicolored needles—dark green above with two white bands beneath—give the tree a silvery blue-green appearance from a distance. Introduced in 1979, this cultivar can be expected to reach a final height of 25 feet with a width of 12 feet (7.6 × 3.7 m).

Picea omorika 'Nana'

Introduced by Goudkade, a Boskoop, Netherlands, nursery in 1930, 'Nana' has a tight globose form and short, glossy green needles that press flatly against its stems. Over time, the plant will probably develop one or more leading shoots that you will need to remove if you want it to retain a globe shape. 'Nana' reaches a mature size of 6 feet × 6 feet (1.8 m).

Picea omorika 'Pendula'

'Pendula' tends to be a catch-all name for a range of weeping *Picea omorika* forms in the trade. Many are extremely pendulous and eventually grow into large specimens. Your local garden center may offer some of the more garden-worthy forms of this cultivar. If you find an appealing specimen, it may be less expensive than some of the other named selections. Expect plants to reach a height of 25 feet (7.6 m). Most selections of 'Pendula' will remain narrow and are therefore useful in tight spots.

Picea omorika 'Pendula Bruns'

Selected by the American Conifer Society as a Collectors Conifer of the Year in 2007, this is a very narrow form. All of its branches cascade downward and the branching remains tight from top to bottom, making 'Pendula Bruns' a truly stunning narrow tree. A specimen growing at Jackson Nursery in Belvedere, Tennessee, performs well in full sun with little care. For some reason, we have seen several large specimens suddenly die. As the jury is still out as to why this happens, we recommend you purchase the plant in containers no larger than 3–5 gallons and then train it to grow straight for a few years. It will reach a final height of 15 feet (4.6 m). Germany's Bruns Nursery introduced this cultivar in 1955.

Picea omorika 'Peve Tijn'

For those gardening in Zone 6, 'Peve Tijn' is a bright-foliaged selection worthy of a spot in a dwarf conifer collection or among interesting small garden plants.

This cultivar was selected at Vergeldt Nursery in the Netherlands and named for the owner's son. Unfortunately, plants in Zones 7 and 8 have not performed well.

Picea omorika 'Pimoko'

Like its Oriental spruce counterpart *P. orientalis* 'Bergman's Gem', 'Pimoko' is an easy plant to design around. It is slow growing, and its short gray-green needles have silver undertones. Because of the way the shoots are arranged, 'Pimoko' offers the best silver color of the smaller globe-shaped forms. This is a great plant for contrasting the color of green-needled conifers and grows to approximately 3 feet × 3 feet (0.9 m). Found as a witch's broom on a *Picea omorika* in Germany.

Picea omorika 'Pimoko'

Picea orientalis Oriental Spruce

Oriental spruce is native to the Caucasus and northern Turkey. Along with the Serbian and Taiwan spruces, this is one of the better species for the South and should be tried in Zone 8. Oriental spruce is perhaps the most picturesque of all spruces. Visitors to Tom's arboretum rate it their favorite. It grows moderately fast and in time becomes a dense, compact, narrow pyramidal tree. It can ultimately grow to 60 feet (18 m). The short ascending branches sweep to the ground. Enhancing this effect are its dark green needles—four-sided with a blunt tip—set tightly on their stems. Cylindrical cones appear on short stalks at the branch ends, emerging with a reddish purple color that turns medium brown at maturity. Oriental spruce has the shortest needles in the genus, and the species has produced some of the best cultivars found in the world of conifers.

Picea orientalis 'Atrovirens'

If one is searching for a full-size specimen evergreen tree, this pyramidal selection should be high on the list. Like the species, it holds its shape well with no pruning and is trouble free. It is shorter than the species and also differs in its exceptionally dark green needles. Expect this plant to grow to 30 feet tall × 15 feet wide (9 × 4.6 m). 'Atrovirens' was developed before 1911 by den Ouden Nurseries, Boskoop, Netherlands.

Picea orientalis 'Aureospicata'

'Aureospicata' is slower growing than most other larger selections. Its branches sweep to the ground gracefully, and in spring the new growth is a buttery yellow that matures to dark green in about two weeks. Probably the only reason to grow this cultivar instead of 'Early Gold' is that it flushes about two weeks later, thus making it possible to extend the spring bonanza. 'Aureospicata' was first described in 1909.

Picea orientalis 'Bergman's Gem'

Growing to around 3 feet tall (0.9 m), this dense, rounded dwarf becomes conical with age. The needles are short and an exceptionally dark green. Because of its shape and size, this plant easily fits into the landscape and is one of our favorites. Kristick Nursery of Wellsville, Pennsylvania, first introduced 'Bergman's Gem' in 1980.

Picea orientalis 'Bergman's Gem' (photo by Joe DeSciose)

Picea orientalis 'Early Gold'

Picea orientalis 'Early Gold'

Of all the conifers in Tom's arboretum, no plant garners more excitement from spring visitors than 'Early Gold'. This is the one "where-can-I-buy-it now?" spruce. When the tree is situated in semishade, the needles are as dark green as those of any conifer and the habit is classic *P. orientalis*. For about two weeks in April, the new growth emerges bright yellow, making a striking contrast against its otherwise dark green, dense foliage. 'Early Gold' gives its spring performance about two weeks earlier than 'Aureospicata' and is much showier. As with all the cultivars of Oriental spruce, it flushes late enough to never suffer late spring frosts. Vermeulen Nursery of New Jersey introduced 'Early Gold' in 1979.

Picea orientalis 'Gowdy'

A narrow selection with a slower growth rate than the species, this tall, dark green, and handsome Oriental spruce has an elegant stature. The branches radiate from the main trunk in a recurved sweeping manner that brings subtle dignity and stateliness to the landscape. This cultivar was first described in 1961.

Picea orientalis 'Nutans'

As with other Oriental spruce selections, the foliage of 'Nutans' is a shiny, rich dark green all year. One of the larger cultivars, with a pleasing, irregular, weeping form, it grows slowly to a mature height of 20 feet (6 m). We consider 'Nutans' the best of the weeping forms of Oriental spruce. Found in Hungary, this cultivar was introduced in 1905 by Hesse Nursery of Weener, Germany.

Picea orientalis 'Shadow's Broom'

This beautiful selection produces bright, spring-green new growth that quickly matures to a rich dark green. As a young plant it displays a slight depression in the center, but in time it will produce a leader and slowly become a broad, mounding specimen to around 6 feet tall (1.8 m). Winchester, Tennessee, nurseryman Don Shadow discovered the plant as a witch's broom and gave it to Jean Iseli of Iseli's Nursery in 1984.

Picea orientalis 'Skylands'

The broadly pyramidal 'Skylands' continues to grow in popularity. Unlike the dark green foliage for which Oriental spruce is so noted, 'Skylands' needles are

Picea orientalis 'Skylands'

Picea orientalis 'Tom Thumb'

bright yellow year-round. Several nice specimens reside in the South where it requires partial shade, especially when young. While we have seen specimens growing over 25 feet tall (7.6 m) in Oregon, this is a slow grower, and a large specimen in the South would be around 15 feet (4.6 m). This tree is especially dramatic during the winter months when it glows like a golden statue. Unfortunately, in the South, this cultivar will never exhibit the same vivid color it displays in the Pacific Northwest or as pictured in gardening catalogs. The original plant was found at Skylands Manor House and Gardens (now Ringwood State Park) near the town of Ringwood, New Jersey. The cultivar 'Tom Thumb' is a globose, dwarf form with attractive yellow new growth. 'Tom Thumb' grows best in the upper South when grafted as a standard and placed where it can be protected from the afternoon sun.

Picea pungens Colorado Blue Spruce

Colorado blue spruce is native to the mountains of Colorado, New Mexico, Utah, Wyoming, and Idaho. Most trees in the wild are gray green, but the most popular forms of Colorado blue spruce in cultivation have been selected for blue color. The species does best in full sun in Zones 6 and 7; we do not recommended it beyond Zone 8a. Where it can be successfully cultivated, it provides unique blue color in the landscape, and some spectacular selections are available. These vary in size, color, and growth habit. In terms of adaptability, there are better spruces for the South, but none provide the same color variations that Colorado blue spruce does. To maintain its vivid blue, maintain soils on the slightly acid side and keep them moist. It is

Picea pungens

paramount that newly planted specimens receive regular water for the first year of root establishment. A nice specimen grows in Westview Cemetery in Atlanta, Georgia; several cultivars have done well at the J. C. Raulston Arboretum in North Carolina; and the plant is common in Lexington, Kentucky, landscapes.

Picea pungens 'Iseli Fastigiate'

Because of its good color and strongly ascending side branches, this plant can be used as a blue exclamation point in the landscape. Given its consistent blue color and fastigiate form, 'Iseli Fastigiate' makes a great accent plant. Expect the final size of this cultivar to be 15 feet tall × 5 feet wide (4.6 × 1.5 m).

Picea pungens 'Iseli Fastigiate'

Picea pungens 'Iseli Foxtail'

This stately blue conifer is aptly named for its tapered needles, which are longer at the shoot base than at the shoot tip. According to the late Dr. J. C. Raulston of North Carolina State University, this selection shows greater adaptability in the South than other Colorado blue spruce selections. Iseli Nursery introduced 'Islei Foxtail' in 1965 and described it in 1981. It can be expected to reach a height of 20 feet (6.1 m).

Picea pungens 'Montgomery'

Picea pungens 'Montgomery'

This dwarf, broad, globe-shaped cultivar is our favorite of the blue spruce cultivars. It is slow growing, with silvery gray-blue needles and closely set branches
that angle outward and upward from the center. During cool months, the color
is restrained, but the spring flush creates a dazzling display of blue color that
lasts until late summer. While some blue-foliaged plants are difficult to incorporate into the landscape, 'Montgomery' is perfect for today's smaller gardens.
It would work well in a rock garden, in a mixed conifer bed, or interplanted with
perennials. To maintain the desired globose habit, prune out any upright or vigorous shoots. Attains a mature height and width of 5 feet × 3 feet (1.5 × 0.9 m).

Picea pungens 'Spring Ghost'

This plant generally appears only in collections curated by people "in the know."
It has attractive light gray-green foliage with new growth that emerges buttery
yellow in spring. This color juxtaposition covers the entire tree. By June, the
needles return to light grayish green. 'Spring Ghost' probably grows to no more
than around 10 feet (3 m) in 15 years.

Picea pungens 'The Blues'

Each year, the American Conifer Society selects two conifers as Collectors
Conifers of the Year. One is an intermediate to large selection and the other a

miniature or dwarf. Both are chosen on the basis of rarity and unique features. In 2008 'The Blues' was the ACS's intermediate size selection. With strongly weeping branches and irregular spreading habit, no two plants are exactly alike. When staked to the desired height, the top will droop—a feature for which it is prized. The color is a bright silvery blue. Larry Stanley of Oregon's Stanley and Sons Nursery selected 'The Blues' from a side sport on 'Glauca Pendula'.

Given the prodigious number of introductions and with new selections being made all the time, it was a challenge to limit the number of Colorado blue spruces we cover here. In addition to those mentioned above, other good selections include 'Baby Blueyes', 'Dietz Prostrate', 'Donna's Rainbow', 'Fat Albert', 'Mrs. Cessarini', and 'St. Mary's Broom'.

Picea smithiana Himalayan Spruce

Anyone who has gardened for any length of time realizes that surprises are common. What we expect to prosper will sometimes die, and what we don't expect to live will make it, sometimes flourishing. Such is the case with this species. With origins in the western and Tibetan Himalayas and in Afghanistan, this is an unlikely spruce for the South. After first seeing several magnificent full-grown specimens at the Hoyt Arboretum in Portland, Oregon, Tom planted a specimen in 2000. It came as a pleasant surprise that the Himalayan spruce turned out to

Picea smithiana

be one of the most vigorous in his collection. Since then, several other conifer enthusiasts have also grown the species and found it adaptable.

Himalayan spruce has the longest needles of all the spruces. As it matures, the branches become quite long, and the young light green branchlets weep vertically, creating a pendulous effect.

This should be a good selection for Zones 7 and 8, though we don't recommend it for Zone 6. Give it full sun with a western exposure, and plant it in its permanent home, as it does not transplant well. It will mature to 35 feet tall and 10 feet wide (11 × 3 m).

Pinus Pines

Along with junipers, no group of plants is more underappreciated in the South than pines. Typically, what comes to mind when one thinks of pines are 60-foot (18 m) loblollies that too frequently blow over in storms. For this reason, homeowners shy away from planting pine trees, and garden centers, therefore, tend not to carry them. We are convinced that once some of the unique pine selections are better known, customer demand and retail availability will change.

With more than 100 species, pines are among the most adaptable and widespread of all conifers, and there are a number of eye-popping selections. With the exception of *Pinus merkusii* (occurring south of the Equator to 2°6'S), all pines are native to the Northern Hemisphere. They occur as trees, shrubs, and dwarf plants and are a highly variable group, even at the species rank. Because of this variability, correct taxonomic identification is sometimes difficult. One common way to distinguish certain pines is by the number of needles found in a bundle. Where pine needles arise from the stem, a scaly sheath holds them together in bundles of two, three, or five needles depending on species. The lone exception is *Pinus monophylla*, which has a single needle wrapped in a sheath of scales at its base.

All pines are monoecious. The pollen cones are small and often quite ornamental, and many of the female cones add a high degree of interest to the landscape. Pines are wind pollinated, and as anyone living in the South knows, they are capable of producing copious pollen in the spring. The female cones differ widely by species; no other conifer on earth possesses anything like the cone variability of the pine. Cones normally mature in their second year. In some species, cones drop from the tree soon after releasing their seed; on others, the cones may persist for years. Some species rely on fire to open their cones. Because such species tend to be fire resistant, fire gives their young seedlings an advantageous head start by keeping at bay other species that will compete with them for light, moisture, and nutrients. Cones of this group remain scaled by a wax substance that melts under heat, allowing the cone scales to open and release seed. In some pines, the seeds are edible (pine nuts) and found in food stores. Some seeds have a small wing to facilitate dispersal by the wind.

Propagation of the species is usually from seed, and almost all cultivars are grafted, though certain clones can be rooted. All pines prefer full sun and well-drained soil. They are adaptable to a range of soil types. Mature plants usually produce a deep taproot and may be difficult to transplant without special equipment. The further south one gardens, the more challenging it becomes to grow the five-needled species—except those from Mexico. Pines have numerous pests. John has conducted trials on more than 20 species in South Georgia and this is evident: the Nantucket pine tip moth devastates most two- and three-needled pines, whereas five-needled pines such as *P. armandii* and *P. wallichiana* do not seem bothered by this pest.

Pinus bungeana Lacebark Pine

Some collectors consider this Chinese species the holy grail of pines. Its chief attribute is the trunk's multicolored bark, reminiscent of that on our native sycamore trees. The trunk of the lacebark pine exfoliates to reveal a mosaic- or camouflage-like bark pattern of browns, rusts, greens, and creams. Needles are three to a bundle and 2–4 inches (5–10 cm) long. You can see noteworthy specimens at the National Arboretum in Washington, D.C., the Rowe Arboretum in the Village of Indian Hill, Ohio, Spring Grove Cemetery in Cincinnati, Ohio, and the Dawes Arboretum in Newark, Ohio. A beautiful specimen on the campus of the University of Georgia died in 2011 after being ravaged by bark beetles. One of the mysteries surrounding the species is that lacebark pines in China produce a vivid, almost chalk-white variation on the characteristic multicolored bark pattern. This white variation isn't seen in the United States. Some experts theorize that trunk whiteness is a function of age or that something particular in the soils or weather of the United States precludes the formation of white bark. No one knows yet the precise reason for this striking difference. Discounting its frustratingly slow growth, this is a great pine for situations where one needs a medium-sized evergreen. This one should reach a height of 25 feet (7.6 m). Best results are obtained with a multitrunk specimen, and bottom limbs

*Pinus
bungeana*

should removed to highlight the trunk. We recommend lacebark pine through-out Zones 6 and 7. The species is named after its discoverer, Dr. Bunge, who found it near Beijing in 1831.

Pinus bungeana 'Diamant'

This compact dwarf selection is one of the true gems of the garden plant realm. Its foliage is a rich bright green, and in spring, the even lighter green new growth provides a beautiful contrast. A wonderful plant for smaller spaces, expect 'Diamant' to reach a mature height and width of 3 feet × 4.5 feet (0.9 × 1.4 m).

Discovered and introduced in Germany, Diamant Nursery discovered the cultivar as a witch's broom, and Jeddeloh Nursery introduced it in 1990.

Pinus bungeana 'Rowe Arboretum'

This highly desirable selection of lacebark pine hails from the Rowe Arboretum in the Village of Indian Hill, Ohio. The cultivar has a more compact habit, with uniform growth, and reaches a final height and width of 20 feet × 10 feet (6 × 3 m). Like the species, this beautifully shaped tree also has impressive bark. 'Rowe Arboretum' may be the same cultivar as 'Compacta' mentioned in some literature.

Pinus bungeana 'Silver Ghost'

Dawes Arboretum of Newark, Ohio, introduced this gray-and-silver-barked selection. The original plant grows at the Dawes and may well be the best selection in the United States for beautiful bark color. Resembling the vivid white bark of very old trees in China and Japan, the bark on this cultivar is noticeably lighter at a younger age.

Pinus densiflora Japanese Red Pine

This species is so named because of the orange-red color of its bark, especially toward the top on mature trees. Native to Japan, China, Korea, and the Russian Far East, this is one of the better-performing pines for the South. The small cones—varying in length from 1–2 inches (2.5–5 cm) and frequently clustered in groups of three to five—remain on the tree for two to three years. Japanese Red pine typically grows with a curved trunk and becomes broadly spreading, which makes it a favorite for use in bonsai. Left untouched, it should grow to around 30 feet (9 m). Unless one is a purist, we see no reason to insist on growing only the species, as breathtaking selections are readily available. Needles on this species are two to a bundle and up to 5 inches (12 cm) long. John is working with a very nice compact selection that has performed well in Zone 8b. Spider mites can be a problem with this species. In the East, cultivars do well when grafted onto seedlings of *P. thunbergii*, though plants on the West Coast are often grafted onto *P. sylvestris*.

Pinus densiflora 'Burke's Red Variegated'

This newer introduction to the mix of variegated (Dragon's Eye) Japanese Red pines is similar to the better-known *P. densiflora* 'Oculus-Draconis' but, in our view, a better plant. For starters, the yellow-banded needles become almost white with age, and the variegation is more prominent in the winter months. Also, it has a better form than 'Oculus-Draconis' that is not as rangy as it matures. Oregon's Mitsch Nursery introduced the cultivar in 1988.

Pinus densiflora 'Golden Ghost'

This variegated Japanese Red pine is an excellent choice for those seeking a unique plant as a focal point. Besides being smaller than other variegated selections—it reaches a final height and width of about 7 feet × 5 feet (2.1 × 1.5 m)—it arguably has the best variegation. In the cooler months, the needles are bright yellow with green margins. As Mother Nature dials the thermostat above 85 degrees (29°C), the foliage begins to assume a brilliant yellow-gold color. This golden hue, which lasts throughout the fall, is created by prominent gold bands that highlight each green needle. As an added bonus, the needles seem impervious to sunburn. Given all its attributes, 'Golden Ghost' is our personal favorite among the variegated forms.

'Golden Ghost' is among a number of variegated pines in cultivation sometimes collectively called "dragon eye" pines. Though it takes some imagination,

Pinus densiflora 'Golden Ghost'

if you picture a stem in cross-section with needles radiating out from it in a circle (like the top of a bottlebrush), you can get some idea of where the term "dragon's eye" comes from. Like the iris of an eye, the white to yellow banding on the needle ends forms a pale ring around the darker green circle of the growth bud, while the brown stem end in the middle resembles an eye pupil. Taken together, they conjure up the image of a dragon's eye. The degree of banding and the vividness of the dragon's eye effect vary among cultivars.

Pinus densiflora 'Little Christopher'

Globe-shaped 'Little Christopher' is similar in form to 'Umbraculifera', except smaller. This small gem is perfectly symmetrical, with orange-red, flaky bark. The best forms we've seen are multitrunked and have had their lower limbs pruned to accentuate the contrast between the bark and the slender, bright green needles. Discovered by the late Ed Rezek and previously named 'Rezek's Witch's Broom Seedling', it was renamed and introduced in 1991. Expect a final height and width of 5 feet × 4 feet (1.5 × 1.2 m).

Pinus densiflora 'Low Glow'

The late Dr. Sydney Waxman of the University of Connecticut introduced a number of excellent pine cultivars that he grew from seed collected from witch's brooms. This low mounding form with dense green needles is, in our opinion, one of his best cultivars and was introduced in 1990.

Pinus densiflora 'Oculus-Draconis'

This selection most typifies the "dragon eye" pine. Marked with alternating yellow and green bands, the needles when viewed from above form the concentric circles of dark in light green that, for those with vivid imaginations, resemble dragons' eyes. The yellow color dulls and recedes during winter but becomes brighter and more prominent during the dog days of summer and well into fall. Strictly a collector's plant, 'Oculus-Draconis' can develop an unkempt look unless it is carefully trained. Introduced in 1890, this cultivar can reach a final height and width of 15 feet × 25 feet (4.6 × 7.6 m).

Pinus densiflora 'Pendula'

'Pendula' is a strong weeper that needs training to maintain an upright form. If left alone, it will become a prostrate creeper. A note of caution: this selection is extremely brittle and therefore difficult to reshape, so early training is essential. 'Pendula' is especially popular when grown as a low weeper that can trail over walls or when staked to form a mounded weeper. The needles are deep green and make a nice complement to the orange-red bark.

Pinus echinata Shortleaf Pine

The mention here of the species *echinata*, *elliottii*, and *taeda* is intended to acquaint the reader with a group of southern species that are almost never listed in plant catalogs or carried in nurseries. The reasons for this are fourfold. First, unlike other species, they are not prolific producers of witch's brooms. Second, they grow naturally in the region's wildlands, where they are quite common. Third, traditionally harvested for lumber, they tend to be viewed as commercial rather than as ornamental species. Last, until recently, conifers have been underappreciated, and practically all knowledge of grafting them existed *outside* the South.

Shortleaf pine is a long-lived species that in favorable conditions can attain

Pinus echinata

heights of 70–100 feet (21–30.4 m). At first glance, *P. echinata* can be confused with Virginia pine (*Pinus virginiana*). Unlike Virginia pine, however, the needles on shortleaf pine are not twisted, and its crown is more regular whereas Virginia pine's habit is scraggly. Shortleaf pine is an important source of lumber although not nearly to the extent of loblolly pine (*P. taeda*) and slash pine (*P. elliottii*). Shortleaf pine is sometimes used in naturalized plantings, in screens, and in parking lots as ornamental accents. It has two needles per fascicle with the random occurrence of a third. The species occurs naturally on clay soils in Georgia and North Florida.

Pinus elliottii Slash Pine

Slash pine is another medium to large pine, 60–100 feet tall (18–30.4 m), that is native to the South. It is indigenous to the Coastal Plain of Georgia and surrounding states, with its greatest incidence in Florida. It often occurs with longleaf pine (*P. palustris*) and with loblolly pine (*P. taeda*). It is difficult to tell the difference between loblolly and slash pine without counting the needles: slash has two needles per fascicle, with an occasional third, whereas loblolly is always three-needled. While slash pine occasionally makes an appearance in naturalized plantings, in screens, and as ornamentals in parking lots, its principal use is for lumber, pulpwood, and plywood.

Pinus flexilis Limber Pine

Limber pine is so named because of the flexibility of its branches: the twigs are so flexible, they can be tied into knots. Naturally a high-elevation pine, it must be limber to survive the weight of heavy snow. It is native to the Rocky Mountains from Canada to New Mexico at elevations of 5,000 to 12,000 feet. It typically grows 25–60 feet tall (7.6–18 m) with a pyramidal habit that rounds as the tree matures. In the South, this species will probably grow no taller than 25 feet (7.6 m). This species' needles are 1.5–4 inches long (1.3–10 cm) and come five to a bundle. Note, however, that limber pine is not the only five-needled pine with flexible twigs and branchlets, so these needle characteristics are not a reliable key in its identification. In cultivation, limber pine is known mostly through its cultivars. Because it prefers cooler climates, it is not recommended south of Zone 7b.

Pinus flexilis 'Cesarini Blue'

This is the bluest form of limber pine we have evaluated in our trials. The needles' brilliant powder blue color is most intense from midsummer through winter. Perfect for smaller yards and large planters, this moderately slow grower reaches a size of about 15 feet tall × 6 feet wide (4.6 × 1.8 m). In the event you want to keep it smaller, it takes well to pruning. Joe Cesarini of Maryland originally made this selection.

Pinus flexilis 'Vanderwolf's Pyramid'

For good reason, this is perhaps the most popular of the limber pines in commercial production. While not possessing the intense blue of 'Cesarini Blue', this compact dense pyramid has handsome, closely spaced, twisted, silver-blue-green needles that retain their color well. It has demonstrated high resistance to both insects and diseases. Vermeulen Nursery of New Jersey first introduced the cultivar in 1972 and apparently named it after the nursery's general supervisor, Rein W. Vanderwolf. Expect a final size of 20 feet tall × 12 feet wide (6 × 3.7 m).

Pinus glabra Spruce Pine

In the upper portions of the South, Virginia pine and Table Mountain pine are the dominant short-needled species. As one moves into the Deep South, a different short-needled species dominates. Only rarely seen in cultivation, spruce pine is nonetheless an alluring tree where it appears. The tree's name relates to its bark, which, as the tree matures, resembles that of a spruce more than that of a pine. Spruce pine has several unique characteristics, such as an ability to tolerate moderate shade and wet soil. In its native range, it grows near blackwater streams in the Coastal Plain region of the southeastern United States, which probably accounts for its adaptability to shaded, moist soils. Spruce pine also retains its lower limbs better than most pines and produces a straight trunk. Combined, all these attributes make it a versatile evergreen landscape tree. North Carolina

Pinus glabra

Arboretum in Asheville features a beautiful grove, and stunning specimens grow at the Bartlett Tree Research Arboretum in Charlotte, North Carolina, the Kanapaha Botanical Garden in Gainesville, Florida, and the Coker Arboretum on the University of North Carolina campus.

In its native habitat, the species can grow quite large, but in cultivation it grows slightly larger than Virginia pine, to around 35 feet (10.6 m). Some specimens appear shorter and fuller, more like Virginia pines; others grow tall and narrow, more like trees typically found in the wild. Spruce pine is a must-have pine for Coastal Plain landscapes, both for its sheer beauty and because it doesn't drop tons of large pine cones in the landscape. Needles of this species are two to a bundle and 1½–3½ inches long (3.8 × 8.9 cm).

Pinus heldreichii Bosnian Pine

In the literature, the Bosnian pine is often called *P. leucodermis* var. *heldreichii*. Because several leading taxonomists such as Aljos Farjon and David M. Richardson no longer treat *P. leucodermis* as a valid species, we have chosen to go with *P. heldreichii*.

The Bosnian pine has consistently been one of the top performers at Tom's arboretum in Zone 7. Based on its disease and pest resistance, needle retention, and ease of care, this pine should adapt well across Zones 6–9a. Bosnian pine has produced a number of excellent cultivars, valuable from an ornamental perspective. For this reason, we see no reason to grow the conventional species, though it is, nonetheless, a wonderful pine with many good qualities. Its dark green needles tend to persist for five to six years, giving it a full appearance. It is native to the Balkan Peninsula from Bosnia and Herzegovina to northern Greece, Bulgaria, and Albania. Despite its natural occurrence on dry, alkaline soil, it is adaptable to many soil types as long as there is adequate drainage. For this species, needles are two to a bundle and 2½ inches (6 cm) long.

Iseli Nursery in Boring, Oregon, has introduced a number of stunning cultivars, which they selected from seed-grown plants. While some are similar, all have their own special allure, and the fact that they are easy to grow puts them high on our list. All are salt-tolerant. Most nurseries are using *P. sylvestris* (Scots pine) as the understock.

Pinus heldreichii 'Emerald Arrow'

Possessing rich, dark foliage, this beautiful selection has a compact habit and a generally upright spire form that makes it a stately landscape specimen. Expect a mature height and spread of 15 × 6 feet (4.6 × 1.8 m). Iseli Nursery in Oregon introduced this cultivar.

Pinus heldreichii 'Green Bun'

'Green Bun' presents a more compact, dwarf form that is slower growing than the species. The densely held needles are dark, glossy green. Expect this selection, similar to 'Compact Gem', to reach a final size of 4 feet × 4 feet (1.2 m). Iseli Nursery introduced 'Green Bun' around 1982.

Pinus heldreichii 'Indigo Eyes'

Several years ago, Tom was visiting Rich's Foxwillow Pines Nursery in Woodstock, Illinois, and stumbled upon a pine with distinctive blue cones. So breathtaking was the color that other visitors immediately heard his heart palpitations and the multiple clicks of his camera shutter. The plant label read, 'Indigo Eyes'. This cultivar's form is similar to that of 'Emerald Arrow', which means that it will remain upright with dark green foliage. The real showstopper is the indigo-blue of its cones, which are especially dramatic against the dark, dense needles. We know of no other pine with cones this color. The cultivar is another introduction from Oregon's Iseli Nursery.

Pinus heldreichii 'Indigo Eyes'

Pinus heldreichii 'Irish Bells'

This new cultivar from Iseli Nursery will form a small, sturdy tree. 'Irish Bells' grows wider than it does tall: 10 feet tall × 12 feet wide (3 × 3.7 m). The stiff, deep green needles tuft the upper portion of the shoots, allowing the silver-white stems to show prominently through the foliage.

Pinus heldreichii 'Mint Truffle'

This new cultivar was selected for its especially dense, mint-green foliage and broad, teardrop shape. This introduction from Iseli Nursery should mature to a height and width of around 10 feet × 6 feet (3 × 1.8 m).

Pinus heldreic
'Smidtii'

Pinus heldreichii 'Smidtii'

Although a bit tricky to grow, this plant is another of the must-have conifers for the crazed collector willing to give it a good site. Eugene Smidt found it in 1926 as a seedling variant in the mountains near Sarajevo, Yugoslavia (now Bosnia and Herzegovina). Though very slow growing, it is well worth the wait. Over time, it forms a dense, compact mound of bright green needles that is perfect for a rock garden, container, or mixed bed. The new growth appears in neat, tightly tufted candles of ivory, pale brown, or light green color. The American Conifer Society selected 'Smidtii' as the dwarf Collectors Conifer of the Year for 2009. (It is incorrectly listed in a number of nursery catalogs as 'Schmidtii'.) You can expect the cultivar to grow slowly to around 3 feet × 3 feet (0.9 m).

Pinus koraiensis Korean Pine

Recognized mainly by several great cultivars we would choose over the species, the little-known Korean pine is underutilized in the parts of the South where it could grow well: Zones 6 and 7. It is painfully slow to grow for the first five years, which might be a plus for those with limited space. The pollen cones are crimson—unusual in the male strobili for pines. Korean pine is native to northeast China, Far East Russia, Korea, and Japan and has needles five to a bundle, 2.4–5 inches (6–13 cm) long. This species performs better in the Louisville, Kentucky, area than the native *P. strobus*.

A newer selection that is certain to make a big splash once it is better known is 'Gee Broom', which was discovered as a witch's broom at Gee Farms nursery in Stockbridge, Michigan. The needles are shorter than the species and remain a bluish green with silver undertones. We like this plant and rate it as the best of the dwarf Korean pines.

Pinus koraiensis 'Morris Blue'

Originating from the Morris Arboretum in Pennsylvania, this tall-growing tree of 40 feet (12 m) is a real beauty. It was chosen primarily for a stately, pyramidal growth habit and silver-blue color, both of which are superior to the species. The two-toned needles are similar to those of the cultivar 'Silveray'. Pay close attention to annual candle pruning, because 'Morris Blue' has a tendency to become open with age. Having seen the mother plant, we consider this selection highly desirable if one has the time and space to let it develop. A handsome specimen is thriving at Lockerly Arboretum in Milledgeville, Georgia, and a healthy 12-year-old tree is growing at Tom's arboretum. This suggests that Korean pine is adapted to a fairly wide range of growing conditions. Plants can be observed in Zone 7 in the South, but older specimens can also be found in Philadelphia, Pennsylvania, and on Long Island in New York. Another

Pinus koraiensis 'Morris Blue'

nice upright selection worth searching for is 'Jack Korbit' which, though slow growing, is exceptional for its soft, lush, blue-green needles and tight form.

Pinus mugo Swiss Mountain Pine, Mugo Pine

The Swiss Mountain pine is a highly variable species that has produced numerous cultivars. Owing to its native environment, its growth habit ranges from shrub-like to prostrate. Native primarily to subalpine regions in Spain and across central Europe to Ukraine, Italy, and Romania, this is not the best selection for most of the South, especially for Zones 7b and higher. Nonetheless, garden centers continue to stock these pines by the thousands, partly because nursery managers are uninformed and partly because they remain in demand. Some of the more ornamental dwarf pine selections originate from this species, so home gardeners seem to favor them. And in the cooler parts of the South, including Zone 7a, they do moderately well.

For those who insist on purchasing a Swiss Mountain pine, make sure to give it absolutely perfect drainage. It also may benefit from light shade after 2:00 p.m., so keep this in mind when selecting a planting site. Finally, because mugo pines best adapt to transplantation at smaller sizes, start with a plant in a #1 container.

Needles, two to a bundle, are 1–2 inches (2.5–5 cm) long and slightly twisted. For those wanting a variegated form, consider 'Carnival'.

Pinus mugo 'Mini Mops'

'Mini Mops' is a very slow-growing, tight globose form with evenly spaced needles on short branchlets. At maturity it forms a deep green ball probably no wider than 2 feet (0.6 m). A good rock garden plant, this cultivar is especially attractive in spring when it produces a profusion of dwarf candles.

Pinus mugo 'Winter Gold'

As the name suggests, this selection turns golden yellow during the colder months. Though the shrub has a spherical form, its habit tends to be more open. There are a number of similar forms in the trade, and most are indistinguishable to the untrained eye.

Pinus nigra Austrian Pine

This species is widely distributed throughout Europe. As with many of the pine species described here, we recommend you stick to the cultivars unless you are a purist. That said, the species forms a nice tree with a straight trunk and beautiful light gray to dark brown bark. Etched in our memories are several huge old trees with almost white, deeply fissured bark growing beside the administration building at the Scott Arboretum of Swarthmore College in Pennsylvania. *P. nigra* is best suited to Zones 6 and 7a, as it does not handle heat and humidity well.

This pine's needles are two to a bundle, 3–4 inches (7.6–10 cm) long, and slightly twisted.

Pinus nigra 'Oregon Green'

We are quite enamored of this selection, found and introduced by Van Meter Nursery of Gresham, Oregon. It is an unusual selection with much shorter, stiffer needles and a smaller, more compact growth habit than the species. In the spring, pale green to white candles shoot up in various lengths from the dark green needles. All who observe it at Tom's arboretum rate it as one of their favorites. 'Oregon Green' makes a great stand-alone specimen. Expect a final height of 10–12 feet and a width of 8–10 feet (3–3.7 × 2.4–3 m).

Pinus nigra 'Oregon Green'
(photo by George Bradfield)

Pinus palustris Longleaf Pine

This three-needled species enjoys the distinction of having some of the longest needles of all pines—up to 17 inches (43 cm) on young trees. As the tree ages, the needles shorten to around 8 inches (20 cm). Longleaf pine is a fire-successional species that starts out in a "grass stage." That is, the stem of the young seedling elongates little during the first several years and bears many long, curved leaves. At this stage, the plant resembles a dense clump of grass. It remains in this stage

Pinus palustris

for three or more years, during which time it spends most of its energy developing a deep taproot. As the tree begins to grow, it will be sparsely branched but retain a particular charm. At maturity, Longleaf pine is a graceful tree with a straight trunk and long cones up to 10 inches (25 cm). This beautiful pine is the state tree of Alabama, and, before extensive logging, it was the dominant tree in the South, estimated to have once covered at least 60 million acres (24 million ha). In the southern portion of its range, it overlaps with *Pinus elliotii* var. *elliotii* (slash pine); the two are easily confused as the needles of the latter are almost as long. On longleaf, the ends of branches are thick and stocky, and on slash, they are slender. Old-growth stands provide habitat for the endangered red-cockaded woodpecker.

Pinus parviflora Japanese White Pine

This species has produced some of the best conifer selections available in the trade. We have never seen one we didn't like, and deciding which ones to feature here was a challenge. Native only to Japan, the Japanese white pine has blue-green needles and is an early cone bearer. Given the large number of excellent cultivars, the species itself is seldom used in gardens, even in Japan. Japanese white pine does best when grown in Zones 6 and 7. Needles of this species are five to a bundle and 4–7 inches (1.6–2.8 cm) long.

Pinus parviflora 'Glauca Brevifolia'

A tall, fast-growing tree of pyramidal habit, it is quite similar to 'Glauca' except with shorter, upcurved needles. The undersides of the needles are silver and glisten in sunlight. 'Glauca Brevifolia' produces numerous cones that remain on the tree for several years. This selection's only negative is a tendency to form long internodes along the main trunk, which can give it a gangly appearance. Judicious candle pruning in spring can mitigate this. First described in 1890, it is also known as 'Brevifolia'.

Pinus parviflora 'Goldilocks'

'Goldilocks' is an excellent choice for a distinctive accent where one has some high afternoon shade. This dense, smaller-growing gem is advertised as having bright gold leaves, but in the South, count on the yellow to be muted. The color is most vivid in the spring and enhanced by the small colorful cones produced near the top. For particularly striking landscape applications, try growing it in a blue pot or near a water feature with Japanese iris.

Pinus parviflora 'Kinpo'

A 1976 introduction, 'Kinpo' is a slow-growing, compact bush form that will likely not exceed a height and width of 4 feet (1.2 m). The blue-green needles are quite short and hug the stems. This selection's main features are its tight growth and intense needle color. We like this plant.

Pinus parviflora 'Miyajima'

Named for its place of origin, Japan's holy Miyajima Island, this beautiful plant is one of the best of the *P. parviflora* selections. With short, slightly curved, two-tone needles, its foliage is similar to that of 'Brevifolia' but without the pyramidal, tree-like habit. Contrary to what most references state, this is a semidwarf upright shrub with a spreading habit. It cones freely at a young age, with most cones forming near the top in clusters of four or more right next to the stem. The color contrast created by the young roseate cones set among the short, blue-white needles is very striking. Often used in bonsai, this is an old cultivar dating from 1890.

Pinus parviflora 'Tanima-no-uki'

'Tanima-no-uki' is an uncommon selection of Japanese white pine and a favorite of all who see it. The creamy-white needle clusters at the stem tips cap the green needles below. This pattern coupled with the appearance of orange-red buds and stems in spring makes 'Tanima-no-uki' a very interesting plant. It is extremely slow growing, though. This cultivar does best when given a bit of shelter from hot afternoon sun. Kristick Nursery of Wellsville, Pennsylvania, introduced 'Tanima-no-uki' in 1990.

Pinus pseudostrobus False White Pine

Endemic to Mexico, false white pine gets its name from the fact that its cones and long, slender needles in bundles of five resemble those of eastern white

Pinus pseudostrobus

pine (*P. strobus*), even though the two plants occupy different subgenera. John has conducted trials of numerous Mexican and Central American pines, and *P. pseudostrobus* is the standout winner. After 10 years in the field, John's pine reached a height of 32.5 feet with a spread of about 25 feet (9.9 × 7.6 m). Initial growth was very pyramidal, but with age the canopy has become more flat-topped. The long, pendulous needles are very attractive, and most visitors exclaim that they have never seen such a beautiful pine before. Plants grown from seed are variable in form and pest resistance. Seedlings are attacked by tip moths, but older trees do not seem to be bothered. Several older specimens grow at the University of Florida campus in Gainesville (Zone 9a), and the tree is definitely worth a try in the Coastal Plain, but we are not sure of its hardiness north of Zone 8.

Pinus pungens Table Mountain Pine

An Appalachian Mountain species that grows on rocky, dry ridges, this pine will probably remain confined to specialty collections, botanical gardens, and arboreta. The species would have escaped our notice had we not observed several specimens at the Dawes Arboretum in Newark, Ohio. Even from a distance, they beckoned us to come closer for a better view. Besides the tree's irregular growth, flat top, and stout branches, the unusual cones caught our attention. Attached directly to the branches, the cones are barbed with stout, curved and hooked prickles. We decided to collect one and later discovered the botanical meaning of the word *pungens*: "sharply pointed, spiny." The cones are virtually impossible to remove from the tree with bare hands. Table mountain pine's native range extends from Pennsylvania down into the northern fringe of Georgia. Whereas the Virginia pine (*Pinus virginiana*) is native to the Piedmont, this species, native to Appalachia, is a stiff cousin. It has its own unique, stunted charm that, like some of the western pines, speaks to its harsh surroundings. Expect a final height of 20–30 feet (6–9 m). Best suited to Zones 6–7a, this species' needles are 2–3 inches (5–7 cm) long in bundles of two.

Pinus strobus Eastern White Pine

Ranked the tallest growing tree in the eastern United States, *P. strobus* is the only five-needled pine native to that region. Capable of growing to 200 feet (61 m), it is second in size only to the West Coast's sugar pine (*P. lambertiana*), which does not prosper in the Southeast. The 2½–5-inch (6.3–12.7 cm) blue-green needles are noticeably slender and soft to the touch, and the 4–8-inch (10–20 cm) slender cones are unique among eastern species. The handsome eastern white pops up sporadically in Zone 6 and 7 landscapes. In Zone 7, it may benefit from light afternoon shade. We do not recommend this pine south of Zone 7, however, because in more southerly regions it dies suddenly from root rot at 15–20 feet.

Pinus strobus 'Angel Falls'

Several years back, this cultivar was the rage among conifer collectors: a one-gallon plant sold at an American Conifer Society live auction for more than $250. The original plant came from seedlings started at Iseli Nursery in 1981. The growers were astute enough to recognize a special pine and named it for the world's tallest waterfall: 'Angel Falls' in Venezuela. The plant has a graceful, weeping habit that requires staking to the desired height. It works best as an eye-catching focal point for that special place in the landscape.

Pinus strobus 'Angel Falls'

Pinus strobus 'Blue Shag'

Selected by the late Sydney Waxman of the University of Connecticut, this is a nice dwarf form introduced in 1978. Those familiar with Dr. Waxman's work appreciate the beauty of his selections, many of which derive from seed collected from witch's brooms. 'Blue Shag' produces long, soft, blue-green foliage and an outstanding, compact, reliably

Pinus strobus 'Diablo'

rounded form. This is a slow-growing selection whose height and width will probably not exceed 4 feet (1.2 m). Another dwarf selection we like is 'Diablo'.

Pinus strobus 'Contorta'

This pine is an oddity in the plant world, because its needles and stems are twisted. It almost looks as if it received a dose of herbicide! While all who see 'Contorta' are enamored of its uniqueness, we are not sure that admiration is the same thing as actual landscape merit. Left alone, it will assume an open pyramidal form and slowly grow to around 25 feet high × 6 feet wide (7.6 × 1.8 m). In the South, specimens are on display at the J. C. Raulston Arboretum in Raleigh and the Bernheim Arboretum and Research Forest in Clermont, Kentucky. This cultivar reportedly originated at Seneca Park in Rochester, New York, during the 1930s.

Pinus strobus 'Niagara Falls'

At the time of this writing, 'Niagara Falls' is the buzz among conifer nuts. It is also the American Conifer Society's 2009 Collectors Conifer of the Year for full-size selections. A slower-growing cultivar, its dense foliage cascades as the tree mounds and sprawls to look quite like the famous Niagara Falls on the border of New York and Ontario. This may be the best-ever introduction of a weeping form of white pine and is another Iseli Nursery selection that began as a mutation on *Pinus strobus* 'Pendula'.

Pinus strobus 'Stony Brook'

Selected by Gregg Williams at Vermont's Kate Brook Nursery, this is our top pick among the numerous pendulous forms. 'Stony Brook' is distinctive in its long needles and undulate branches that twist and turn as they assume a pendant attitude. An exceptional accent plant, 'Stony Brook' makes a great display beside a water feature or overhanging a stone wall.

Pinus strobus 'Winter Gold'

This is one of two pine cultivars suitable for the South that reliably turn bright yellow in winter. This full-size selection displays a softer, light golden yellow than the other selection, *P. sylvestris* 'Gold Coin'. Also known as 'Hillside Winter Gold', this cultivar was first described in 1985. If you are searching for the perfect tall, slender-growing white pine, consider the selection 'Stowe Pillar'.

Pinus sylvestris Scots Pine

Scots pine is the national tree of Scotland. It has the twin distinctions of being the most widely distributed pine in the world and one of only three conifers native to the United Kingdom. It ranges from Spain across northern Europe, through Siberia nearly to the Pacific coast, and as far south as Mongolia. Given this span, Scots pine is a highly adaptable species that has produced a significant number of gardenworthy cultivars. Needles occur in pairs of 1½–2½ inches (4–7 cm) long. Scots pine grows best from Zone 7b northward.

Pinus sylvestris 'Gold Coin'

Certain to brighten the winter countryside, this is one of the most reliable of all conifers for bright gold color in the winter. As soon as the first freeze occurs, the thick needles seem almost magically to transform from light green to an intense yellow that lasts until mid-spring. Its intermediate size and upright, broadly conical form make it a wonderful accent plant for landscapes of all varieties.

Pinus sylvestris 'Gold Coin'
(photo by Courtenay Vanderbilt)

Pinus sylvestris 'Green Penguin'

Every once in a while a plant comes our way that really grabs our attention. This is certainly true of the diminutive pine, 'Green Penguin'. Slow growing to a height and width of around 6 × 4 feet (1.8 × 1.2 m), its very dense, rich green needles overlap to create a layered effect, which we predict will make it a future star.

Pinus sylvestris
'Green Penguin'

Pinus taeda Loblolly Pine (NCSU dwarf group)

Loblolly pine is a common tree in the Piedmont and Coastal Plain of the southeastern United States. It occurs in pure stands and is one of the first plants (pioneer species) to colonize an area after its disturbance by fire, heavy grading, or the like. One of the tallest pines in the region, it can grow to 100 feet (30.4 m). It is also an effective self-pruner, developing an oval, somewhat open, crown with no lower branches on its fairly straight trunk. One of the easiest ways to identify loblolly pine is by the presence of sharp, downturned prickles on its cones. Loblolly also consistently has three yellow-green needles per fascicle.

With increased home building across the South, residential developers have frequently left loblolly pines in place, and many homeowners have learned the hard way that a 100-foot loblolly next to a house is not a friend. In severe storms, these pines easily shed their thick branches and wreak havoc on roofs. This tendency among loblollies is probably one of the main reasons pines are mostly absent from planted landscapes in the South.

A number of dwarf loblolly pines growing at the J. C. Raulston Arboretum of North Carolina State University (NCSU) were planted under the supervision of the late Dr. Raulston and are among the more treasured plants at the arboretum. (In this specific instance, the term "dwarf" refers to a height of approximately

Pinus taeda NCSU dwarf group

30 feet [9 m] after many years.) These plants are now being labeled as *Pinus taeda* NCSU Dwarf Group. Doremus Nursery near Warren, Texas, offers an illegitimately named cultivar 'Nana' that is propagated by grafting. The nursery's original plant was propagated via scion wood grafts taken from cuttings sent from the Raulston Arboretum. Like the original plants, the tree grown by Doremus features a strongly horizontal branching habit with a tendency to retain lower limbs.

In 1987 (21 years after arriving at NCSU), Dr. Raulston wrote the following: "Among the finest plants in the NCSU Arboretum is a group of about forty-five 30-year-old dwarf loblolly pines which arose as seedlings from cones of witch's brooms originally collected by university forestry researchers. Twenty-three years later, the slow growing seedlings now vary in height from 8 feet to 15 feet (2.4 m to 4.5 m) with beautiful, dense rounded crowns."

The seed for this group reportedly came from a single witch's broom collected in Virginia in 1964 for potential use as a dwarfing rootstock in forestry production. In 1966, Dr. Fred Cochran took cuttings from two trees grown from this seed, and these cuttings were later planted in the Raulston Arboretum. Seedlings from these trees are about 20 percent dwarf, and juvenile material can be rooted at low percentages.

Pinus thunbergii Japanese Black Pine

Endemic to the coastal hills and mountains of Japan and South Korea, the Japanese black pine is at home throughout most of the South. Picturesque when young, with age it develops an open, irregular structure with stiff needles that are not particularly attractive. If one took the time to train it, a handsome specimen might result, but with so many great cultivars to choose from already, we are not keen on growing the straight species. Numerous selected forms are highly recommended, including at least one natural hybrid.

Once established, Japanese black pine is quite drought tolerant and doesn't seem to be fussy as to soil type. Tolerant of salt spray, it is a good candidate for seaside plantings. While it does best in Zones 6 and 7, Japanese black pine grows seaside as far south as Jacksonville, Florida. Needles occur in pairs, 3–5 inches (7.6–12.7 cm) long.

Pinus thunbergii 'Banshoho'

This excellent Japanese pine is a dense plant with dark green foliage. Over time, it will form a nice, uniform mound about 10 feet (3 m) wide. As dark a green as that of any pine cultivar we have observed, the foliage is accented by numerous white buds in spring. 'Banshoho' was first described in 1975.

Pinus thunbergii
'Beni Kujaku'

Pinus thunbergii 'Beni Kujaku'

This attractive upright form is similar to 'Torabu Matsu', with foliar variegation occurring at the base of the needles rather than out toward the tips. Individual shoots can be quite stunning on a cloudy day. Some authorities consider this selection a hybrid between *P. densiflora* and *P. thunbergii*.

Pinus thunbergii 'Thunderhead'

Whoever came up with this name did an excellent job. Spring's new candles set within tight, beach ball–sized clusters of dark green foliage suggest lightning

Pinus thunbergii 'Thunderhead'

darting through a looming thundercloud. The habit is broadly spreading to a height and width of 8 × 10 feet (2.4 × 3 m). Vermeulen Nursery of New Jersey introduced this cultivar in 1987. We consider it a top-tier plant.

Pinus thunbergii 'Torabu Matsu'

If you're looking for a fast-growing selection with the most unusual variegation of any of the variegated pines, this might just be the best ticket. Overall and down to each needle, 'Torabu Matsu' looks as if it were spray painted with flecks of gold. This long-needled selection has good form for a taller-growing cultivar and glimmers like a beacon in the afternoon sun. Because it lacks aesthetic subtlety, site this plant where it can provide contrast without overpowering its neighbors.

Pinus thunbergii 'Torabu Matsu' (photo by Joe DeSciose

Pinus virginiana Virginia Pine

Beyond its frequent cultivation for the Christmas tree trade in the Deep South, Virginia pine gets no respect. Ranging naturally from the Piedmont as far south as northern Alabama and Georgia, this pine can be identified by its scraggly, dense appearance and slightly twisted needles. With twisted trunks and numerous twigs, the more interesting forms are typically small trees that may become broad and flat-topped with age. Virginia pine cones heavily and retains its cones for several years. Needles are two to a bundle, reaching lengths of 1½–3 inches (3.8–7.6 cm).

Pinus virginiana 'Ancient Wonder'

Reminiscent of Monterey cypress along the California coast, 'Ancient Wonder' is best described as having a windswept appearance with long branches that sweep all the way to the ground. In an old cow pasture in Canton, Georgia, Tom discovered a specimen whose age various authorities have estimated at more than 150 years. While all surrounding trees had long since been removed, the various

Pinus virginiana 'Ancient Wonder'

property owners apparently appreciated this one pine's beauty and spared the ax. Propagation efforts are under way both here and in Europe, and we expect this selection to be available within a few years. 'Ancient Wonder' grows to 20 feet tall with an equal spread (6 m).

Pinus virginiana 'Bernie'

Though difficult to locate, 'Bernie' is certainly worthy of a place in southern landscapes. Growing to a height and width of about 6 feet (1.8 m), it forms a dense plant with bright green needles. One of the few named selections of Virginia pine arising from a broom, it was found growing at the Bernheim Arboretum and Research Forest in Clermont, Kentucky.

Pinus virginiana 'Driscoll'

To quote the well-known Oregon nurseryman Larry Stanley, "best of the series." We first saw this tight-cushioned pine at the Bartlett Arboretum in Charlotte, North Carolina, and were immediately captivated by its light green color, rounded form, and dwarf size. Because of its slow growth, 'Driscoll' will not soon overwhelm its neighbors. We agree with Larry, adding that of all the globose forms of pines we've seen, 'Driscoll' is in the top five.

Pinus wallichiana Himalayan White Pine

Indigenous to the Himalayan region where it is an important timber tree, this species and its cultivars are among the stateliest of all pines in the world. Though the straight species is rarely available, we nonetheless find ourselves captivated by its charm. At maturity, it becomes a graceful, broadly pyramidal tree with wide sweeping branches. Himalayan white pine tends to retain its lower branches as it matures. With age, the older needles droop and impart softness to the landscape. In the South, expect a moderate height and width to 30 × 20 feet (9 × 6 m). The blue-green needles, up to 8 inches (20 cm) long, occur in bundles of five. John has an unnamed selection growing well in Tifton, Georgia (Zone 8b).

Pinus wallichiana 'Frosty'

Some confusion surrounds this cultivar: in several well-respected collections, we have observed specimens labeled 'Frosty' that looked like the straight species while others so labeled are variegated. The true cultivar does not grow as large as the species and produces a denser crown. During winter, its grayish green needles develop a cream yellow cast that gives them the appearance of being frosted. This selection's best features are its soft texture and dense rounded canopy. Introduced to the trade in 1986, 'Frosty' can be expected to grow to 20 feet high and wide (6 m).

Pinus wallichiana 'Zebrina'

This variegated selection of the beautiful Himalayan pine has the same long, thin, straight needles of the species but with bands of blond yellow that create a

Pinus wallichiana 'Zebrina'

lovely warm yet misty effect both up close and at a distance. Still very popular, 'Zebrina' is an old selection from 1889.

Pinus yunnanensis Yunnan Pine

A Chinese endemic species, Yunnan pine, like so many plants from southwest China (Sichuan, Yunnan, Guizhou, Guangxi), adapts well across the American South. Considered hardy in Zones 6b–8, Yunnan pine, when young, closely resembles our native longleaf pine (*P. palustris*). Because all of its lower branches are pendulous, Yunnan sometimes resembles "Cousin It." The needles usually occur in bundles of two, sometimes three, and grow as long as 11 inches (30 cm).

Pinus yunnanensis

Platycladus orientalis Oriental Arborvitae

Though sometimes treated as a member of genus *Thuja* (*Thuja orientalis*), Oriental arborvitae is now classified by most authorities as a separate genus. It has been cultivated for centuries in Asia, where many old trees are valued as national treasures. Outside an arboretum or botanical garden, you are unlikely to encounter the straight species, which can grow to be a magnificent tree of large proportions. Numerous cultivars can be found, however, particularly in cemeteries and on old home sites throughout the southern and southwestern United States. The plants' longevity is due to their drought tolerance and ability to grow in the poorest of soils. Oriental arborvitae adapts well to chalky or alkaline soils, making it useful in areas such as Dallas, Texas, and Miami, Florida, where some conifer selections will not prosper. It has also proven adaptable to the heat of the Deep South, even as far south as Miami. You can easily distinguish *P. orientalis* from *Thuja* by the vertical arrangement of its foliage, which, unlike *Thuja*'s, is the same color on both sides and has no scent when crushed.

Hardwood or softwood cuttings are relatively easy to propagate at any time of year. There have been some reports that deer are fond of its foliage. John has some nice dwarf forms and several selections from the Xian Shan Mountains outside Beijing, China, that he is evaluating for potential release. Variegated forms that deserve consideration for the Upper South include 'Nana Fleck' and 'Van Hoey Smith'. In recent years, many selections have been infected with *Cercosporidium* blight, and many older plantings have therefore been removed. This unfortunately happened to most of the selections at Tom's arboretum.

Platycladus orientalis 'Aurea Nana'

One of the dwarf golden arborvitaes in the trade, this is an exceptionally compact-growing, dense conical bush with foliage to the ground. The leaves, yellowish green in the summer, turn orange with cooler weather before turning brownish during cold winters. 'Aurea Nana' is an old cultivar first introduced in 1868.

Platycladus orientalis 'Blue Cone'

This upright medium-growing, oval-shaped shrub will attain a height of 5–8 feet (1.5–2.4 m) with a spread of 3–6 feet (0.9–1.8 m). Its main attribute is its uniform green foliage that remains tight without the need for pruning. This is a rarely offered selection that, once better known, will become popular. We consider it a top-tier conifer. Besides its habit and foliage, it also produces bright, glaucous blue cones that contrast beautifully against the green foliage. While 'Blue Cone' can be used effectively as a hedge, its best application is as a specimen plant.

Platycladus orientalis 'Conspicua'

This small conical to columnar shrub grows to 6 × 3 feet (1.8 × 0.9 m) and features densely branched yellow-green vertical sprays with a yellow-gold cast at the tips. This is the golden Berckman's arborvitae seen in the trade and synonymous with 'Berckmans Golden Biota'. Often confused with the cultivar 'Aurea Nana', 'Conspicua' differs in its more upright, fastigiate growth habit. The two selections resemble each other when young but mature to assume different habits. Years ago, while visiting a large container nursery operation, John noticed two distinct forms, one upright ('Conspicua') and the other more broadly conical ('Aurea Nana'). John has since seen this several times, where the two cultivars get mixed up in production—a problem if you prefer one over the other or want to be precise in your collection. 'Conspicua' was first described by nurseryman-horticulturist Prosper Berckmans of Augusta, Georgia, in 1902. Founded in 1858, Berckmans Nursery, also known as Fruitland, was the first large-scale horticultural nursery in the southeastern United States. The nursery later became the site of the famous Augusta National Golf Club.

Platycladus orientalis 'Fruitlandii'

For some reason this old cultivar is seldom offered. Like 'Blue Cone', it is a medium-growing upright shrub to 8 feet tall with a spread of 3–6 feet (2.4 × 0.9–1.8 m). It will ultimately form a small cone-shaped plant with medium green foliage. California's Monrovia Nursery Company introduced it in 1987.

Platycladus orientalis 'Morgan'

In the sphere of dwarf conifers, 'Morgan' is simply one of the best. Its first best feature is the dwarf size and tight pyramidal form that make it easy to incorporate into myriad landscape applications. Its second is color: because it is known for stunning year-round color changes, 'Morgan' has been described as a "woody chameleon." In spring, the chartreuse outer sprays of new growth contrast vividly with the darker

Platycladus orientalis 'Morgan'

green interior foliage. In summer, the color turns a lime green that, in winter, morphs into a stunning purple-orange color. Then, as the weather warms, the show repeats itself. 'Morgan' will grow between 2 and 4 inches per year (5–10 cm), reaching around 3 feet (0.9 m) at maturity. This selection was discovered by John Emery in Australia around 1989.

Platycladus orientalis 'Van Hoey Smith'

This great Oriental arborvitae is appropriately named to honor the late J.R.P. van Hoey Smith, the former director of the Trompenburg Arboretum in Rotterdam and former president of the International Dendrology Society. As far as we have observed, no other conifer has bright orange-gold vertical foliage flecked with green and white—a tricolor pattern that makes 'Van Hoey Smith' a conifer easy to identify. Its only drawback is its tendency to present a thin appearance, which can be somewhat remedied by an annual light shear of the foliage. This selection has a vertical growth form to 12 feet tall × 5 feet wide (3.7 × 1.5 m).

Platycladus orientalis
'Van Hoey Smith'

Podocarpus Yellowwood

While *Pinus* is the largest genus in the Northern Hemisphere, *Podocarpus* is the largest in the Southern Hemisphere. Numbering between 80 and 105 species (depending on the authority), most yellowwoods have a subtropical to tropical distribution and are seldom if ever seen outside greenhouses or U.S. Zones 9–10. Several species are native to Southeast Asia and Malaysia and are hardy as far north as Zone 7.

Those unfamiliar with their fruiting characteristics or broader foliage (more leaf-like than spray- or needle-like) typically do not recognize them as conifers. This is because of their atypical dark, shiny, lanceolate leaves and the berry-like, brightly colored red to purple fleshy fruits (arils) produced on female trees. John has evaluated several small-leaved species over the years and found none to be overly exciting for landscape use.

Podocarpus macrophyllus
Buddhist Pine

One of the most frequently encountered conifers in the Coastal Plain and seen everywhere in towns like Savannah, Georgia, and Charleston, South Carolina, Buddhist pine is not commonly seen in landscapes further north. We attribute this to the notion that the species is not hardy in Zone 7. Nonetheless, Buddhist pine is a tough tree adaptable to a wide range of conditions, including salt spray, high temperatures, and drought. Aside from being subject occasionally to scale, it does not appear to have any serious pest or disease problems. *Podocarpus* also takes well to pruning into various hedge forms, although we recommend leaving it alone to grow into its natural beauty. Buddhist pine performs best in well-drained,

Podocarpus macrophyllus

acidic soils in either full sun or medium shade. Avoid planting it in wet soils. Its one drawback is a slow growth rate. A handsome large specimen grows in the town of Meigs, Georgia. John is working on the development of fastigiate (upright) growing forms, and the United States National Arboretum has a selection that has been cold hardy in Washington, D.C. Expect a mature height and width of 20 feet × 6 feet (6 × 1.8 m).

Podocarpus macrophyllus var. *maki*

This variety is similar to the species except much shorter and shrubbier with narrower leaves. Adaptable in Zones 7–9, this plant in our opinion does best grown in full sun to medium shade. Other *Podocarpus* selections that will survive as far north as Zone 7 include 'Pringle's Dwarf', a shrubby form with bluish leaves, and 'Gold Crown', which, as the name suggests, has yellowish leaves. For Zones 8–9a, two silvery blue cultivars we recommend are *P. elongatus* 'Monmal' Icee Blue® from California's Monrovia Nursery and 'Blue Chip' from Oregon's Cistus Nursery. Both are slow growing and can easily be maintained at a desired size.

Pseudolarix Golden Larch

Together with *Glyptostrobus*, *Larix* (which we exclude here), and *Metasequoia*, this genus completes the list of deciduous conifers indigenous to China. *Pseudolarix* provides yet another example of the complete adaptability of certain Asian flora to portions of the southeastern United States. Fossil remains of the golden larch have been found in the Cretaceous strata of eastern and western Siberia and in Paleocene-Pliocene strata in Europe, central Asia, northeast China, Japan, and the western part of the United States. Rapid climate changes brought about by the last ice age resulted in the disappearance of the golden larch from all but a few locations in eastern and central China. Native stands are rare and do not always produce fertile seeds.

Obtained as liners (in general, a trade term for immature plants), several golden larch were planted at Tom's arboretum in 1994, and all are now 15-foot-plus specimens and prospering. A tree in John's trials reached a height of 22 feet (6.7 m) in 10 years. All grow in full sun and receive no special attention. Several have also been transplanted with no problems. Large trees growing at the J. C. Raulston Arboretum have produced beautiful cones that are always special to view in the fall. A somewhat crowded specimen is growing at the Atlanta Botanical Garden, while Duke Gardens in North Carolina has several nice specimens.

Pseudolarix amabilis fall color

Pseudolarix amabilis leaf arrangement

American Conifer Society regional director Tom Neff has several large trees growing in his conifer collection in Marietta, Georgia.

The golden larch displays the most prominent fall color of all the deciduous conifers. Aptly named, it was originally called the golden pine in China. The best color develops in Zones 6 and 7; in Zone 8 the tree shows hints of yellow, then quickly turns brown as needles fall off. That said, golden larch is well worth growing in all areas of the South for form and interest—consider the fall color a bonus.

While golden larch tops out over many years at around 50 feet (15 m), given its slow growth rate it will not soon be out of scale in most landscapes. With few exceptions, deciduous trees seldom provide much in the way of winter interest. By contrast, golden larch's outline of wide-spreading branches and its grayish furrowed bark create visual interest, making for a good winter tree. When foliage is present, the coin-shaped needle clusters radiating from central points along the branches offer a leaf arrangement unique in the conifer world.

Provide golden larch with supplemental watering for the first two years during periods of drought. Pruning is unnecessary unless you wish to maintain a smaller size tree; in that case, prune only in late winter. For the best fall color, plant this species in full sun. A well-maintained golden larch is truly a spectacular tree.

Our decision not to include *Larix* along with *Pseudolarix* stems from our trying and losing virtually all species of *Larix* and determining, as a result, that they are not adaptable throughout much of the South. Notable exceptions are plants of *L. decidua* and *L. kaempferi*, which are doing well in the Louisville, Kentucky, area. We have also seen healthy specimens growing at East Tennessee State University in Johnson City and in Ellijay, Georgia, so pockets exist where they adapt.

Pseudotsuga Douglas-Fir

The Douglas-firs have a disjunct distribution of several species occurring in western North America and eastern Asia (China, Japan, and Taiwan). The genus consists of four species and three varieties. The North American species, *P. menziesii* and *P. macrocarpa*, are commonly referred to as Douglas-fir. The hyphen in the common name denotes that this is not a true fir in the genus *Abies*. The two Asian species, *P. sinensis* and *P. japonica*, are very similar in appearance.

Pseudotsuga menziesii Douglas-Fir

Douglas-fir is one of the most important timber trees in the world and also popular in the western United States as a Christmas tree. The leaves grow to 1¼ inches (3 cm) long and occur in two horizontal ranks. The cones grow to 4 inches (10 cm) long and are easily distinguished by the three-forked papery bracts that appear between the scales. Several interesting cultivars are worth trying in Zones 6–7. *P. menziesii* var. *glauca*, a blue-foliaged form native to the central Rocky Mountains, is not recommended for the South because of our heavy summer rains. A Mexican form recognized by some authorities as *P. lindleyana* is currently being evaluated for hardiness and adaptability.

We believe it is still too early in the evaluation process to deem *P. menziesii* a recommended species. Like several other western conifers, such as *Thuja plicata*, it may prove to be at home in parts of the South. Several nice specimens have been growing for more than 15 years in the Marietta, Georgia, area, and healthy specimens have also been seen in Tennessee. According to the owner in Marietta, he collected some small seedlings from his son's property in Oregon and planted them when he returned to Georgia. They are now more than 20 feet (6 m) tall. Several selections have also been growing at Tom's arboretum for five years and show no signs of stress. We expect that this species will have limited suitability in the Coastal Plain region. David Douglas, a Scottish botanist, first introduced the Douglas-fir in 1827, and the plant received its common name in his honor.

Pseudotsuga menziesii 'Emerald Twister'

'Emerald Twister' may take the prize for the most bizarre of conifers. If plants had a circus, this one would be the contortionist. Each branch exhibits an irregular wave-like (or undulate) pattern; some branches even appear to have been tied in knots. A specimen growing in Tom's arboretum has demonstrated a medium growth rate. Its new growth is a pleasing light green that contrasts handsomely with the older dark green foliage. This cultivar is likely to reach a height of 20 feet (6.1 m), growing well in full sun or light shade.

Pseudotsuga menziesii 'Graceful Grace'

'Graceful Grace' is a narrow form with drooping branches and bluish needles that are longer than those of the species. This moderate grower does not require staking to produce an upright weeping specimen. Expect this cultivar to mature at a height and width of 10 feet × 6 feet (3 × 1.8 m). The effect of 'Graceful Grace' in the landscape can be dramatic: some plants grow to resemble dancing figures with arms outstretched. Where it can be successfully cultivated, this is an exciting plant.

Pseudotsuga sinensis Chinese Douglas-Fir

Little information is available on this species. Native to mainland China, where its status is listed as "vulnerable," it is a close cousin of the North American

Pseudotsuga sinensis

species *P. menziesii*, except smaller. Several plants growing in Zone 7 have proved well adapted, and we surmise that this species will prosper in Zones 6–8. While it will take some searching to locate garden-ready plants, this is a good species for the South. Where you can find it, plant it in favor of *P. menziesii*. John has a Chinese Douglas-fir in the field that was grown from seed; its development has been more like that of a *Microbiota*, with a spreading habit and no central leader. One southern specialty nursery we know of, Camellia Forest Nursery in Chapel Hill, North Carolina, offers this species for sale.

Sciadopitys verticillata   Japanese Umbrella Pine

Japanese umbrella pine is not, in fact, a true pine, nor is it even in the same family. This primitive species has no close relatives. Its common name derives from the arrangement of its pine-like needles, which radiate from the center of each stem tip like the spokes of an umbrella. The species name *verticillata* translates as "whorled." Each needle contains a center groove and, in reality, is actually two needles fused in a pair. As the common name further denotes, this monotypic genus is native to southern portions of the Japanese archipelago. Millions of years ago, it had a much wider distribution throughout the Northern Hemisphere. It was originally named *Taxus verticillata* and later reclassified in 1842 by Siebold and Zuccarini as *Sciadopitys verticillata*.

Sciadopitys verticillata

In the wild, Japanese umbrella pine forms a pyramidal to conical tree with heights up to 75 feet (23 m). Mature trees bear cones up to 4 inches (10 cm) long, which take approximately 18 months to ripen. The cones resemble those of some of the true pine species. The tree grows naturally on steep hillsides where there is abundant rainfall and humidity in the summer.

In youth, this tree is painfully slow growing, which accounts for the high price it commands in specialty catalogs and nurseries. While it can be a finicky plant to grow in the South, a well-grown specimen is as good as it gets in the plant world. *Sciadopitys* has produced a number of distinct cultivars that are well worth searching for. Though more seem to be added each day, don't expect to find most of them in local garden centers. This is definitely a connoisseur's plant and one for adding a special touch to the collector's garden.

In the South, Japanese umbrella pine benefits from afternoon shade and demands well-drained, non-alkaline soil. Avoid planting sites where the tree may be exposed to high winds. We have also found that if you can site it on a slope, its chances of success are increased. During the first several years of root establishment, water generously each week, and continue this practice during periods of sustained drought. Propagation is from seed while cultivars are always grafted. Little or no pruning is required. While there will always be exceptions, we recommend that *Sciadopitys* be planted only in Zones 6–7.

When it comes to cutting-edge *Sciadopitys* cultivars, perhaps the most renowned mail-order nursery in the United States is Bethlehem Nursery in Bethlehem, Connecticut. When asked about his favorites, owner Dennis Dodge named 'Yellow Dream' and 'Moon Light'. Both are golden yellow selections, and each has interesting variations in its needles.

Sciadopitys verticillata 'Golden Rush'

'Golden Rush' is a yellow-needled selection that requires some afternoon shade in the South. One of the slower-growing and more open selections, it will mature into a short conical and shrubby plant. In three years of trials, it has always produced bright yellow needles in the summer; the winter color is a dull orange that fails to excite.

Sciadopitys verticillata 'Green Star'

This selection from the Netherlands has thick short needles and a tight dwarf habit. While the leaves have a tendency to bronze in winter, the robust and glossy deep green of its summer foliage is reason enough to grow this plant. 'Green Star' was first introduced in 1987.

Sciadopitys verticillata 'Joe Kozey'

This 1986 Sidney Waxman introduction from the University of Connecticut is a top echelon cultivar. Best used where an unusual vertical accent plant is needed, its main attribute is its tight narrow form, with upright branches held tightly against the main trunk. The color is a consistent lush green, and it retains its columnar form as it ages. Plants grow slowly to 15 feet tall × 4 feet wide (4.6 × 1.2 m).

Sciadopitys verticillata 'Monolith'

Like 'Joe Kozey', this is another upright growing, fastigiate form that can hold its own among the standouts of the genus. It was introduced by Rob Means, owner of the Yadkin Valley Nursery in North Carolina.

Sciadopitys verticillata 'Ossorio Gold'

Of the yellow-needled forms we have seen, 'Ossorio Gold' is among the best. Its growth habit is tight, and it can tolerate more sun than many conifer selections planted in the South. 'Ossorio Gold' also holds its color well during periods of cold. Introduced from the estate of the late Long Island conifer collector Alfonso Ossorio, it was first described by Coenosium Gardens in Washington State in 1990.

Sciadopitys verticillata 'Ossorio Gold'

Sciadopitys verticillata 'Sternschnuppe'

This selection has short, very thick needles on a dwarf upright plant, 5 feet tall × 2.5 feet wide (1.5 × 0.75 m). 'Sternschnuppe', which translates to "meteor" or "shooting star," was supposedly created by using the chemical colchicine to alter its genetic composition. Kurt Wittboldt Muller of Verden, Germany, introduced this unusual conifer, first described in 1992.

Sciadopitys verticillata 'Wintergreen'

Perhaps the finest form of the larger growing selections, this plant features a narrow conical habit and bright green foliage that does not discolor in winter. The plant grows slowly and often looks so pristine that one could mistake it for a plastic replica. Sidney Waxman of the University of Connecticut developed 'Wintergreen' and released it in 1985.

Sciadopitys verticillata 'Wintergreen'

Sequoia sempervirens Coast Redwood

Attaining heights approaching 400 feet (122 m), this regal tree is the world's tallest. It is the only remaining species of this genus and among the oldest living trees on earth: specimens more than 2,200 years old have been documented.

Sequoia sempervirens

The coast redwood is native to the coastal range of northern California into the southwestern portion of Oregon. Precipitation determines its southern limit and temperature its northern limit. Along this narrow fog belt, where moisture is plentiful, trees reach enormous heights.

Because of the similarity in scientific names, coast redwood gets confused with the giant sequoia (*Sequoiadendron giganteum*), a tree that is not recommended for anywhere in the South. Whereas the coast redwood is a coastal species, the giant sequoia grows far from the coast on the western slopes of the Sierra Nevada mountain range. Coast redwood forms groves, whereas the giant sequoia's numbers are more scattered. While coast redwood is the world's tallest tree, giant sequoia, as its name suggests, is the world's largest tree in terms of overall biomass. Also, in mature trees, the giant sequoia's crown is more obviously rounded than the crown of a coast redwood.

Two forms of leaves are present on mature coast redwoods. Lower leaves are two-ranked and grow in a linear fashion similar to that of yews, an adaptation that probably facilitates the capture of sunlight in shaded areas. Leaves on the tree's upper portions, where more light is available, are scalelike and overlapping. On young trees and likely all trees in ornamental applications, the leaves are linear, opposite facing, and slightly upcurved. The purplish brown, egg-shaped cones are about an inch (2.5 cm) long and mature in one season. They may remain on the tree after seed release.

Given its natural habitat, it is somewhat surprising that coast redwood would prosper in the South. It is not uncommon to find large specimens in Zones 7–8, and several gardens have begun featuring some of the more interesting cultivars suitable for smaller spaces. Old trees can even be found growing as far south as Magnolia Plantation in Charleston, South Carolina. We suspect that coast redwood is probably not a good selection for the mountain regions of western North Carolina and northward. 'Aptos Blue', 'Chapel Hill', and 'Soquel' have been growing in Tifton, Georgia, since 1997. Ten-year growth ranged from 15 to 21 feet (4.6–6.4 m). Very large specimens (60+ feet; 18 m) grow in Hawkinsville, Georgia, and Marshallville, Georgia. Some of the best specimens on the East Coast grow near the ocean in the Norfolk, Virginia, area. Aside from its beauty, coast redwood makes an interesting conversation piece—you can amaze people by pointing to this tree and explaining that it is both the tallest and one of the longest-lived on earth.

The genus name honors Sequoia, son of a British merchant and Cherokee woman, who became a Cherokee chief and created the first Indian alphabet.

S. sempervirens requires moist, well-drained soil and regular watering in summer (particularly when young). Foliage tends to burn during hot, dry spells in Tifton. The species is suitable for full sun or light shade, but avoid planting it in areas where cold drying winds are frequent. Where winter temperatures drop into the low teens, it is not uncommon for the top leader to be killed. While this can be a bit unsightly, a new leader quickly forms in the spring and, by the end of most years, no evidence of dead wood is visible. Remember to mulch, mulch, mulch: coast redwood groves are generally cool and moist, so mulching will keep tree roots happy. Propagation is from seed; cultivars are from cuttings. Seed does not store well, so sow as soon as possible. No pruning is required except to remove unwanted branches, which is best done in mid-spring. Basal suckers can be removed any time of year. Coast redwood is one of the few conifers that will resprout from dormant buds when cut down.

Sequoia sempervirens 'Filoli'

Discovered at the famous Filoli estate just south of San Francisco, this is one of the better blue selections. The form and habit are typical of the species. This selection will probably grow no more than 30 feet tall (9 m) in the South. As a side note, Filoli is the mansion seen from the air in the opening credits of the former television series *Dynasty*.

Sequoia sempervirens 'Soquel'

The cultivar 'Soquel' is one of the better coast redwood selections for good pyramidal habit. This selection also holds its fine-textured gray-green color during winter. Once established, it can grow more than 1 foot (0.3 m) per year, to 50 feet (15 m) at maturity. As mentioned, during severe cold it may lose the top of its central leader, but a replacement leader will quickly grow. It can also experience significant branch dieback from cold, but by May, new growth has replaced it and little visible sign of damage remains. A 1981 introduction from Monrovia Nursery, 'Soquel' performs best in Zones 7b and above.

Gilbert's Nursery in Chesnee, South Carolina, has propagated a clone of 'Soquel' found growing in South Carolina. A 5-foot plant at Tom's arboretum experienced no cold damage during the terrible winter of 2009–2010. The foliage is bluer than the species, and the form is more open, with arching branches. It shows promise as a plant for the future.

Taiwania cryptomerioides Taiwan Cedar

To see a well-grown Taiwan cedar is to recognize many of the best attributes conifers have to offer. With drooping branch tips, blue-green curtain-like foliage, and a conical form, this is a strikingly beautiful tree. Its only drawbacks are its prickly foliage and tendency to turn a rust color during below-freezing temperatures. Like *Sequoia*, during extreme cold spells, Taiwan cedar may lose the

Taiwania cryptomerioides

Taiwania cryptomerioides (photo by George Bradfield)

top of its central leader. This is not a problem as it quickly forms a new one, and such freeze damage becomes less of an issue as the tree matures. *Taiwania* is not bothered by pests or diseases and seldom requires any pruning. Its species name, *cryptomerioides*, is based on its resemblance to the genus *Cryptomeria*. Being indigenous to the mountainous areas of Taiwan, southeast China, and northern Vietnam, the tree shows remarkable hardiness in Zone 7 and is well adapted in Zone 8. *Taiwania* is not particularly drought tolerant and performs best with supplemental watering during prolonged dry periods. Nice specimens started in the 1960s grow at Dodd and Dodd Nursery in Semmes, Alabama. John's plant in Tifton, Georgia, reached a height of 26 feet (7.9 m) in 10 years and in his test plots is rivaled only by *Pinus pseudostrobus* for ultimate "wow" factor. Tom also has several nice specimens and has selected one with the potential to become the most beautiful conifer at his arboretum.

    Taiwania is treated by most taxonomists as a monotypic genus (*Taiwania cryptomerioides*). Some authorities recognize a second species, *T. flousiana*, whereas others treat it as a variety (*Taiwania cryptomerioides* var. *flousiana*) originating from mainland China. *Taiwania* should be grown in full sun to moderate shade. Propagation is from seed (if you can get it) or cuttings (use only vertical shoots). Plants grow slowly to around 40 feet tall × 20 feet wide (12 × 6 m) in cultivation. *Taiwania* was selected as the 2010 Tree of the Year by the International Dendrology Society.

Taxodium Swamp Cypress

Under the current taxonomic treatment, *Taxodium* is a monotypic genus with three distinct varieties. It is one of only five conifers to shed its foliage each fall. All *Taxodium* share the common trait of being tolerant of swampy or damp situations, though Montezuma cypress will not tolerate long periods of inundation. While each has the word "cypress" in its common name, none is, in fact, a "true" cypress (of the genus *Cupressus*), but all three are members of the Cupressaceae, or cypress family. Swamp cypress's closest relative is *Glyptostrobus pensilis* (Chinese swamp cypress). The genus name comes from the Greek words *taxos*, meaning yew tree, and *edios*, meaning resemblance. *Taxodium* has a wide distribution, mainly across the southeastern United States. Its range extends from Delaware Bay south to Florida and west to southern Texas and into Mexico and Guatemala. It also grows inland along the Mississippi and Ohio rivers north to southern Illinois and Indiana. Old trees growing along rivers or in seasonal ponds or lakes often have large, buttressed stems and root systems.

Taxodium fall color

Though all varieties prefer a heavy soil rich in organic matter, they will grow in any garden soil and can be variously sited in shallow water (all except the Mexican variety), on pond or stream margins, or on dry sites. Plants growing on dry soil tend to form deep taproots, making them difficult to transplant after a few years in the ground. One advantage of planting swamp cypress on average soils is that they grow faster because of increased oxygen to their roots. A new tree planted in an upland situation should receive regular water until its root system becomes established. After that, the tree is essentially care free. Dwarf cultivars should be watered at least weekly for the first year until their roots are established; after that, all should perform well in the South and over time become gardenworthy plants.

All three varieties are produced from seed. Most cultivars are propagated by grafting onto *Taxodium* understock. *Taxodium* also roots rather easily from juvenile shoots, but older plants can be difficult to root. Prune as desired to improve shape and form at any time of year.

Trying to stay current on new *Taxodium* cultivars is like trying to paint a moving train. Several newer ones that have caught our attention are 'Jim's Little Guy', a semidwarf upright form, 'Twisted Logic', a highly contorted form to around 15 feet (4.6 m), and 'Little Twister', a dwarf selection with twisted leaves. Lindsey's Skyward™ is a new introduction selected for its tight, upright form. The parent plant is more than 20 years old and is only 23 feet tall × 6 feet wide (7 × 1.8 m). Aside from these attributes, it has shown no propensity to produce surface knees, making it a good candidate for home landscapes.

Taxodium distichum var. *distichum* Bald Cypress

Whether one is talking about native North American conifers or hardwood trees, bald cypress is one of the truly majestic beauties found in the southern landscape. To see a towering virgin stand of these great trees in parks such as Francis Beidler Forest in Harleyville, South Carolina, or Corkscrew Swamp in west Naples, Florida, is the southern equivalent of seeing the giant redwoods in northern California. In either park, it is not uncommon to see trees more than 1,000 years old and some as tall as 100 feet (30 m).

In its natural environment, bald cypress grows in deep swamps that are usually flooded for long periods of time and on wet stream banks and bottomlands. Contrasted with its close relative, the pond cypress (*Taxodium distichum* var. *imbricarium*), bald cypress occurs naturally where water is flowing or where there is seasonal flooding. Its trunk grows straight with numerous ascending branches. At maturity, the tree generally has a broad fluted or buttressed base. In

Taxodium distichum var. *distichum*, dry site

late fall the leaves turn a pleasing russet red and then abscise; it is from this annual shedding of its leaves that the tree derives its common name, bald cypress. Depending on the weather, during a period of several weeks to sometimes as long as a month before leaf fall, the tree goes through a color metamorphosis from green to light tan to orange brown.

In cultivation, bald cypress grows faster and suffers no ill effects when grown on drier sites. In an evaluation conducted at Tom's arboretum, two specimens in #1 containers were planted in 1996—one on a dry site and the other at the

Taxodium distichum var. *distichum*, wet site

margin of a pond. The one on dry site is now approximately 35 feet (10.6 m) tall and the other is approximately 20 feet (6 m). The fact that bald cypress occurs naturally only in wet locations may be attributed to its preference for noncompetition from other plants as well as to the fact that the seed will germinate only when exposed to constant moisture. It is also observed that bald cypresses are thin barked and therefore susceptible to destruction by forest fires. Since fires do not travel through wet swamps, it appears that bald cypresses trees have adapted to avoid one threat by surviving in less than optimal conditions.

When grown in or near water, bald cypress develops a series of root protuberances (or "cypress knees") around its base. These may occur as a mechanism to buttress or help anchor the tree in mucky soil. Another theory is that the knees act as weirs to trap nutrients in the moving water. Yet another popular explanation is that they provide oxygen to the roots that grow in swamp waters low in dissolved oxygen. This last explanation appears to be off target: in experiments involving the removal of cypress knees, the tree still survived. Whatever their function, the knees can occur some distance from the tree and attain a height of 3 feet (1 m); the height is usually related to the high-water mark in the swamp. Trees grown on dry sites rarely produce knees, and the bases of their trunks are much less fluted. They will produce large surface roots on dry land that are difficult to mow around, so it's best not to plant *Taxodium* in lawn areas or near walkways. At the Coastal Plain Research Arboretum in Tifton, Georgia, John planted several trees above the creek bank in 1993. No knees have formed at the planting site, but they *have* developed in the creek bed, 6 feet (1.8 m) below the original level of planting.

A common question is how one easily distinguishes bald cypress from the dawn redwood (*Metasequoia glyptostroboides*). Aside from growth habit, the leaves on the stems of bald cypress are alternate, whereas those of the genus *Metasequoia* are opposite. The easiest way to remember this is to use the ABC rule: Alternate = Bald Cypress. Bald cypress has two types of leaves: scalelike on the stems that bear the cones and flat on nonbearing shoots. Their two-ranked, flat leaf arrangement is similar to that of yews (*Taxus*), hence the derivation of the genus name *Taxodium*. A unique feature of this genus is that the twigs that bear the flat leaflets are also deciduous and fall with the leaflets still attached.

Taxodium distichum var. *distichum* 'Cascade Falls' (PP12296)

This cultivar ranks as one of the best new conifer introductions in the past 10 years. It has everything going for it: strong weeping habit, tolerance of various soils, sufficient resistance to pests and diseases, and perfect adaptations to the South. 'Cascade Falls' was found as a chance plant growing near a pond on the property of Graeme and Rosemary Platt in Auckland, New Zealand. Graeme had originally purchased several malformed specimens to place near a small stream because they were cheap, and, from these, 'Cascade Falls' was selected. The world-famous Cedar Lodge Nursery in New Plymouth, New Zealand, introduced the plant.

Growers commonly use two methods to train this cultivar. The first is to continue to stake the central leader in a vertical direction to produce a tall weeper. A specimen grown in this manner at Tom's arboretum is now approximately 15 feet (4.6 m) tall, and the central leader has now begun to grow skyward without staking. The other method is to graft high, then train the tree to arch over. This is normally carried out at around the 5-foot (1.5 m) mark. Depending on the desired effect, either method produces a strong accent tree for the landscape. 'Cascade Falls' makes an especially striking water-garden feature. Stanley and Sons Nursery of Boring, Oregon, introduced this selection into the United States.

Taxodium distichum var. *distichum* 'Cave Hill'

This tight bun of a plant was found at Cave Hill Cemetery in Louisville, Kentucky. Aptly described as a rounded dwarf, 'Cave Hill' best shows its garden merit when grown on a standard where it can mature into a dense round lollipop on a stick. Grown in this fashion, the plant affords four seasons of interest. The foliage is similar to that of the species and is dark green throughout the spring and summer. We expect it to grow slowly to around 3 feet (0.9 m). 'Cave Hill' was introduced in 2002.

Taxodium distichum var. *distichum* 'Cave Hill'

Taxodium distichum var. *distichum* 'Fallingwater'

A selection named by the great plantsman Don Shadow of Winchester, Tennessee, from an unnamed plant he observed at a plant trade show in Essen, Germany. Don managed to take some cuttings, and his story of the hoops he had to jump through is quite amusing. Readers who know Don should ask him to recount it. After much consideration, he named this special plant 'Fallingwater' after the famous Pennsylvania residence of noted architect, Frank Lloyd Wright. Unlike the similar selection 'Cascade Falls', which tends to have a somewhat upright, serpentine form, 'Fallingwater' has an upright central leader with strongly cascading side branches. A mature plant is reminiscent of a curtain of water. It must be trained to grow upright and is then best left to its own devices. This is a plant you can look forward to seeing grow larger in the landscape, as it should just get better each year.

Taxodium distichum var. *distichum* 'Gee Whiz'

Another dwarf selection found by Gary Gee, 'Gee Whiz' is one among the Harper Collection of Dwarf and Rare Conifers at Tipton, Michigan's Hidden Lake Gardens, that is beginning to make its way into the marketplace. This plant appears to be more spreading in habit than 'Cave Hill'.

Taxodium distichum var. *distichum* 'Gee Whiz'

Taxodium distichum var. *distichum* 'Hursley Park'

This witch's broom cultivar is a favorite of Tom's. In the landscape it grows into a dwarf dense shrub with slightly twisted foliage. Though it has yet to reach its ultimate size in Tom's arboretum, we expect it to mature at around 3 feet × 3 feet

(0.9 m). Even though the plant is deciduous in winter, its dwarf size and tight branching make a nice foil to dwarf needled conifers, especially dwarf mugo pines such as *Pinus mugo* 'Mini Mops'. Hillier Nurseries first introduced 'Hursley Park' in 1971, describing it in *Hillier's Manual of Trees and Shrubs*. The cultivar arose from a broom found in 1966 at nearby Hursley Park in Hampshire, UK.

Taxodium distichum var. *distichum* 'Mickelson' (PP3551 Shawnee Brave®)

This Earl Cully selection from Johnson County, Illinois, forms a narrow pyramidal to columnar tree with a dense crown. It is fast growing, reaching 16 feet (4.8 m) in 10 years. The central trunk is straight with numerous lateral branches arching out at a 45–50-degree angle. The parent tree is 75 feet tall × 18 feet wide (23 × 5.5 m). The plant patent for this selection was issued in 1974.

Taxodium distichum var. *distichum* 'Peve Minaret'

Along with *Metasequoia* 'Ogon' and several others mentioned in this book, this amazing bald cypress is one of the best new introductions over the past 10 years. Its symmetrical, tidy form conjures the image of a miniature railroad garden where it would look perfect. Unlike some dwarf plants that never seem to be in scale, 'Peve Minaret' looks like a perfect miniature tree. It develops a main leader that is straight as an arrow, with dense side branches and a very narrow habit. As a dwarf, it will work in the very smallest of gardens and stay much smaller than the species. This cultivar lends itself to myriad forms through

Taxodium distichum var. *distichum* 'Peve Minaret'

selective pruning. One creative method is to create a pole-like effect by removing all side branches. Though art is always in the eye of the beholder, one of the most artful forms in our opinion is created by allowing several main side branches and then coppicing the tree each spring to a height of around 5 feet (1.5 m). In this form, the plant resembles a giant redwood in miniature. Further south in John's collections, 'Peve Minaret' has proven highly susceptible to spider mite damage. A relative newcomer, 'Peve Minaret' was introduced to cultivation in 1990.

Taxodium distichum var. *distichum* 'Secrest'

This is another of bald cypress's captivating dwarf cultivars now making their way into the trade. 'Secrest' arose as a witch's broom at the Secrest Arboretum in Ohio. The needles are smaller than the species and slightly twisted. Like those of other cultivars, the leaves will turn a bronzy orange before falling in the autumn. A mature specimen growing in the Harper Collection at Hidden Lake Gardens in Michigan is enough to make one skip a car payment in favor of buying a fully grown plant. Fortunately, the plant *is* available and at a price considerably less than a car payment. Expect this form to maintain a rounded habit in the height and width range of 3 feet × 5 feet (0.9 × 1.5 m). Coenosium Gardens of Eatonville, Washington, introduced 'Secrest' in 1992.

Taxodium distichum var. *imbricarium* Pond Cypress

This variety, often confused with bald cypress, is smaller than bald cypress, has a narrower crown, is slower growing, and has differently constituted foliage. Whereas the leaves of bald cypress appear more or less in a flat plane, the leaves of pond cypress are spine-shaped on woody twigs and arranged in a spiral configuration. John teaches that, in appearance, bald cypress = bird feather, and pond cypress = rattail. Until only recently, the species was known as *Taxodium ascendens*, which no doubt came from the fact that the twigs grow in an ascendant fashion instead of in the spreading fashion of bald cypress. Pond cypress offers a unique form in the landscape, and some would argue that it is the most architecturally appealing of the three cypress varieties.

The two most frequently asked questions about pond cypress are (1) Where does pond cypress occur? and (2) Does it produce knees? Pond cypress usually occurs on wet sites, primarily sandy pond or lake margins. You can think of the comparison this way: bald cypress occurs where water is either moving or the water table is seasonally shifting, whereas pond cypress grows where the water is still or slow moving—hence its common name. While the occurrence is rare, when grown near water pond cypress will sometimes produce knees. These are more rounded that the knees of bald cypress, which are pointed.

Taxodium distichum var. *imbricarium*

A very nice specimen grows next to the administration building at the University of Georgia–Tifton on a high, dry site without supplemental irrigation. The tree is attractive and easily half the size of most bald cypress seen in South Georgia. A very nice native population grows in the Alapaha River swamp on Highway 319 from Tifton to Ocilla, Georgia. Mature specimens of both bald and pond cypress are growing together beside a pond at Callaway Gardens in Pine Mountain, Georgia. While both are outstanding, we rank the pond cypress as the more graceful of the two. Borrowing from this theme, Tom planted both species directly into approximately 1 foot of water in a pond where the water level remains constant. The bald cypress has grown somewhat slowly, and the pond variety has grown extremely slowly. The pond cypress has not produced any knees, but the bald cypress has. A specimen growing at Bernheim Arboretum and Research Forest in Claremont, Kentucky, is a must-see for visitors.

If you have the space next to a pond or a lake, pond cypress is one of the top choices for landscape "wow." At least one nursery—Moon's Tree Farm in Loganville, Georgia—is producing a selection of pond cypress that is not yet named. We hold the opinion that pond cypress is a vastly underrepresented conifer that should be offered more often.

Taxodium distichum var. *imbricarium* 'Morris' (PPAF Debonair®)

Somewhat similar to 'Nutans', Debonair® is more narrowly pyramidal and the branch tips droop. In fact, you might at first identify it as a cultivar of *Platycladus orientalis* if you were to go by one of its long, string-like branches alone. This may well be the finest textured of the many clones of pond cypress. It should mature to a height and width of around 50 feet × 12 feet (15 × 3.7 m). The original scion was given to Earl Cully in the early 1960s from a plant growing at the Morris Arboretum in Philadelphia, Pennsylvania.

Taxodium distichum var. *imbricarium* 'Nutans'

Over time, this cultivar will grow into a medium sized tree with a trunk that is very wide at the base. The branch structure is very short, and the thin, adpressed, awl-shaped needles are notably upright. As the foliage tends to be both dense and airy, 'Nutans' is one of the best of the pond cypress forms. Its autumn color transitions from russet to an eye-popping golden brown before leaf fall. Along with 'Debonair', 'Nutans' offers a distinct form in the landscape, especially if planted near a pond or lake where its reflection can be seen in the water. When planting, allow for a tree 50 feet high × 16 feet wide (15 × 4.8 m). This cultivar was first described in 1926.

Taxodium distichum var. *imbricarium* 'Prairie Sentinel'

As its name implies, this upright form brings a striking vertical accent to the landscape. Its short lateral limbs lie somewhat close to the main trunk, a feature that makes this a good four-season tree. Its small, pointed green needles arch upward from the twig in a threadlike manner, further enhancing the tree's vertical aspect. The original tree discovered by Earl Cully in 1968 in Illinois is now more than 60 feet tall × 10 feet wide (18 × 3 m). Since then, 'Prairie Sentinel' remains the standard by which all fastigiate forms of pond cypress are measured. It was registered by the Arnold Arboretum in 1971.

Taxodium distichum var. *mexicanum* Montezuma Cypress, Mexican Swamp Cypress

First described in 1853 and endemic to Guatemala, Mexico, and the southern tip of Texas, Montezuma cypress remains evergreen to semi-evergreen in its native habitat but, when planted toward the northern limit of its hardiness, is tardily deciduous. It does not grow as tall as bald cypress but with age achieves enormous diameter and girth. One of the most famous champion trees in the world is a giant Montezuma cypress growing in the town of El Tule, approximately nine miles (15 km) from the city of Oaxaca, the capital of the southern Mexican state of the same name. A 1987 sign gave the tree's dimensions as 137 feet (42 m) tall, 190 feet (58 m) in circumference, and 48 feet (14.6 m) in diameter. Assuming this is one tree, it has the thickest trunk of any tree on earth.

In terms of its appearance, Montezuma cypress is more weeping than var. *distichum* or *imbricarium* and, as a result of its long, pendulous branches, resembles var. *distichum* 'Pendens'. Reminiscent of American beech (*Fagus grandifolia*), its short shoots and thin needles tend to remain on the tree throughout the winter months, detaching when the new leaves emerge in the spring. In summary, Montezuma cypress differs from its northern cousin, the bald cypress, by being more compact and having shorter leaves and smaller cones. The Montezuma cypress is faster growing than the bald or pond cypress, partly because its foliage drops later in the fall and develops earlier in the spring. This schedule can pose a problem when there is a late spring frost of significant magnitude, as occurred in 2007, because the cold can damage or kill the new growth.

Though several specimens in Zone 7b have survived brief cold snaps as low as 14°F (-10°C), their overall performance has been unspectacular. Montezuma cypress is therefore a better choice for landscapes in Zone 8b and above. As with a number of conifers that are marginally hardy in the upper portions of the South, provenance plays a major role in their adaptability. A tree in John's trials is growing 2 feet (0.6 m) per year after three years in the ground. This species performed very well in Auburn University's Shade Tree Trials, growing to a height and width of 22.7 × 21 feet (6.9 × 6.4 m) after nine years. Our observations indicate that this variety will grow wider than the other two varieties of cypress.

Taxodium 'Nanjing Beauty' Nanjing Cypress

Dr. David Creech introduced this new plant through the Nanjing Botanical Garden and the Chinese Academy of Science. It is the first-ever reported intervarietal cross between two *Taxodium*: var. *distichum* and var. *mexicanum*. Indicating that it is a fast-growing tree, 'Nanjing Beauty' grew 3 feet (0.9 m) the first year in John's trials and, so far, has a very open growth habit. The hybrids are believed to be tolerant of alkaline soils, and several newer clones—reportedly improvements over the original introduction—should become available over the next several years. It is hardy at least through Zones 7 and 8.

Taxus Yew

Yew is a widespread genus. It is found across eastern and western North America and, in the East, ranges from southwestern China westward to northern Burma, Nepal, and northern India, then southeastward into the Philippines and southward to the Celebes. It is important to point out that not all species are suitable for the South. As a general rule, *Taxus* from Europe and North America grow at higher latitudes than do the Asian taxa and are therefore less adaptable to the heat and humidity of warmer climates. We therefore cover only four here: two Asian species, *Taxus wallichiana* and *T. cuspidata*; the hybrid, *Taxus ×media*; and the Florida yew, *Taxus floridana*. It is unfortunate so few yews adapt well to the South, because the vast majority of cultivars derive from the English yew, *Taxus baccata*. Specialty nurseries sometimes offer a third Asian species, *T. mairei*, which is reportedly well adapted to Zone 7.

All yews make great foundation plants and integrate well into mixed borders. Their rich green needles are short and remain on the plant for many years. The deep green contrasts well with the reddish brown bark that exfoliates with age. Yews can survive the cruelest pruning and come back strong. Plus, they are devoid of major pests or diseases. Yews prefer high afternoon shade but, with adequate moisture, will survive in full sun.

With the exception of the aril, all parts of the yew are poisonous, especially to horses. Yews are almost always dioecious, so you may never see fruit on the plants. Propagation is from seeds; most cultivars are produced from cuttings or by grafting. Pruning can be done at any time of the year, with the best time being late winter or early spring.

Taxus cuspidata Japanese Yew

This species is hardier than the other yews treated here and is unquestionably well adapted to the South. Japanese yew's distinguishing feature is the V-shaped orientation of its needles. While chiefly known as one of the parents of *Taxus × media*, it has produced several gardenworthy cultivars.

Taxus cuspidata 'Dwarf Bright Gold'

For most of the year, this Iseli Nursery selection differs little from other good forms. In midspring, though, it comes alive with bright yellow new foliage that retains a shiny green striation along the length of each needle. Not recommended for full sun, this selection is perfect for the semishade garden where its new yellow foliage plays off azaleas and other spring-flowering shrubs. The cultivar grows slowly to a height and width of 5 feet × 3 feet (1.5 × 0.9 m). A similar selection, named 'Aurea Nana', is also worthy of a place in southern gardens.

Taxus cuspidata 'Aurea Nana'

Taxus floridana Florida Yew

Florida yew is one of the most endangered trees in the world and listed as an endangered species by state and federal agencies. It occurs only along forested bluffs and in ravines scattered along a 15-mile reach on the east side of the Apalachicola River between Chattahoochee and Bristol in Florida's Gadsden and Liberty counties. In cultivation, Florida yew should attain a height of around 10 feet (3 m), but it is hard to find in nurseries and can be difficult to grow. Its bushy form lends a certain air of openness to a shade garden and contrasts well with its thin, irregular, flaking bark. If you can, get a seed-grown specimen in order to ensure an upright form instead of a sprawling horizontal, or plagiotropic, form that may take years to develop a dominant central leader. The species grows naturally in the shade in Zone 8b but has proven hardy as far north as Zone 7b. Winter browning can be a problem in full sun.

Taxus ×media Anglojap Yew

Developed in the United States around 1900 from a cross of English yew (*Taxus baccata*) and Japanese yew (*T. cuspidata*), the Anglojap yew has given rise to a seemingly endless array of cultivars, and all seem to adapt well to the South. In appearance they most resemble *T. cuspidata*, with ornamental features including compactness, slow growth rate, stem and foliage density, and summer or winter color. Form varies according to selection. We feature three different cultivars, each with a distinct form: spreading, rounded, and upright columnar. Anglojap yews are recommended for Zones 6–7a.

Taxus ×media 'Dark Green Spreader'

This Monrovia Nursery introduction is an excellent yew where one is looking for a low-maintenance plant that will grow 4 feet tall × 6 feet wide (1.2 × 1.8 m). As its name suggests, 'Dark Green Spreader' has dark green foliage that emerges light green in spring. It is slow growing and, like all yews, forgiving of heavy pruning.

Taxus ×media 'Densiformis'

This female form requires a male pollinator to produce fruit. It is a semidwarf, dense selection that typically grows into a mound 3–4 feet (1.2 m) tall. A popular cultivar first introduced in 1951.

Taxus ×media 'Hicksii'

Introduced in 1923, this older cultivar is no stranger to southern gardens—for good reason. It tolerates a variety of well-drained soils; it can handle deep shade; it has no serious insect or disease problems; and because 'Hicksii' retains its lustrous, dark green foliage, it almost never appears disheveled. All these features add up to an attractive, low maintenance plant. Dense and narrowly columnar in form with ascending branches, 'Hicksii' grows in time to a height of around 12 feet (3.7 m).

Taxus wallichiana Himalayan Yew

Several Asian species of *Taxus* can be seen in various arboreta and botanical gardens, but not all authorities agree on their taxonomy. We have seen this species listed as *Taxus wallichiana* var. *chinensis*. Specimens prosper at the J. C. Raulston Arboretum, the Atlanta Botanical Garden, and the Stephen F. Austin State University Arboretum. It has been successful in John's trials, and Tom has

Taxus wallichiana

grown it for more than 12 years with no problem. Himalayan yew grows best as an understory specimen in light shade—just as it occurs naturally. All the specimens we have observed have become large spreading shrubs in the range of 6 feet × 6 feet (1.8 m) or more.

Thuja Arborvitae

Native to North America and eastern Asia, all *Thuja* are characterized by fan-shaped, flattened branchlets. The common name "arborvitae" is Latin for "tree of life": it was once believed the tree's resins contained curative properties. As a group, the arborvitae have produced a significant number of highly desirable cultivars, and all perform well in the South. Propagation of the species is from seeds. Most cultivars are produced either from cuttings or by grafting. Pruning can be done at any time of the year, but the best time is late winter or early spring. As discussed in the entry on *Chamaecyparis obtusa*, the foliage of some *Thuja* are hard to distinguish from *Chamaecyparis*, particularly among those sections with permanently juvenile foliage.

Thuja koraiensis

Thuja koraiensis Korean Arborvitae

This gem of a small tree or large shrub is mainly absent from gardens and nurseries. This is unfortunate, because Korean arborvitae brings a certain cottage charm to a woodland setting. It has lacey foliage, a conical form with gently weeping branches, and tiny new yellow-green cones that mature to reddish brown. It is most often seen as a sprawling plant but in time will develop a central leader. Its branchlets are trailing with flat shoots. The scalelike leaves are diamond shaped on young shoots, triangular on older shoots, and bright green on top with silvery stomatal wax bands underneath. This silvery underside attracts the most attention as it appears to have been spray painted with a high-gloss silvery white pigment.

Where offered, Korean arborvitae is usually sold under the cultivar name 'Glauca Prostrata'. In our opinion, 'Glauca Prostrata' is likely the straight species that in time will form a leader. Some clones exhibit a glaucous appearance on the top side of the foliage, and occasionally you will come across selections with irregular white bands on the top. All are gardenworthy plants for Zones 6–7 and may even thrive further south if given shade and excellent drainage. Korean arborvitae is native to Korea and extreme northeast China.

Thuja occidentalis Northern White-Cedar, Arborvitae

Northern white-cedar is a highly adaptable conifer and aptly classified as low-maintenance. Unless you collect species, we recommend you opt for one of the cultivars instead. Numerous cultivars have been selected, demonstrating a wide range of formal variations that translate into hosts of different landscape applications. While northern white-cedar grows naturally in wet forests and swamps, it is adaptable to dry areas. Like bald cypress, it may be happiest where there is little competition. Its main nemesis appears to be deer, which enjoy browsing its foliage. The plant is also unforgiving of fire. Given favorable conditions, though, this is a long-lived species, with the oldest known plant being more than 1,100 years old. Northern white-cedar is frequently called arborvitae, Latin for "tree of life." This name was given to the plant by the French explorer Jacques Cartier, whose men used the vitamin C in its foliage to combat scurvy during the winter of 1535–36.

Thuja occidentalis 'American Pillar' (PP20209)

Discovered as a sport of 'Hetz Wintergreen' by the late John Houser when he was 80 years old, this stand-out selection is perfect as a lone specimen or as a screening tree. Houser named it 'American Pillar' because—strong, tall, and trim—it reminded him of a soldier standing at attention. It grows rapidly to around 30 feet tall × 4 feet wide (9 × 1.2 m). Because of its height and narrow base, it is highly suitable for screening pools or for providing a privacy blind on lot lines where a narrow plant is preferable to Leyland cypress or 'Green Giant', both of which can grow considerably wider. 'American Pillar' has good disease resistance and an excellent root system that sustains it in high winds. This is a plant with a future.

Thuja occidentalis 'Conabe' (PP19009 Fire Chief™)

It can be easy at first glance to mistake Fire Chief™ for the older cultivar, 'Rheingold'. On closer inspection, though, you will see that Fire Chief™ displays brighter orange and flame-red foliage on the growing tips and in our view is a more dazzling plant in both winter and spring. The rounded, almost perfect globe form is perfect for the mixed bed, in a rock garden, or grown with other conifers such as dwarf pines. It resists sun and winter burning and is not fussy as to soil type as long as not planted in standing water. While suitable for full sun to part shade in Zone 7 and higher, it appreciates some light afternoon shade. Expect the final size of this cultivar to be 4 feet high × 4 feet wide (1.2 m). Maryland

Thuja occidentalis 'Conabe' Fire Chief™

nurseryman Gabe Cesarini originally found this plant as a branch sport of *Thuja occidentalis* 'Rheingold'.

Thuja occidentalis 'Degroot's Spire'

This is one of the better conifers for the South where one is looking for a tall, narrow, dark green exclamation point. The tightly whorled foliage is thick enough not to be wimpy and does not tend to break apart like that of conifers of similar form such as Italian cypress (*Cupressus sempervirens*). To ensure a strong specimen that will hold together, purchase only plants with a single leader or, if it is already in the landscape, remove all competing leaders. This seedling selection from Sheridan Nursery of Ontario, Canada, can be expected to reach a mature height and width of 20 feet × 4 feet (6 × 1.2 m).

Thuja occidentalis 'Golden Tuffet'

Reminiscent of an igloo top, this is a highly desirable and unique cultivar: there is no mistaking it for any other plant. The golden orange two-toned foliage

Thuja occidentalis 'Golden Tuffet'

reminds one of braided ringlets and never fails to draw attention. This Iseli Nursery introduction should mature at 1 foot tall × 2 feet wide (0.3 × 0.6 m).

Thuja occidentalis 'Hetz Wintergreen'

This is another fine dual-use selection that is good as a specimen plant or for use in screening. With a narrow, upright form and a moderately fast growth rate, it is ideal for use as a narrow hedge or privacy screen, and, where space allows, a well-grown specimen is an object of beauty. 'Hetz Wintergreen' retains its soft, glossy, dark green foliage all year and is extremely attractive during the winter. Because it tolerates lower light conditions than most arborvitae, 'Hetz Wintergreen' is a versatile selection. It matures to a height and width of 30 feet × 12 feet (9 × 3.7 m).

Thuja occidentalis 'Linesville'

'Linesville' has a dense globose habit with soft, pastel blue-green, juvenile foliage. The foliage is an ericoides type that is soft to the touch. The habit is tight and compact, and it retains its shape without pruning. 'Linesville' is also notable for resisting winter discoloration. Given its soft color and texture, this arborvitae

Thuja occidentalis 'Linesville'

works very well in group plantings or as a foreground plant with larger upright evergreens as a backdrop. It would also make a handsome low border along paths, walkways, and sidewalks. Conifer enthusiast and propagator Joe Stupka of Pennsylvania apparently discovered 'Linesville' as a witch's broom in the Linesville cemetery around 1985. Also sold under the name 'Mr. Bowling Ball', this cultivar should reach a mature size of 4 feet × 4 feet (1.2 m).

Thuja occidentalis 'Rheingold'

Fantastic in form and color, 'Rheingold' features a dense compact globe shape with soft gold-tinged top foliage that transitions into green below. It puts on its best show in spring and summer when the orange-yellow of the foliage intensifies. This vivid shade changes to a dark golden copper in winter, providing seasonal interest and a gentle change of pace. This popular cultivar should reach a mature size of 4 feet × 4 feet (1.2 m).

Thuja occidentalis 'Smaragd'

Commonly called emerald arborvitae in the trade, this attractive cultivar has a compact conical habit and retains its lustrous green color throughout the seasons. While somewhat common in the South, 'Smaragd' makes a great landscape plant nonetheless and deserves its place in the garden. At maturity, it reaches a height of about 12 feet and a width of 4 feet (3.6 × 1.2 m). 'Smaragd' originated as a sport growing on *Thuja occidentalis* 'Kelleriis Viridis', and the D. T. Poulsen nursery in Denmark introduced it around 1950.

Thuja plicata Western Red-Cedar

The western red-cedar is not actually a cedar (*Cedrus*) but belongs in the Cupressaceae family, along with cypresses. It is one of two arborvitaes (*Thuja*) native to North America and is the principal source of many outdoor products, including cedar decking, shingles, and siding. Its native range in the northwestern United States and southwestern Canada extends south from southern Alaska and British Columbia to northwest California and inland to western Montana. Given its geographic distribution, it was a surprise to discover that it adapts so well to the growing conditions of the southeastern United States.

Western red-cedar has long been used by indigenous peoples of the Pacific Northwest for building timbers, totem poles, medicine, dug-out canoes, and ceremonial objects. In its native habitat, it grows to immense proportions—150 feet tall (45 m)—and is considered one of the major trees of the region. In the South, a large specimen might be half that size.

While it is not unusual to see the straight species planted in the South, most trees of this type are *Thuja* × 'Green Giant'. Left on its own, it will grow rather quickly into an upright tree with a pyramidal silhouette and strongly horizontal branches. It tolerates pruning quite well and can be maintained at a much smaller size. It is ideal for use as a hedge or screen or as a specimen where space is not an issue. Best in Zones 6–7.

Thuja plicata 'Daniellow' (PP20267)

'Daniellow' came to our attention in 2009 while we were visiting nurseryman Rick Crowder at Hawksridge Farms in Hickory, North Carolina. We were immediately taken by its bright yellow color and narrow, upright pyramidal form. This is definitely a plant for the future, and we see more and more growers offering it. 'Daniellow' originated from Nijerk, Netherlands, in 1997 as a branch sport from *T. plicata* 'Gelderland'.

Thuja plicata 'Grune Kugel'

A somewhat new introduction from Germany, 'Grune Kugel' is perhaps the smallest of all *T. plicata* cultivars. It requires little or no pruning, and the dark green color of its handsome shiny foliage is enhanced in winter by a purple cast on the leaf tips. An excellent border plant, 'Grune Kugel' is also good for filling small niches in the landscape. This diminutive cultivar should reach a mature height and width of 1 foot × 2 feet (0.3 × 0.6 m). The cultivar name of this German-found sport translates as "green ball."

Thuja plicata 'Sunshine'

'Sunshine' slowly reaches a mature height of 20 feet (6 m). A slender columnar form with branches that ascend narrowly, it has profuse short branches and makes an excellent exclamation point in the landscape. The bronze and orange winter coloration is normal and adds to its landscape interest.

Thuja plicata 'Whipcord'

This selection receives our vote for looking the least like a *Thuja* of any *Thuja* we know. Nothing we can find in its appearance offers a clue to its parentage. For gardeners seeking a conversation piece, 'Whipcord' may fit the bill. It is a multibranched shrub with long tendrils of foliage that present a droopy, mop-like appearance. Glossy green in summer, the foliage acquires a bronze cast in the winter. At maturity, the shrub is 5 feet high × 4 feet wide (1.5 × 1.2 m).

Thuja 'Green Giant'

Now one of the mainstays in the southern landscape along with *Cryptomeria*, 'Green Giant' has largely replaced Leyland cypress for screening purposes. It has all the attributes one desires in a plant of this size: vigorous growth; a tall, pyramidal shape; and rich evergreen color that endures throughout the seasons. 'Green Giant' is equally at home in full sun or light shade. It has no serious pest or disease problems and is widely available at a respectable price. 'Green Giant' cannot well tolerate prolonged drought when it is young, so keep it watered during dry spells.

'Green Giant' reportedly made its debut in 1967 from a single plant reputed to be *Thuja* (*standishii* ×*plicata*). D. T. Poulsen of Kvistgaard, Denmark, gave the plant to the U.S. National Arboretum. After some evaluation, 'Green Giant' was distributed to nurseries, and the name was selected to signify its landscape qualities. Expect mature plants to reach a height and width of 50 feet × 15 feet (15 × 4.6 m). The cultivar 'Steeplechase' (PP16094) does not appear adaptable to container production in the lower parts of Zone 8, though it seems to perform fine in field nurseries in Zone 8a.

Thuja 'Green Giant'

Thujopsis dolobrata Hiba or False Arborvitae

Thujopsis is a monotypic genus having only one species. This underutilized conifer is slowly making its way into home gardens. Its bold, flattened, scalelike green foliage seductively sports bright silvery stomatal patches underneath. Unlike most silvery conifers, which demand strong light, this one does best in light shade but will tolerate full sun; it is thus less likely to be smothered by surrounding plants. It has a Christmas-tree shape and once established grows 4–8 inches (10–20 cm) a year. In the South, it probably won't get any larger than 18 feet tall (5.5 m) × 5 feet wide (1.5 m), although nursery catalogs may forecast more substantial dimensions. Pruning can be done at any time of the year, though the best times are late winter or early spring. *Thujopsis* has good color year-round.

After several years, specimens of *Thujopsis dolobrata* var. *hondae* growing in trials in Zones 7a and 8b have grown quite slowly to only 3 feet (0.9 m) tall. This may be because *hondae* is a northern variety that occurs naturally in Japan. It differs little from var. *dolobrata,* except that its leaves are slightly

Thujopsis dolobrata

smaller. A nice specimen of var. *hondae* grows in the Asian Valley at the U.S. National Arboretum in Washington, D.C. One of the most outstanding specimens we have seen is growing in the late Jane Platt's garden in Portland, Oregon. Several newer forms are making their way into the trade, including 'Cristata', which displays white markings on both sides of the leaves, and 'Latifolia', a low shrubby form.

Thujopsis dolobrata 'Nana'

This often-ignored dwarf selection is perfect for the shade garden. With yellow-green scale-like leaves and a lacy texture, everything about the selection is bright, delicate, crisp, and diminutive. As if this were not enough to recommend it, 'Nana' is also maintenance free. In the South, we anticipate a mature height and width of no more than 3 feet × 4 feet (0.9 × 1.2 m).

Thujopsis dolobrata 'Variegata'

This cultivar is almost identical to the species except that its leaves are variegated. A number of clones are available in the trade, but some are not stable and will revert. A specimen we received from Mountain Meadows Nursery of Weaverville, North Carolina, is the best we have evaluated so far: it is now more than 10 feet tall (3 m) and perfectly formed.

Torreya

Like a number of conifers, torreya has a disjunct distribution in eastern and western North America and eastern Asia (China and Japan). These members of the yew family (Taxaceae) are primitive plants. Each species is restricted to a small geographical area, particularly so in North America. While most are adapted to the South, we have chosen the two that perform best here. All can be pruned at any time of the year, though the best times are late winter or early spring. When grown well, *Torreya* can make beautiful landscape specimens. All produce plumlike green fruit and differ from the similar *Taxus* and *Cephalotaxus* by having stiff spine-tipped leaves.

Torreya taxifolia Florida Torreya, Stinking Cedar

Occurring in the same general area as Florida yew (*Taxus floridana*), Florida torreya is a rare and endangered species that is in a serious state of decline in its

Torreya taxifolia

native habitat. Florida torreya is not an abundant species and is found only in widely scattered populations along the Apalachicola River in northern Florida and in one county in southwest Georgia. It became one of the first federally listed endangered plant species in the United States in 1984. These populations are threatened because of habitat destruction and fungal pathogens that kill young trees before they reach sexual maturity.

Florida torreya is an evergreen tree that can reach heights of 30 feet (9 m) in cultivation. Its two-ranked needles are a bright glossy green that glistens in sunlight. A mature specimen growing at the State Botanical Garden in Athens, Georgia, offers living proof of how beautiful this tree can be, especially in a woodland setting. The leaves and cones have a strongly pungent resinous odor when crushed—hence the names "stinking yew" and "stinking cedar." The champion Florida torreya grows in Madison, Florida.

The species is much hardier than its current status would suggest. Thanks to conservation efforts by individuals and by institutions such as the Atlanta Botanical Garden, this species is now being successfully cultivated in locations north of its native range. Florida torreya seems to prefer light shade and is potentially adaptable throughout the South. This is an excellent conifer with its only drawbacks being slow growth and sharp needle points. Tom has found that liberal applications of lime improve the appearance of torreya at his arboretum.

Torreya nucifera Japanese Torreya

Japanese torreya is a moderately slow-growing conifer that will eventually reach heights up to 30 feet (9 m) in cultivation. With a pyramidal silhouette and long, glossy, dark green branches, this is a conifer that deserves more attention in the South. The down-curved needles are two-ranked and reminiscent of *Taxus* (yew). They are smaller than those of the Florida torreya and give off a sage-like aroma when crushed. The tree's biggest draw are its glossy green leaves that shimmer in the sun; in fact, no conifer has a shinier leaf. The 1½-inch green fruits follow the insignificant flowers and persist on the tree for several years. Its main use would be as a specimen tree where it has room to grow. This species should grow best in filtered to moderate shade.

Tsuga Hemlock

One of the first assumptions about "hemlocks" is that they are poisonous. Quite the contrary, the poisonous plant mistakenly called hemlock is, in fact, the biennial weed *Conium maculatum*, native to Europe. *Tsuga* is the Japanese name for hemlock. Depending on the source, there are somewhere between 9 and 14 species. In this book we treat the genus as having nine species, one subspecies, and three varieties. Four species are native to North America, and the other five are native to the Himalayas and eastern Asia. With the exception of the two western species, *T. mertensiana* and *T. heterophylla*, all do well in some parts of the South but are generally best suited to Zones 6 and 7. Though *Tsuga* will survive in Zone 8, the species is not regularly used in Zone 8 landscapes. Two trees are known to be growing in Tifton, Georgia, both under the shade of tall pine trees, in a setting similar to that for growing camellias. Irrespective of species or where in the South you garden, hemlocks will benefit from afternoon shade: hemlocks are highly shade tolerant.

A sap-sucking insect, the hemlock woolly adelgid (*Adelges tsugae*), now threatens the two species that occur naturally in the Southeast. This insect was introduced accidentally from eastern Asia. Current reports indicate that the Asian hemlocks as well as the two western American hemlocks are relatively resistant to this pest. In the near future, the U.S. National Arboretum plans to conduct trials of *T. chinensis* and hybrids resistant to the hemlock woolly adelgid. In the wild, Canadian hemlock shades mountain streams, helping keep the water cool and ideal for trout. Since no other tree fills this environmental niche, loss of hemlocks could mean demise of trout populations in the southeastern United States. Imidacloprid, a systemic insecticide, does a good job of controlling the adelgid in landscape situations where individual trees can be drenched, but it is difficult to treat large natural areas with this product. Propagation is from seeds; most cultivars are propagated from cuttings or by grafting. Plants are intolerant of high pH soils. Pruning can be done at any time of the year, but the best times are late winter or early spring.

Tsuga canadensis Eastern Hemlock

Eastern hemlock is native to the eastern United States, from Maine west to Minnesota and south to northern Alabama and Georgia. It also extends into portions of eastern Canada, most notably New Brunswick and Nova Scotia. While it is highly unlikely that any of us will be around to witness it, after many years the tree can attain a height of 175 feet × 20 feet (53.3 × 6 m). The U.S. champion hemlock is found in the Great Smoky Mountains National Park and is 165 feet (50 m) tall with a trunk almost 6 feet (1.8 m) in diameter, suggesting that under good conditions, this is a long-lived tree.

The dark green evergreen needles are short and linear and arranged horizontally on the branchlets. The needles reach about half an inch (1.3 cm) in length, with two distinct whitened stomatal bands on the underside. The cones are among the smallest of any conifer. In its natural habitat, the tree casts dense shade, and few plants (other than its own seedlings) are able to survive under its canopy. It can be difficult to sort out the more than 200 cultivars, many of which have only minor differences. We have nonetheless observed the following cultivars as noteworthy and possessing unique traits:

Tsuga canadensis 'Bennett'

This plant appears to be more compact than most of the other low-growing forms. As its graceful arching branches mature into a plant that is wider than high, it serves as a great addition to the mixed shade garden. In winter, it provides evergreen interest, and in the spring and summer it provides great contrast with herbaceous perennials such as hosta. In the fall, its dark green foliage accents the changing leaf colors of deciduous trees. Discovered by Mr. Bennett in Atlantic Highlands, New Jersey, this cultivar was first described in 1965.

Tsuga canadensis 'Cole's Prostrate'

'Cole's Prostrate' is still the standard for prostrate forms of Canadian hemlock, and, on occasion, older specimens are encountered in the South. A particularly beautiful specimen was seen at the former Evergreen Nursery in Leicester, North Carolina, the summer home of former American Conifer Society president Jordan Jack, who sadly passed away in the spring of 2010. When well grown, this is a plant of distinction that remains small enough to work in any shade garden. It would be especially effective used in combination with stone to accent its layer of green carpet. This selection was first collected by H. R. Cole in 1929 near Mt. Madison, New Hampshire, and subsequently introduced by Gray and Cole Nursery, Haverhill, Massachusetts.

Tsuga canadensis 'Curly'

This densely compact cultivar grows upright with an irregular zigzag form, and it is one of our favorites. The leaves are dark green and curl downward and away from the main stem. 'Curly' is guaranteed to provide architectural interest throughout the seasons. It was first described in 1969 after being discovered by H. Epstein of Larchmont, New York.

Tsuga canadensis 'Dawsoniana'

If one is looking for a hemlock of intermediate size—in the range of 8–12 feet (2.4–3.7 m)—'Dawsoniana' is a fine choice. It has many desirable features for today's landscapes: a dense, bushy form and wide needles that are dark green throughout the year. As the plant matures it maintains a restrained form with little or no pruning. Found in 1933 by Harry S. Dawson of Holliston, Massachusetts.

Tsuga canadensis 'Frosty'

'Frosty' is the template for dwarf, white-foliaged hemlock cultivars. Given its frosted color and thin branches, 'Frosty' can be a bit temperamental: this plant must be grown in shade to survive in the South. Based on our experience, it is best planted in Zones 6 and 7. Sited properly, this cultivar complements any shady site and is worthy of the effort to find a source. It grows slowly to approximately 5 feet (1.5 m) and was first described in 1984.

Tsuga canadensis 'Gentsch White'

This is a mostly green form that produces white tips on new growth. While some reference books and catalogs list it as a "dwarf globe," it is anything but. A specimen growing at Tom's arboretum is more than 12 feet tall × 5 feet wide (3.7 × 1.5 m). This is one of the better intermediate forms and is not temperamental. It also can be placed in more shaded environments while still offering some variation in color. Like all hemlocks, 'Gentsch White' accepts heavy shearing, after which new growth comes out silvery white on the branch tips, making a good color contrast with the remaining green foliage. Found by Otto Gentsch, a nurseryman on Long Island, New York, and described in 1984.

Tsuga canadensis 'Jeddeloh'

This cultivar is easy to identify as no other has the same curious form. 'Jeddeloh' is often described as having a bird's nest–like center, because its center is lower than the outsides, and the branches arch out and then over. It will eventually form a rather dense and somewhat uniform plant that should max out at around 5 feet high × 6 feet wide (1.5 × 1.8 m). 'Jeddeloh' is non-temperamental, moderately fast growing, and relatively trouble free. Like all the dwarf and intermediate hemlocks, because of its size, 'Jeddeloh' is easy to spray for control of the woolly adelgid. This cultivar is an introduction from Jeddeloh Nursery Company of Germany, circa 1965.

Tsuga canadensis 'Pendula'

Based on numerous observations, we have determined that 'Pendula' is a catch-all name for any number of weeping forms of Canadian hemlock first described in 1891. All possess a certain charm and will develop into a mound of overlapping, pendulous branches. All forms need to be staked to the desired height, unless you want the plant to assume a prostrate habit. Most plants that one comes across in a garden center are staked to a height of 3–6 feet (0.9–1.8 m). When a leader is continually staked, the height can easily be manipulated. All selections will continue to spread, and a mature specimen can easily be 5 feet (1.5 m) in width. A well-sited specimen presents a green accent of weeping beauty that can be incorporated into any number of landscape applications. For example, on a slope, it could be trained to cascade downhill; near a stream or pond, it could be trained to hang over the water. Several nice forms occasionally come across our radar screen, including 'Ashfield Weeper' (from Watnong Nursery, 1984) and 'Sargentii', a wide-spreading and weeping large shrub form (10 feet tall × 20 feet wide [3 × 6 m]), with many pendulous branches. Old specimens growing at the New York Botanical Garden are as breathtaking as any conifer on earth.

Tsuga canadensis 'Slenderella'

Another of the intermediate forms, 'Slenderella' is unique. What sets it apart from other similar cultivars are its slender needles, which have an open effect. This is one cultivar that garden enthusiasts either love or hate. At maturity it should grow to around 15 feet high × 5 feet wide (4.6 × 1.5 m). It would be a splendid selection paired against a dense dark green upright conifer such as *Thuja* × 'Green Giant'. 'Slenderella' was named in 1984 after a plant growing at Longwood Gardens in Pennsylvania.

Tsuga canadensis 'Vermeulen Wintergold'

This selection is a gem of a plant that never fails to turn bright yellow at the start of cold weather, even in shade. Too often, plants advertised as turning gold in the winter fail to live up to their billing in the warmer parts of the South. If one is looking for that attribute, this cultivar—along with several others such as *Pinus strobus* 'Hillside Wintergold' (also known as 'Wintergold')—is a surefire winner. Where one has the room, a grouping of 'Vermeulen Wintergold', 'Summer Snow', and 'Dawsoniana' would be interesting in light shade. We expect it to attain a height of around 15 feet (4.6 m).

Tsuga diversifolia Northern Japanese Hemlock

Northern Japanese hemlock is perfectly at home in the Southeast's Zones 6 and 7b if grown as an understory tree with adequate moisture. This species is not bothered by the insect pests that plague many of our native eastern hemlocks and is the first hemlock to produce new growth in the spring. *T. diversifolia* has a conical habit and is often a multitrunked tree growing to a height of about 30 feet (9 m). This plant's only drawback is its slow growth, around 6 inches (15 cm) per year.

Tsuga sieboldii Southern Japanese Hemlock

This narrow-leaved hemlock from moist mountain sites in southern Japan often forms a multistemmed small tree in the range of 30–35 feet tall × 20–25 feet wide (9–11 × 6–8 m). Its branch habit is horizontal with nodding tips. The shiny dark green needles are densely arranged in irregular flat rows and have two minute, not very bright, white stomatal bands on the lower surface. The chief difference between it and its northern cousin (*T. diversifolia*) is in the appearance of the stomatal bands; those of *T. diversifolia* are much more distinctly white and it has pubescent young stems. The needles of *T. sieboldii* are more densely set in irregular flat rows than those of the more northern species. No hemlock native to North America resembles this species. In those areas where the woolly adelgid has become a problem, this species would make a good small landscape substitute as it, along with the other Asian species, does not seem affected by this pest. Southern Japanese hemlock should be adaptable in Zones 5–8a.

Tsuga sieboldii 'Greenball'

To date, very little mention has been afforded this dandy little cultivar of the southern Japanese hemlock. The few plants we have observed are tight buns of congested dark green foliage that at first glance resemble a dwarf *Chamaecyparis*. Everything about the plant is small, including its needles. As it is one of a handful of conifers that prosper in the shade, this cultivar is quite useful and pairs well with any number of herbaceous perennials, especially those exhibiting variegation. We believe that 'Greenball' will not get any larger than 5 feet × 5 feet (1.5 m).

Wollemia nobilis Wollemi Pine

Like several other conifers, *Wollemia* is a monotypic genus having only one species. One of the most recent finds in the conifer world, the Wollemi pine was first discovered 93 miles (150 km) northwest of Sydney, Australia, in 1994 by David Noble, a New South Wales National Parks and Wildlife officer. There are only about 100 trees growing in the wild, and these are in Wollemi National Park.

Wollemi pine is in the family Araucariaceae. Young trees are fast growing in full sun and can reach heights of more than 100 feet (30 m) in their native habitat. Plants should be adapted to Zones 8 and 9 in the southeastern United States. This species appears to be susceptible to Phytophthora root rot, so planting on a well-drained site is recommended. Conservation efforts in Australia have been successful, and numerous trees have been propagated via cuttings for sale to the public.

Wollemia nobilis

Appendix 1

AHS Heat Zone Map

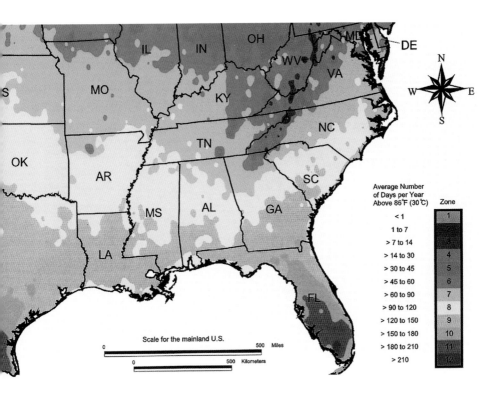

Appendix 2

USDA Hardiness Zone Map for the South

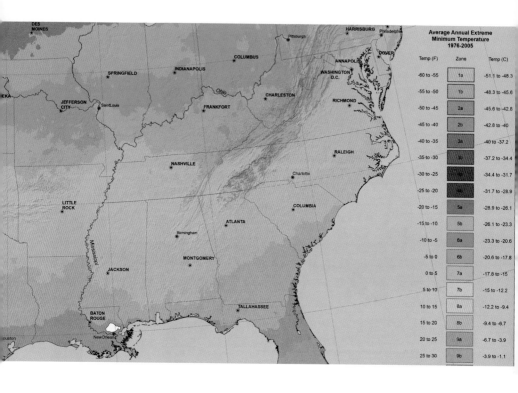

Average Annual Extreme
Minimum Temperature
1976–2005

Temp (F)	Zone	Temp (C)
-60 to -55	1a	-51.1 to -48.3
-55 to -50	1b	-48.3 to -45.6
-50 to -45	2a	-45.6 to -42.8
-45 to -40	2b	-42.8 to -40
-40 to -35	3a	-40 to -37.2
-35 to -30	3b	-37.2 to -34.4
-30 to -25	4a	-34.4 to -31.7
-25 to -20	4b	-31.7 to -28.9
-20 to -15	5a	-28.9 to -26.1
-15 to -10	5b	-26.1 to -23.3
-10 to -5	6a	-23.3 to -20.6
-5 to 0	6b	-20.6 to -17.8
0 to 5	7a	-17.8 to -15
5 to 10	7b	-15 to -12.2
10 to 15	8a	-12.2 to -9.4
15 to 20	8b	-9.4 to -6.7
20 to 25	9a	-6.7 to -3.9
25 to 30	9b	-3.9 to -1.1

Appendix 3

Conifer Sizes

In this book we use the American Conifer Society's mature size designations. See http://www.conifersociety.org.

Growth per year	Approx size at 10 years
MINIATURE	
<1 inch	<1 foot
<2.5 cm	<30 cm
DWARF	
>1–6 inches	>1–6 feet
>2.5–15 cm	>0.3–1.8 m
INTERMEDIATE	
>6–12 inches	>6–15 feet
>15–30 cm	>1.8–4.5 m
LARGE	
>12 inches	>15 feet
>30 cm	>4.5 m

In the world of conifers, plants that grow to be more than 1–6 feet tall (0.3–1.8 m) in 10 years are sometimes listed as dwarf selections. In fact, so-called dwarfs are sometimes merely selections that grow much more slowly than the species. Terms such as "dwarf" are relative, and references to "ultimate height" and "ultimate spread" are often estimates based on our experience with a plant. As we have learned, the majority of size and growth designations in reference books and nursery catalogs are based on plant performance in areas outside the South. Growth rates may also vary within the region based on cultural practices, soil type, rainfall amount, and so on. In his book, *The*

Year in Trees, the late J. C. Raulston makes the following observation: "Among some of the early plantings that were to be significant in following years was the 'dwarf conifer' (some of which are now 20 feet tall!) collection, which successfully demonstrated that conifers could indeed grow happily and well in the South, eventually spurring interest by growers and landscapers to add these superb and eminently useful plants to their program."

Appendix 4

Conifer and Ginkgo Selection Based on Landscape Application

Conifers for Full Sun

Abies spp. and all grafted cultivars
   using *A. firma* as the rootstock
Cedrus
Chamaecyparis
Cunninghamia
Cryptomeria
Cupressus
Ginkgo
Glyptostrobus
Juniperus
Keteleeria
Microbiota
Metasequoia
Picea
Pinus
Platycladus
Pseudolarix
Pseudotsuga
Sequoia
Taiwania
Taxodium
Thuja
Torreya

Conifers for Light to Moderate Shade

Abies spp. and all grafted cultivars
   using *A. firma* as the rootstock
Cephalotaxus
Chamaecyparis
Cryptomeria
Fokienia
Ginkgo
Microbiota
Metasequoia
Platycladus
Podocarpus
Pseudotsuga
Sciadopitys
Sequoia
Taxodium
Taxus
Thuja
Thujopsis
Torreya
Tsuga

Conifers for Full Shade

Tsuga

Conifers and Ginkgo with Fall Foliage Color

Ginkgo
Glyptostrobus
Metasequoia
Pseudolarix
Taxodium

In addition, numerous selections of plants such as pines, junipers, yew, and spruce turn an amazing array of colors in winter and spring.

Drought-tolerant Conifers

Cupressus (many, not *C.* ×*leylandii*)
Juniperus
Platycladus
Thuja

Conifers for Wet Soil

Chamaecyparis thyoides
Glyptostrobus
Metasequoia
Taxodium

Appendix 5

Nursery Sources and Conifer Gardens in the South

Alabama

Bellingrath Gardens and Home
12401 Bellingrath Gardens Road
Theodore, Ala. 36582
(251) 973-2217

Birmingham Botanical Gardens
2612 Lane Park Road
Birmingham, Ala. 35223
(205) 414-3903

Donald E. Davis Arboretum
101 Life Sciences Building
Auburn University, Ala. 36849-5407

Green Nurseries and Landscape Design
415 North Greeno Road
Fairhope, Ala. 36532

Huntsville Botanical Garden
4747 Bob Wallace Avenue Southwest
Huntsville, Ala. 35805-3390
(256) 430-3572

Mobile Botanical Gardens
5151 Museum Drive
Mobile, Ala. 36608
(251) 342-0555

University of Alabama in Huntsville
Huntsville, Ala. 35899

Florida

Alfred B. Maclay Gardens State Park
3540 Thomasville Road
Tallahassee, Fla. 32309
(850) 487-4115

Harry P. Leu Gardens
1920 North Forest Avenue
Orlando, Fla. 32803-1537
(407) 246-2620

Kanapaha Botanical Gardens
4700 Southwest 58th Drive
Gainesville, Fla. 32608-0808
(352) 372-4981

University of Florida–North Florida
    Research and Extension Center
155 Research Road
Quincy, Fla. 32351-5677
(850) 875-7100

Georgia

Arthur A. "Buck" Jones Nursery
Various locations in the Atlanta metro area
(770) 345-5506

Atlanta Botanical Gardens
1345 Piedmont Avenue Northeast
Atlanta, Ga. 30309
(404) 876-5859

Callaway Gardens
P.O. Box 2000
Pine Mountain, Ga. 31822-2000
(800) 225-5292

Cox Arboretum and Gardens
1621 North Lake Drive
Canton, Ga. 30115
(770) 772-9747
By appointment only

Just Add Water Rare Plant Nursery
3062 East Hightower Trail
Conyers, Ga. 30012
(770) 761-8882
By appointment only

Lockerly Arboretum
1534 Irwinton Road
Milledgeville, Ga. 31059
(478) 452-2112

Piccadilly Farm
1971 Whippoorwill Road
Bishop, Ga. 30621-6227
(706) 769-6516

Smith-Gilbert Arboretum
2382 Pine Mountain Road
Kennesaw, Ga. 30152
(770) 919-0248

Specialty Ornamentals
3650 Colham Ferry Road
Watkinsville, Ga. 30677
(706) 310-0143

The State Botanical Garden of Georgia
2450 South Milledge Avenue
Athens, Ga. 30605
(706) 542-1244

Thompson Mills Forest
State Arboretum of Georgia
Braselton, Ga.
(706) 654-2666

Twin Branch Nursery
1169 Wiley Bridge Road
Woodstock, Ga. 30188
(770) 926-8566

The University of Georgia Tifton Campus
Ornamental Horticulture Research Area
    and Coastal Plain Research Arboretum
2360 Rainwater Road
Tifton, Ga. 31793-5766
(229) 386-3355

Waddell Barnes Botanical Gardens
Macon State College
100 College Station Drive
Macon, Ga. 31206
(478) 471-2780

Kentucky

The Baker Arboretum
4801 Morgantown Road
Bowling Green, Ky. 42102
(270) 846-2397
By appointment only

Bernheim Arboretum and Research
    Forest
2499 Old State Highway 245
Clermont, Ky. 40110
(502) 955-8512

Cave Hill Cemetery
701 Baxter Avenue
Louisville, Ky.
(502) 451-5630

Chris Summers Nursery
6702 Old Zaring Road
Crestwood, Ky. 40014
(502) 241-5818

Yew Dell Gardens
6220 Old LaGrange Road
Crestwood, Ky. 40014
(502) 241-4788

Mississippi

The Crosby Arboretum
370 Ridge Road
Picayune, Miss. 39644
(601) 799-2311

North Carolina

Appledorn Landscape Nursery
1251 Jonestown Road
Bostic, N.C. 28018
(828) 245-6475

Biltmore Estate
1 Approach Road
Asheville, N.C. 28803

Daniel Stowe Botanical Garden
6500 South New Hope Road
Belmont, N.C. 28012

Hawksridge Farms Nursery
4243 South N.C. 127 Hwy
Hickory, N.C. 28603
(828) 294-2081
Wholesale Only

The Hobbit Garden
9400 Sauls Road
Raleigh, N.C.
(919) 772-6761
By appointment only

North Carolina (*continued*)

J. C. Raulston Arboretum
4415 Beryl Road
Raleigh, N.C. 27695
(919) 515-3132

Juniper Level Botanic Garden
9241 Sauls Road
Raleigh, N.C. 27603
(919) 772-4794

Mountain Meadows Landscaping and
   Nursery
40 Elkins Branch Road
Weaverville, N.C. 28787
(828) 301-2184

Sandhills Horticultural Gardens
3395 Airport Road
Pinehurst, N.C. 28374

Sarah P. Duke Gardens
426 Anderson Street
Duke University West Campus
Durham, N.C. 27708

Tarheel Native Trees
616 Hood Farm Road
Clayton, N.C. 27520
(919) 553-5927

The Unique Plant Nursery
4207 Oak Hill Road
Chapel Hill, N.C. 27514

South Carolina

Gilbert's Nursery
4675 Peachtree Road
Chesnee, S.C. 29323-9143
(864) 592-1734

Head-Lee Nursery
2365 Blue Ridge Boulevard
Seneca, S.C. 29672-6619
(864) 882-3663

South Carolina Botanical Garden
150 Discovery Lane
Clemson, S.C. 29634
(864) 656-3405

Tennessee

East Tennessee State University
Arboretum
East Tennessee State University
Department of Biological Sciences
Johnson City, Tenn. 37614
(423) 439-8635

Knoxville Botanical Garden and
Arboretum
2743 Wimpole Avenue
Knoxville, Tenn. 37914
(865) 862-8717

Shadow Nursery
254 Shadow Nursery Road
Winchester, Tenn. 37398-3247
(931) 967-6059

University of Tennessee Arboretum
901 South Illinois Avenue
Oak Ridge, Tenn.

University of Tennessee
Gardens-Jackson
West Tennessee Research and
Education Center
605 Airways Boulevard
Jackson, Tenn. 38301
(731) 424-1643

University of Tennessee Gardens
252 Ellington Plant Sciences Bldg.
2431 Joe Johnson Drive
Knoxville, Tenn. 37996
(865) 974-8265

Texas

SFA Mast Arboretum
Stephen F. Austin State University
Nacogdoches, Tex. 75962
(936) 468-4404

Virginia

Blandy Experimental Farm
The State Arboretum of Virginia
400 Blandy Farm Lane
Boyce, Va. 22620
(540) 837-1758 Ext. 0

The Hahn Horticulture Garden at
Virginia Tech University
Blacksburg, Va. 24061
(540) 231-5451

Lewis Ginter Botanical Garden
1800 Lakeside Avenue
Richmond, Va. 23228
(804) 262-9887

Norfolk Botanical Garden
6700 Azalea Garden Road
Norfolk, Va. 23518-5537
(757) 441-5830

Washington, D.C.

The U.S. National Arboretum
3501 New York Avenue, Northeast
Washington, D.C. 20002-1958
(202) 245-4539

In addition to this list, members of the American Conifer Society (http://www. conifersociety.org) can access a directory of elaborate gardens that are open by appointment.

Appendix 6

Growth Data for Conifers in Tifton, Georgia (USDA Zone 8b)

Name[a]	Number of years in field	Height (ft)	Width (ft)
Abies firma	10	8.7	11.2
Afrocarpus falcatus	10	13.9	15.2
Araucaria angustifolia[c]	7	8.6	9.2
Callitris columellaris	10	20.4	-
Callitris oblonga	10	14.7	5.7
Calocedrus formosana	10	19.5	13.8
Calocedrus macrolepis	10	17.4	16.0
Cedrus deodara 'Kashmir'	10	24.4	16.2
Chamaecyparis obtusa (1-12)	10	7.1	6.6
Chamaecyparis obtusa 'Crippsii'	10	16.3	11.2
Chamaecyparis obtusa var. *formosensis*	10	22.2	15.5
Chamaecyparis pisifera 'Boulevard'	10	16.0	12.5
Chamaecyparis pisifera 'Plumosa Aurea'[b]	7	14.3	10.8
Chamaecyparis thyoides 'Okefenokee'[b]	7	11.7	7.4
Chamaecyparis thyoides 'Rachel'	10	14.5	15.4
Chamaecyparis thyoides 'Twombly Blue'	10	13.4	11.6
Cryptomeria japonica 'Araucarioides'	10	12.2	10.9
Cryptomeria japonica 'Ben Franklin'	10	27.1	15.9
Cryptomeria japonica 'Black Dragon'	10	10.1	4.5
Cryptomeria japonica 'Cristata'	10	12.4	8.6
Cryptomeria japonica 'Globosa'[b]	7	4.8	5.1
Cryptomeria japonica 'Gyokuryu'	10	11.8	9.1
Cryptomeria japonica 'Ikari'[b]	7	5.2	9.3
Cryptomeria japonica 'Rasen'	10	20.1	9.8
Cryptomeria japonica 'Rein's Dense Jade'[b]	7	2.7	4.1
Cryptomeria japonica 'Sekkan'	10	18.5	12.7
Cryptomeria japonica 'Tansu'	10	15.9	9.9
Cryptomeria japonica 'Tarheel Blue'	10	27.1	15.8
Cryptomeria japonica 'Yaku'	10	20.4	-
Cryptomeria japonica 'Yoshino'	10	26.9	18.5

(continued)

(continued) Name[a]	Number of years in field	Height (ft)	Width (ft)
Cryptomeria japonica var. *sinensis*	10	21.1	18.7
Cunninghamia konishii	10	15.5	-
Cunninghamia lanceolata 'Samurai'	10	35.0	20.8
Cupressus arizonica var. *arizonica* 'Arctic'	10	34.1	16.8
Cupressus arizonica var. *glabra* 'Blue Pyramid'	10	24.3	12.7
Cupressus arizonica var. *glabra* 'Blue Streak'	10	27.4	12.2
Cupressus arizonica var. *glabra* 'Carolina Sapphire'	10	28.8	-
Cupressus arizonica var. *glabra* 'Chaparral'	10	17.4	10.4
Cupressus arizonica var. *glabra* 'Silver Smoke'	10	26.6	11.7
Cupressus assamica	10	23.0	12.6
Cupressus cashmeriana[c]	7	32.4	18.5
Cupressus duclouxiana	10	12.0	8.9
Cupressus gigantea	10	31.9	12.6
Cupressus ×*leylandii* (Augusta form)	10	32.5	20.0
Cupressus ×*leylandii* 'Gold Cup'[b]	7	21.2	14.7
Cupressus ×*leylandii* 'Gold Rider'	10	24.4	12.4
Cupressus ×*leylandii* 'Naylor's Blue'	10	27.2	19.8
Cupressus ×*leylandii* 'Robinson's Gold'[b]	7	21.9	14.9
Cupressus ×*leylandii* 'Silver Dust'[b]	7	21.0	12.4
Cupressus lusitanica (3-23)	10	29.3	28.0
Cupressus lusitanica (3-3)	10	28.4	21.2
Cupressus lusitanica (6-18)	10	19.2	14.8
Cupressus macrocarpa 'Fine Gold'[b]	7	18.1	7.9
Cupressus macrocarpa 'Horizontalis Aurea'[b]	7	12.4	11.5
Cupressus nootkatensis 'Pendula'[b]	7	7.4	5.4
Cupressus ×*notabilis*[c]	7	37.3	17.5
Cupressus ×*ovensii*[c]	7	38.2	15.2
Cupressus sempervirens var. *dupreziana*[b]	7	21.1	5.3
Fokienia hodginsii	7	13.2	12.0
Glyptostrobus pensilis	10	16.8	-
Juniperus chinensis 'Angelica Blue'	10	7.6	13.6
Juniperus chinensis, 'Gold Lace' (PP#8202)	10	8.3	16.6
Juniperus deppeana 'McFetters'	10	11.6	-
Juniperus rigida	10	15.9	11.7
Juniperus scopulorum 'Sparkling Skyrocket'[b]	7	5.1	2.6
Juniperus virginiana 'Brodie'	10	25.0	13.1
Juniperus virginiana (1-33)	10	18.4	11.9
Juniperus virginiana 'Corcorcor' (PP#5041)	10	21.9	13.3
Juniperus virginiana 'Silver Spreader'	10	8.3	19.4

Name[a]	Number of years in field	Height (ft)	Width (ft)
Juniperus virginiana 'Staver Blue'	10	24.4	18.2
Keteleeria davidiana	10	20.7	16.0
Metasequoia glyptostroboides	10	34.4	-
Nageia nagi	10	15.2	10.4
Picea chihuahuana	10	2.9	3.9
Pinus pinea	10	13.9	13.3
Pinus pseudostrobus	10	32.1	-
Pinus wallichiana	10	15.9	14.4
Platycladus orientalis 'Bakeri'[b]	7	7.6	6.3
Platycladus orientalis 'Conspicua'	10	10.2	7.4
Platycladus orientalis 'St. Patti's Green'[b]	7	10.0	6.8
Platycladus orientalis (xianshanensis form 1-24)	10	24.3	14.1
Podocarpus lawrencii 'Purple King'[b]	7	4.0	13.0
Podocarpus macrophyllus 'Prostrata'	10	2.3	6.2
Pseudolarix amabilis (4-1)	10	21.1	-
Pseudolarix amabilis (7-11)	10	9.8	14.5
Sequoia sempervirens 'Aptos Blue'	10	19.6	14.5
Sequoia sempervirens 'Chapel Hill'	10	20.7	16.7
Sequoia sempervirens 'Soquel'	10	14.7	18.0
Taiwania cryptomerioides	10	26.0	20.0
Taiwania flousiana	10	22.1	19.4
Taxus floridana[b]	7	5.6	7.5
Thuja occidentalis 'Degroot's Emerald Spire'	10	7.9	3.4
Thuja occidentalis 'Globe'	10	6.1	9.2
Thuja occidentalis 'Golden Globe'	10	7.9	7.9
Thuja occidentalis 'Hetz Midget'	10	2.0	3.5
Thuja occidentalis 'Hetz Wintergreen'	10	23.5	8.9
Thuja occidentalis 'Holmstrup'	10	6.8	5.7
Thuja occidentalis 'Little Giant'	10	3.9	6.6
Thuja occidentalis 'Nigra'	10	8.0	4.4
Thuja occidentalis 'Pumila Sudworth'	10	6.9	8.2
Thuja occidentalis 'Smaragd'	10	11.2	5.9
Thuja occidentalis 'Sunkist'	10	5.8	7.3
Thuja occidentalis 'Techny'	10	7.6	7.9
Thuja occidentalis 'Wansdyke Silver'	10	9.7	7.4
Thuja occidentalis 'Watnong Gold'	10	8.0	7.8
Thuja occidentalis 'Woodwardii'	10	9.7	5.3
Thuja occidentalis 'Yellow Ribbon'	10	6.2	5.8
Thuja plicata	10	14.1	10.3
Thuja plicata 'Atrovirens'	10	14.9	12.2

(continued)

(*continued*)

Name[a]	Number of years in field	Height (ft)	Width (ft)
Thuja plicata 'Hillieri'[b]	7	4.4	3.1
Thuja plicata 'Hogan'	10	14.0	10.1
Thuja plicata 'Hoyt Arboretum'[b]	7	11.5	6.4
Thuja plicata 'Puget Pyramid'	10	10.4	7.8
Thuja plicata 'Rogersii Aurea'	10	8.5	10.6
Thuja plicata 'Stoneham Gold'[b]	7	4.6	4.5
Thuja plicata 'Zebrina Extra Gold'	10	14.1	11.5
Thuja standishii[b]	7	10.6	7.5
Thuja 'Green Giant'	10	25.4	14.4

[a] Numbers in parentheses refer to row locations in Tifton trials
[b] Plants removed due to poor health
[c] Plants blown down by four hurricanes in 2004

Acknowledgments

The experience and learning that made this book possible were not accomplished in a vacuum. Along the way, numerous individuals crossed our paths who contributed to our knowledge. Much of this knowledge came from the sharing of plant material that made it possible for us to evaluate a wide array of conifers at both the species and the cultivar levels.

The space here is insufficient to thank all the nurseries, botanical institutions, and individuals who supported us with their donations of plants, time, and knowledge. We especially thank Ron Determann, Atlanta Botanical Garden, and David Creech, Regent's Professor, Stephen F. Austin State University, for their reviews and suggestions on improving the manuscript. We owe a great deal of thanks to Jo-Evelyn Morris, a master gardener and fellow conifer lover, for her review and continued support of this project; to Bruce Tucker, Nancy Hand, and numerous staff for their assistance over the years taking care of the conifer collection in Tifton; and to Jodi Figgatt for her help with the manuscript.

We want to extend our thanks across the pond for the cooperation and generosity we received from Chris Reynolds and Daniel Luscombe of Bedgebury National Pinetum, Kent, England. Thanks too to Paul Halladin, propagation manager, Iseli Nursery, Boring, Oregon, for his patience with our many questions concerning the history of various cultivars and the selection of rootstocks, and to the Center for Applied Nursery Research, Dearing, Georgia, for its financial support of this project.

Last but certainly not least, we acknowledge our wives, Susan Ruter and Evelyn Cox:

Susan, I thank you for supporting who I am and what I do. Your endurance and support during the development and completion of "that book" have been a true blessing.

Evelyn, I thank you for tolerating all the years of mud as we started an arboretum and for the many trips where we drove from place to place in the "dirtmobile" with plants poking you in the back. Without your patience and support this effort would not have been possible.

Sources

Adams, R. P. 2004. *Junipers of the World: The Genus Juniperus*. Bloomington, Ind.: Trafford.

American Conifer Society. http://www.conifersociety.org/.

Arno, S. F., and R. P. Hammerly. 2007. *Northwest Trees*. Seattle: Mountaineers Books.

Barnard, E. L., and R. M. Leahy. 2004. "Cypress Canker of Leyland Cypress in Florida." Plant Pathology Circular No. 404. Florida Department of Agriculture and Conservation Services. Division of Plant Industry.

Bitner, R. L. 2007. *Conifers for Gardens: An Illustrated Encyclopedia*. Portland, Ore.: Timber Press.

Bloom, A. 2001. *Gardening with Conifers*. London, U.K.: Francis Lincoln.

Burns, R. B., and B. H. Honkala. 1990. *Silvics of North America*. Vol. 1, *Conifers*. Agriculture Handbook 654. Washington, D.C.: USDA Forest Service.

Cope, E. A. 1986. *Native and Cultivated Conifers of Northeastern North America: A Guide*. Ithaca, N.Y.: Cornell University Press.

Cranshaw, Whitney. 2004. *Garden Insects of North America*. Princeton, N.J.: Princeton University Press.

Cutler, S. M. 1997. *Dwarf and Unusual Conifers Coming of Age*. North Kingsville, Ohio: Barton-Bradley Crossroads.

Debreczy, Zsolt, and Istvan Racz. 2011. *Conifers Around the World*. Budapest: Dendropress.

Dirr, M. A. 2009. *Manual of Woody Landscape Plants*. 6th ed. Champaign, Ill.: Stipes.

Earle, C. J., ed. 2010. The Gymnosperm Database. Web site. http://www.conifers.org.

Eckenwalder, J. E. 2009. *Conifers of the World*. Portland, Ore.: Timber Press.

Erhardt, W. 2005. *Namensliste der Koniferen* [List of Conifer Names]. Germany: Eugen Ulmer.

Farjon, Aljos. 2005. *Pines*. 2nd ed. Leiden, Netherlands: Brill.

———. 2005. A Monograph of Cupressaceae and *Sciadopitys*. Cumbria, U.K.: Kew Publishing.

———. 2008. *A Natural History of Conifers*. Portland, Ore.: Timber Press.

Gittlen, W. 1998. *Discovered Alive: The Story of the Chinese Redwood.* Pierside Publications.

Godfrey, R. K. 1988. *Trees, Shrubs, and Woody Vines of Northern Florida and Adjacent Georgia and Alabama.* Athens: University of Georgia Press.

Halfacre, R. G., and A. R. Shawcroft. 1989. *Landscape Plants of the Southeast.* 5th ed. Raleigh, N.C.: Sparks Press.

Hansen, E. M., and K. J. Lewis, eds. 1997. *Compendium of Conifer Diseases.* St. Paul, Minn.: APS Press.

Head, B. H. 2006. *Hutchinson's Tree Book: Popular Landscape Trees.* Hutchinson, Kans.: Hutchinson's Publishing.

Hillier Nurseries. 1991. *The Hillier Manual of Trees and Shrubs.* 6th ed. Newton Abbot, Devon: David & Charles. Reprinted 1994.

Jacobsen, A. L. 2006. *Trees of Seattle.* Seattle: Arthur Lee Jacobsen.

Jensen, E. C., and C. R. Ross. 2005. "Trees to Know in Oregon." Extension Bulletin 1450. Corvallis: Oregon State University.

Johnson, W. T., and H. H. Lyon. 1991. *Insects That Feed on Trees and Shrubs.* 2nd ed., revised. Ithaca, N.Y.: Comstock.

Jones, R. K., and D. M. Benson, eds. 2001. *Diseases of Woody Ornamentals and Trees in Nurseries.* St. Paul, Minn.: APS Press.

Kirkman, L. K., C. L. Brown, and D. J. Leopold. 2007. *Native Trees of the Southeast.* Portland, Ore.: Timber Press.

Krüssmann, Gerd. 1991. *Manual of Cultivated Conifers.* 2nd ed. Portland, Ore.: Timber Press.

Lanner, R. M. 2007. *Conifers of California.* Los Olivos, Ca.: Cachuma Press.

Leahy, R. M. 2000. "Cercosporidium Blight of Leyland Cypress and Related Conifers." Plant Pathology Circular No. 397. Florida Department of Agriculture and Conservation Services. Division of Plant Industry.

Meyer, Frederick Gustav, Peter M. Mazzeo, and Donald H. Voss. 1994. *A Catalog of Cultivated Woody Plants of the Southeastern United States.* Issue 7 of the United States National Arboretum contribution. Washington, D.C.: U.S. Dept. of Agriculture, Agricultural Research Service.

Mitchell, Alan 1978. *A Field Guide to the Trees of Britain and Northern Europe.* London, U.K.: William Collins Sons.

Nguyen, Duc To Luu, and Philip Ian Thomas. 2004. *Conifers of Vietnam.* http://www.ceh.ac.uk/sections/bm/conifer_manual.html

Nixon, E. S. 2010. *Gymnosperms of the United States and Canada.* Bruce Lyndon Cunningham Productions.

Perry, Jesse P., Jr. 1991. *The Pines of Mexico and Central America.* Portland, Ore.: Timber Press.

Price, T. S. 2008. *Forest Health Guide for Georgia.* 3rd ed., revised. Georgia Forestry Commission. http://www.forestpests.org/gfcbook/FHG050108.pdf.

Rouse, Robert J., Paul R. Fantz, and Ted E. Bilderback. 2000. "Descriptions and a Key to Cultivars of Japanese Cedar Cultivated in the Eastern United States." *HortTechnology* 10, no. 2:252–66.

Rushforth, Keith D. 1987. *Conifers*. New York: Facts on File.

Ruter, J. M. 2012. "Conifers for the Southeast." *American Nurseryman Magazine* 212, no. 1:14–16, 18.

Samuelson, Lisa J., and Michael E. Hogan. 2006. *Forest Trees: A Guide to the Eastern United States*. Upper Saddle Ridge, N.J.: Pearson/Prentice-Hall.

Thomas, R. William, Susan F. Martin, and Kim Tripp. 1997. *Growing Conifers: Four-Season Plants*. 21st Century Gardening Series. Handbook #152. New York: Brooklyn Botanical Garden.

Tripp, K. E., and J. C. Raulston. 1995. *The Year in Trees*. Portland, Ore.: Timber Press.

University of Georgia Center for Invasive Species and Ecosystem Health. Web site. http://www.bugwood.org/index.cfm.

van Gelderen, D. M., and J.R.P. van Hoey Smith. 1996. *Conifers: The Illustrated Encyclopedia*. 2 vols. Portland, Ore.: Timber Press.

Vidakovic, Mirko. 1991. *Conifers: Morphology and Variation*. Revised and expanded edition. Croatia: Graficki zavod Hrvatske.

Welch, Humphrey J. 1991. *The Conifer Manual*. Vol. 1. New York: Kluwer Academic.

Welch, Humphrey, and Gordon Haddow. 1993. *The World Checklist of Conifers*. Herefordshire, U.K.: Landsman's Bookshop.

Index

Page numbers in italics refer to illustrations.

Tom Cox is the founder and owner of Cox Arboretum and Gardens in Canton, Georgia. Hosting a premier collection of woody taxa, the arboretum produces research examining the adaptation of conifers in the Southeast. He is past president of the American Conifer Society.

John M. Ruter is the Allan Armitage Professor of Horticulture at the University of Georgia–Athens, where he teaches and conducts research on the breeding and selection of ornamental plants. Previously, Ruter served as the nursery crops research and extension specialist at the University of Georgia–Tifton. He is also working with *Camellia oleifera*, tea oil camellia, to develop it as a new, healthy oil crop suitable for human consumption. Ruter has received numerous awards and coauthored two books.